AUTOCOURSE

CHAMP CAR

OFFICIAL CHAMP CAR® YEARBOOK 2004 2005

CMG
CRASH MEDIA GROUP
WWW.CRASH.NET
motorsport portal
NEW MEDIA
web development
PUBLISHING
books/calendars
PHOTOGRAPHIC
photo agency
RADIO
internet radio
MERCHANDISE
production/retail
GRAND PRIX ARCHIVE
historical database
AUTOCOURSE
CHAMP CAR
OFFICIAL CHAMP CAR YEARBOOK
2004
2005
12th Year of Publication
CRASH MEDIA GROUP
No I SILVERSTONE INNOVATION CENTRE, SILVERSTONE CIRCUIT,
SILVERSTONE, NORTHANTS, NN12 8TN, UNITED KINGDOM.
TEL: +44 (0)870 3505044 FAX: +44 (0)870 3505088
WWW.CRASHMEDIAGROUP.COM EMAIL: INFO@CRASH.NET

CONTENTS

AUTOCOURSE
OFFICIAL
CHAMP CAR
YEARBOOK
2004–2005

is published by:
Crash Media Group,
No.1 Silverstone Innovation Centre,
Silverstone Circuit, Silverstone,
Northants, NN12 8TN
United Kingdom
Telephone: +44 (0)870 350 5044
Fax: +44 (0)870 350 5088

Printed in England by
Butler and Tanner Ltd,
Frome, Somerset
BA11 1NF
United Kingdom
butler&tanner.com

ISBN: 1 905334 00 1

DISTRIBUTORS
Vine House
Waldenbury
Chailey
East Sussex
BN8 4DR
Telephone: +44 (0)1825 723398
email: sales@vinehouseuk.co.uk

REST OF THE WORLD
Menoshire Ltd
Unit 13
21 Wadsworth Road
Perivale
Middlesex UB6 7LQ
Telephone: +44 (0)20 8566 7344
Fax: +44 (0)20 8991 2439

Acknowledgments

The Editor and publishers wish to thank the following for their assistance and encouragement in compiling the Autocourse Official Champ Car Yearbook 2004-05: Kevin Kalkhoven, Paul Gentilozzi, Gerald R. Forsythe, Dick Eidswick; Eric Bachelart, Dale Coyne, Carl A. Haas; Enrique Hernandez-Pons Torres, Mike Lanigan, Paul L. Newman, Dan Pettit, Carl Russo, Jimmy Vasser, Derrick Walker, Keith Wiggins; John Anderson, Justin Anderson, Katie Brannan, Merrill Cain, David Clare, Matt Cleary, Gene Cottingham, Peter Davies, Kevin Diamond, Lee Dykstra, Wendy Gabers, Heather Haupt, Kirsty Kalkhoven, Billy Kamphausen, Gordon Kirby, Chris Kneifel, Kelby Krauss, Kathi Lauterbach, John Lopes, Megan Lundgreen, Cathie Lyon, Nicole Norris, John Oreovicz, Nadia Petrossi, David Phillips, Andrew Punzal, Tara Ragan, Kathi Reichert, Steve Sewell, Steve Shunck, Jeff Swartwout, Melissa Watson; and Tamy Valkosky.

This book is dedicated to all the fans and friends of Champ Car racing.

publisher
BRYN WILLIAMS

editor
JEREMY SHAW

deputy editor
ALEX SABINE

associate editors
ERIC MAUK
TOM McGOVERN

sales director
STUART DENT

design and production
STEVE SMALL

chief photographers
LAT PHOTOGRAPHIC USA

Dust-jacket photograph: Sébastien Bourdais was a dominant force with Newman/Haas Racing's #2 McDonald's Ford-Cosworth/Lola.
Michael Kim/LAT

Title page photograph: Californian A.J. Allmendinger cleaned up the Roshfrans Rookie of the Year honors for the equally new RuSPORT team.
Dan Streck/LAT

Photographs published in The AUTOCOURSE OFFICIAL CHAMPCAR YEARBOOK 2004-2005 have been contributed by: LAT PHOTOGRAPHIC USA (Michael Levitt; Phil Abbott, Greg Aleck, Brad Bernstein, David Chesson, Richard Dole, Greg Feistman, Maria Grady, Leland Hill, Anthony Kent, Michael Kim, Lesley Ann Miller, Al Munger, Phil Sedgwick, Dan Streck, Mark Taylor). Tom Anderson, Dan R Boyd, Ford-Cosworth.

AUTOCOURSE™
www.autocourse.com

FOREWORD
by SÉBASTIEN BOURDAIS
2004 Champ Car World Series Champion

Sébastien and Claire share a special moment with the Vanderbilt Cup.
Michael Levitt/LAT

WHEN I came over from France to test a Champ Car for the first time in December 2002 at Sebring, I would have never imagined that I would be the one writing the Foreword of the Autocourse Champ Car Yearbook just two years later. I was coming out of a Formula 1 test and I didn't feel a lot of desire to see me racing in that series, even though I did pretty well. But when I arrived in Florida everything was different. I felt a true passion for racing within the Newman/Haas team, passion that I cherished ever since the beginning of my career, and just for that I was pumped up as rarely before. I started 2003 with all my energy and my heart, and we were furiously quick right away. For several reasons, it was a roller coaster ride all year long, but my entire crew kept telling me the '04 season would be ours – and guess what, they were right!

A lot of "our" 2004 success is related to that mind-set we all have – enjoy ourselves while working as hard as we can to make us win. I don't pretend to know very much about anything, but I do know one thing: I could have never accomplished so much without everybody's support within the team as well as our sponsors, especially McDonald's.

We've had a lot of opportunities to celebrate during this past season with all the wins and poles. I drove my best race ever in Denver, overcame a lot of adversity, and recorded with Bruno the best season ever for Newman/Haas Racing.

Now, the doors of Formula 1 didn't open yet, and I'm getting ready to try and keep this Vanderbilt Cup driving the McDonald's car #1. So far, it is the biggest challenge of my career for more than one reason. First of all, the quality of the field is stepping up big time, with the emergence of fairly new but nevertheless very strong teams such as RuSPORT. Also, we'll have a few new venues on the schedule with San Jose, Edmonton and Korea. All of these factors should continue the steep rise Champ Car is on, in order to get back to the very top of the world of open-wheel racing.

Finally, the fan support has been greater than I would have ever dreamed. I've received all sorts of awards, and it's amazing to know that most of these have been voted on by the fans. Thank you for sharing with us your love of racing, and I look forward to seeing you at the track during a Champ Car event.

ON THE REBOUND

by Jeremy Shaw

Above: **New champion Sébastien Bourdais and the historic Vanderbilt Cup trophy are flanked by OWRS principals (from left) Kevin Kalkhoven, Paul Gentilozzi and Jerry Forsythe at the awards banquet.**
Michael Levitt/LAT

Far right: **The moment of truth for new champion Bourdais after receiving a check for $750,000 from Bridgestone's Al Speyer and Ford's Anne Stevens.**
Phil Abbott/LAT

IT might be considered trite to describe the 2004 Champ Car World Series season as "pivotal," but that doesn't make the description any less accurate. The fact that there even *was* a 2004 season represented a triumph in of itself. That it provided the usual quota of exciting competition and drew more than two million fans through the turnstiles during a 14-race schedule provided the icing on the cake.

Frankly, in mid-January precious few of even the most hardened Champ Car aficionados would have been prepared to bet much – if anything – on its future. After the previous sanctioning body, Championship Auto Racing Teams, had been driven into the ground and declared bankrupt, rumors of the series' imminent demise were rampant.

But a potential savior had emerged in the form of Open Wheel Racing Series, LLC. The new group, comprised of super-successful businessmen and arch auto racing enthusiasts Kevin Kalkhoven, Gerald R. Forsythe and Paul Gentilozzi, made a firm bid for the CART assets and satisfied a bankruptcy court in Indianapolis that it had both the wherewithal to ensure the series' immediate survival and a credible business plan to secure its future. The ruling in OWRS' favor (which nixed a "hostile" bid from Indianapolis Motor Speedway President and rival Indy Racing League founder Tony George) was handed down on January 28 – or a little less than 11 weeks before the teams' transporters would need to begin their journey to the opening race in Long Beach, California. Much work remained to be done, especially in terms of paperwork and logistics.

Almost three weeks later, OWRS announced that the deal had been finalized and that plans for the new season were properly under way.

"I have been through a number of business dealings in my time," Kalkhoven said at the time. "But this has been one of the toughest. It took a great amount of work and commitment from a lot of people and we are very pleased with the result."

Work continued behind the scenes to finalize plans for the new season, and several important pieces in the puzzle were confirmed in early March when the new ownership group hosted its "2004 Season Premiere" in Long Beach. A 14-race schedule was announced, along with a sassy new television deal ensuring regular nationwide exposure on Spike TV. All the teams present affirmed their commitment to Champ Car, as did its much valued partners Ford-Cosworth and Bridgestone.

Two days later, vaunted Mexican star Adrian Fernandez turned an abrupt volte-face, claiming a lack of confidence in Champ Car's future. One week later, three-time champion Bobby Rahal cited similar reasons for pulling out, despite the fact his team had finished a very strong third in the 2003 title-chase with fast-improving Mexican Michel Jourdain Jr. and already had confirmed plans to continue with funding from the Gigante department store chain. Coincidentally (or not), both Fernandez and Rahal announced they would instead increase their IRL involvement, in which they already

CHRONOLOGY OF THE 2004 SEASON:

JANUARY 28 - After a U.S. Bankruptcy Court hearing in Indianapolis, Judge Frank J. Otte rules in favor of allowing Open Wheel Racing Series, LLC to take over operations of the Champ Car World Series.

FEBRUARY 16 - The 2004 Rule Book is published, incorporating a new point-scoring system and provision for each event to include a minimum of two or three pit stops (depending on the race distance) to be completed under green-flag conditions.

FEBRUARY 17 - OWRS principals announce they have "finalized the acquisition of assets formerly held by Championship Auto Racing Teams and will now commence with the operation of the Champ Car World Series."

MARCH 8 - At the 2004 Champ Car Season Premiere in Long Beach, a schedule comprising 14 events is announced, along with an intention to add two more races (which subsequently fail to materialize).

MARCH 9 - Officials from Ford-Cosworth introduce a "push-to-pass" feature for the requisite XFE motor as a means of promoting overtaking opportunities during the races.

MARCH 11 - Two days after confirming his participation at Long Beach, Mexico's Adrian Fernandez announces his team will withdraw from the series.

MARCH 18 – Bobby Rahal follows suit, but his former driver, Michel Jourdain Jr., affirms his commitment to Champ Car.

MARCH 31 - RuSPORT confirms it will field a second car for Jourdain alongside its existing entry for Toyota Atlantic champion A.J. Allmendinger.

APRIL 2 - Bridgestone proclaims its commitment: "The Champ Car World Series competes in a number of markets that are very important to the Bridgestone brand," says Al Speyer, executive motorsports director for Bridgestone/Firestone North American Tire, LLC. "We recognize and respect the tremendously loyal support from the fan base in those markets."

APRIL 6 - The Champ Car two-seater makes its bow at a media day in Long Beach, with defending series champion Paul Tracy at the wheel. A few days later, Ryan Hunter-Reay creates a buzz of excitement in New York as he drives the car in Times Square.

APRIL 14 - Bridgestone announces plans to produce softer "option" tires (later renamed as "alternate" tires), beginning at Long Beach, as a means of further spicing up the show.

APRIL 18 - The first race under Champ Car's new ownership, the 30th annual Toyota Grand Prix of Long Beach, sees Tracy emerge triumphant in front of more than 75,000 fans.

JULY 7 - Champ Car confirms the addition of a 400-mile race at Las Vegas Motor Speedway on the evening of September 25, to be held in conjunction with a NASCAR Craftsman Truck Series event. (The race originally slated for Korea later was postponed until '05.)

AUGUST 10 - Two days after a confusing race at Road America, Champ Car officials announce a simplification of the pit stop rules. The changes will take effect at Denver.

AUGUST 27 - McDonald's is named the "Official Fast Food Restaurant of Champ Car" through 2006.

AUGUST 29 - Jimmy Vasser breaks Al Unser Jr.'s "iron-man" record by making his 193rd consecutive Champ Car start in Montreal.

SEPTEMBER 24 - Roshfrans is named the "Official Lubricant of Champ Car" – the first time a Mexican company has become an official series sponsor.

OCTOBER 4 - California-based Mojave Aerospace Ventures, LLC claims the $10 million ANSARI X PRIZE Presented by Champ Car after its futuristic SpaceShipOne craft completes the specified two manned flights into space within a two-week period.

OCTOBER 27 - Roshfrans announces it will sponsor the Champ Car Rookie of the Year Award.

OCTOBER 28 - Champ Car ratifies a 14-race schedule for 2005, including new events in Silicon Valley, California (later confirmed as San Jose); Edmonton, Canada; and Ansan, South Korea.

NOVEMBER 7 - Sébastien Bourdais secures a $750,000 bonus at the season-ending awards banquet in Mexico City after winning the final race and securing the 2004 Bridgestone Presents the Champ Car World Series Powered by Ford title and the historic Vanderbilt Cup.

fielded teams with substantial support from Honda...

The withdrawal of two such well-established names caused a massive shock wave, and once again cast the series' viability into grave doubt. How, critics asked, could Champ Car possibly answer the bell for the race at Long Beach – which was now little more than a month away – with the contractually required 18-car field?

Malicious gossip even suggested that Newman/Haas Racing might be the next to jump ship. But that prospect was quickly laid to rest by team co-owner Paul Newman: "Any rumor that Newman/Haas Racing is leaving the Champ Car World Series is a figment of somebody's imagination," said the Academy Award-winning actor who had long since proclaimed his dedication to the cause. "We remain committed to the series and are looking forward to the Toyota Grand Prix of Long Beach season-opener on April 18."

Recently installed Champ Car President Dick Eidswick also sought to stem the tide: "Champ Car has worked diligently during the transition period [from CART to OWRS] in preparation for the 2004 season, in essence accomplishing six months of work in six weeks," he said. "We understand the complexity of the purchase caused some delays in planning for the teams. But the recent release of our 2004 race schedule and television package has allowed numerous teams, drivers and sponsors to move forward with final negotiations. We fully anticipate a series of positive team and driver announcements within the next several days."

In short, it was a case of all hands on deck.

Top: It's business as usual, with packed grandstands at Long Beach to celebrate the street course party's 30th anniversary.

Top right: Paul Newman, now five times a champion team owner, has become the sport's most loyal and fervent advocate.

Photographs: Lesley Ann Miller/LAT

Fortunately, both Jourdain and Gigante remained firmly in Champ Car's corner, and said so publicly. Shortly afterward came confirmation that the fledgling RuSPORT team, which had stepped up to the Champ Car World Series after dominating the 2003 Toyota Atlantic Championship with budding American star A.J. Allmendinger, would enter a second Lola for Jourdain and Gigante. Forsythe, meanwhile, pledged a third car for Patrick Carpentier alongside his already-confirmed entries for defending series champion Paul Tracy and Rodolfo Lavin, who had brought sponsorship from Corona beer. Other commitments were forthcoming from stalwart Champ Car entrants Dale Coyne and Derrick Walker, while another extremely talented young American, Ryan Hunter-Reay, was confirmed as the second driver for Herdez Competition. Then came news that popular young Briton Justin Wilson, who had shown impressive form during his rookie Formula 1 season in 2003, had joined forces with Mi-Jack Conquest Racing.

At last, Champ Car was beginning to gain some momentum.

Another snippet of welcome news came at the end of March, when an independent study conducted by *Sports Business Daily* concluded that the Bridgestone Presents the Champ Car World Series Powered by Ford ranked second among all forms of motorsport in the world in average event attendance, headed only by the NASCAR Nextel Cup series.

"We have always maintained that our fan base is among the best in the world, and never has the passion that the fans have for Champ Car racing been more in evidence than it was during last season," said Champ Car's Eidswick. "Our fans cover the globe and support us in great numbers wherever we go. This is something we have felt all along, and it is great when independent research backs up our feelings. The numbers of fans that follow Champ Car are the reason sponsors come to the series and are therefore the reason we go racing."

Right on cue, the traditional Toyota Grand Prix of Long Beach extravaganza went off with nary a hitch -- under a typically glorious Southern California blue sky and in front of more than 75,000 race-day fans, including such world-renowned celebrities as Paul McCartney and Tom Cruise. The event also showcased the new "push-to-pass" feature that had been introduced by Ford-Cosworth for its turbocharged XFE engines and the softer-compound "option" (later more accurately dubbed "alternate") tires from Bridgestone.

Tracy began his title defense in fine style, using the extra boost (worth around 50 horsepower) to excellent effect by vaulting past front row qualifiers Bruno Junqueira and Sebastien Bourdais immediately after the start. The Canadian never looked back. The stickier Bridgestone tires added to the intrigue, even though the different tire compounds didn't produce quite the disparity in lap times that some people had anticipated. Nevertheless, they enabled Bourdais to post the fastest lap of the race in the closing stages, and the program was "tweaked" to thrilling effect as the season unfolded.

Champ Car officials employed various rule changes during the year – some with more success than others, but all introduced with one goal in mind: to improve the show for the fans.

The quality of the racing, indeed, was at least as good as any in Champ Car's illustrious history, and the caliber of the leading contenders was absolutely top-drawer. Frenchman Bourdais already was recognized as one of the world's most promising open-wheel talents before switching his sights from Europe to North America and claiming Rookie of the Year honors in 2003. The 25-year-old didn't begin the '04 season with quite the same distinction he had exemplified the year before (when he established a new record by winning the pole in his first two races), but his more measured approach quickly paid dividends.

Bourdais realized that consistency would provide the key to a successful challenge for the venerable Vanderbilt Cup trophy. That and a blinding turn of speed. The young man from Le Mans took control of his own destiny by earning eight poles and seven race wins, although a couple of late-season glitches ensured that the championship remained undecided until the final race. Fittingly, Bourdais saved his most dominating performance for last, qualifying on the pole and romping to a resounding victory in front of a bumper weekend crowd of over 345,000 in Mexico City to become the first Frenchman ever to lift the Champ Car crown.

The well-deserved triumph put him among some exalted company, joining Mario and Michael Andretti, Nigel Mansell and Cristiano da Matta in winning the championship for Newman/Haas Racing. The team's joy was further compounded by Junqueira ensuring its first-ever monopoly of the top two positions in the over-

Performance Chart

Driver	Wins	Poles	Fastest laps	Most laps led
Sébastien Bourdais	7	8	6	7
Paul Tracy	2	3	1	4 (1 shared)
Bruno Junqueira	2	1	5	-
Ryan Hunter-Reay	1	1	1	1
Patrick Carpentier	1	1	-	1
Alex Tagiani	1	-	-	1 (1 shared)
Mario Dominguez	-	-	1	-

all point standings.

Bourdais was far from the only man to make his mark during the 2004 season. Allmendinger augmented his burgeoning reputation by scooping Roshfrans Rookie of the Year honors, while his RuSPORT team showed it, too, will be a bona fide championship contender in the years to come. Two other Americans also shone: Hunter-Reay became the first driver in a dozen years to lead every lap of a Champ Car oval race (in Milwaukee), and at season's end was presented with the Greg Moore Legacy Award (as the driver who best typifies the spirit and personality of the gifted Canadian who so tragically lost his life in 1999); while 1996 champion Vasser reached an important milestone in Montreal by making his 193rd consecutive start, eclipsing the previous standard set by two-time champion Al Unser Jr.

"I've been fortunate throughout my career to not get sidelined with any serious injuries, and I'd just like to thank Mr. Kevin Kalkhoven, Mr. Jerry Forsythe and Mr. Paul Gentilozzi for saving this great championship and breathing new life into it," said Vasser, echoing the sentiments of countless drivers and fans around the world who have developed a true passion for the sport. "Without this opportunity I wouldn't have been able to do what I love to do – drive in the Champ Car World Series."

As befits Judge Otte's prescient judgment in January '04, the prospects for Champ Car's future look bright. Three exciting new venues (in San Jose, California; Edmonton, Alberta, Canada; and Ansan, South Korea) will host rounds of the 2005 championship. A new and vastly more attractive domestic television package has been developed in conjunction with CBS, NBC and SPEED Channel. And the sanctioning body's intention of continuing to provide improved value for money to its teams seems to have been assured following the purchase in November by Kalkhoven and Forsythe of the iconic Cosworth Racing brand, which for the past two years has supplied the magnificently powerful and reliable Ford-Cosworth XFE engines.

By any standard, the 2004 Bridgestone Presents the Champ Car World Series Powered by Ford has to be considered an overwhelming success – if for no other reason than its new ownership group confounded the naysayers and survived. In reality it did much more than that. In the space of one short year, Champ Car racing has emerged from the edge of an abyss and now has begun to exhibit perceptible growth.

Jeremy Shaw
Rancho Santa Margarita, California
March 2005

IN MEMORIAM

Photograph: Dan Boyd

DOUG SHIERSON passed away on May 26 at the all-too-young age of 62 following a lengthy battle with cancer.

After graduating from the University of Michigan, Shierson joined his family's Adrian, Michigan-based oil business which distributed Marathon products throughout the Midwest. He was introduced to auto racing in 1965 and enjoyed some success himself in sports car events before beginning a lengthy and hugely satisfying vocation as a car owner. His race team won frequently, initially in Formula 5000 and later in what is now the Toyota Atlantic series, winning the championship with Howdy Holmes in 1978 and Jacques Villeneuve (Sr.) in 1980 and '81. Shierson Racing most famously won the 1990 Indianapolis 500 with Arie Luyendyk at the wheel of its Domino's Pizza Lola-Chevrolet. Luyendyk's winning average speed of 185.981 mph remains unbeaten as the fastest Indianapolis 500 of all.

At the end of that season Doug realized he'd achieved all he possibly could from his hobby and decided to sell his team. But he never tired of the sport, and for several years afterward served with the Champ Car series as a protest judge.

Invariably gracious, he was a man with many virtues who possessed a wide range of interests. He studied architecture at the University of Michigan and, along with his wife Fern, loved to collect art. Their home and life were rich in this way but there was always Doug's other passion: cars and racing.

Shierson was one of the most genuine, unprepossessing men one could ever wish to meet. He is survived by a wonderful family, including Fern and their daughters Sarah, Rebeccah and Molly.

KENNY FERRIS and VITOR PINTO, two experienced and popular members of the Herdez Competition team, were tragically killed in a road accident in Arkansas on December 22. Ferris, 42, originally from South Tidworth in England, worked with the late, great Ayrton Senna at Team Lotus in Formula 1 before moving to the United States. He spent time with Reynard Racing Cars, Jim Hall Racing, Walker Racing, Team Rahal and Mo Nunn Racing before joining Herdez in 2003. Pinto, 44, from Coimbra, Portugal, spent time in the World Rally Championship and, after relocating to the U.S., was a member of the BDJS/Ralt American team with which David Empringham won the 1994 Toyota Atlantic Championship. Pinto spent time with Team Menard and Target/Chip Ganassi Racing before joining Herdez, and for the past three seasons had served on the "over-the-wall" crew as the inside front tire changer for Mario Dominguez.

ART FLORES, one of the most knowledgeable and passionate of all auto racing photographers, passed away suddenly and quietly at his home in Alameda, California, over the weekend of March 8/9. Flores, who was 59, held a particular passion for Formula 1 and Champ Car, and served for many years on the executive boards of both the American Racing Press Association (ARPA) and the American Auto Racing Writers and Broadcasters Association (AARWBA).

RICHARD "DICK" KING, who was a mainstay of the United States Auto Club for many years, serving as its president and chief executive officer from 1976 to 1999, died suddenly on November 8 while vacationing in Mexico. He was 73.

JOHN MARTIN JR. lost his life in a surfing accident in Nassau, Bahamas, on October 29. Martin, whose father was an accomplished racer, worked with a variety of Indy Lights, Toyota Atlantic and Champ Car teams before switching to the IRL with Super Aguri Fernandez Racing. He worked as fueler for 2004 IRL Rookie of the Year Kosuke Matsuura.

RODGER WARD, who won the Indianapolis 500 and the USAC National Championship in 1959 and 1962, died on July 5 in Anaheim, California, at the age of 83. A World War II fighter pilot, Ward was an all-around racer who even competed in a couple of world championship Formula 1 races, most notably at Sebring in 1959 with a Kurtis midget. After the 1960 Indy 500, Ward suggested to Jack Brabham and car owner John Cooper that they should think about modifying a rear-engined Cooper grand prix car to run at Indianapolis. Within a few years, the traditional front-engined "Roadsters" had been rendered obsolete.

DUANE SWEENEY, chief starter of the Indianapolis 500 from 1980 through 1996, died on January 15 at his home in New Berlin, Wisconsin, at the age of 81.

"CACTUS JACK" TURNER, a regular in the Indianapolis 500 in the late 1950s and early 1960s who survived spectacular accidents in three consecutive years from 1961-63, died in Renton, Washington, at the age of 84 on September 12.

LOUIE UNSER, older brother to multiple Indianapolis 500 winners Al and Bobby and the twin brother of Jerry (who was the first of the famed clan from Albuquerque, New Mexico, to qualify at Indianapolis, in 1958), died March 2 in Anaheim, California. Unser, a wonderfully gifted mechanic who suffered from multiple sclerosis and had been confined to a wheelchair since the 1970s, was inducted into the Orange County (California) Hall of Fame in 1987. He was 71.

JOHN "JACK" ZINK, the Tulsa, Oklahoma industrialist whose cars won the Indianapolis 500 in 1955 (with Bob Sweikert) and 1956 (Pat Flaherty) died February 5, aged 75.

BRIDGESTONE
PRESENTS
CHAMP CAR
WORLD SERIES
POWERED BY
Ford

TELM
Banam

BRIDGESTONE
POTENZA

McDonald's

TOP TEN DRIVERS

In accordance with the Autocourse tradition, Editor Jeremy Shaw offers his personal ranking of the best of the best in the 2004 Bridgestone Presents the Champ Car World Series Powered by Ford, taking into account their individual performances, their level of experience and the resources at their disposal.

Photography by LAT Photographic

FROM the moment the 2004 Champ Car World Series contenders arrived in California for the opening race of the new season, Sébastien Bourdais was widely tipped as a likely winner of the coveted Vanderbilt Cup. The studious-looking Frenchman had earned that status by virtue of a string of impressive feats during his rookie campaign, including three wins and a handful of poles. The fact that he remained with Newman/Haas Racing further strengthened his credentials. Even so, perhaps few people were really prepared for the manner in which he won his first Champ Car title, and the fifth for Paul Newman and Carl Haas.

It's true that he only clinched the crown at the final race in Mexico City, but he did so in style, leading all 63 laps from the pole and eventually cruising home well clear of teammate Bruno Junqueira. Bourdais had displayed similarly imperious form on a regular basis, and only a controversial coming-together with top rookie A.J. Allmendinger in Montreal and then a punt from outgoing series champion Paul Tracy two weeks later at Mazda Raceway Laguna Seca prevented him from wrapping up the honors much sooner.

Bourdais' statistics make impressive reading: He won precisely half of the year's 14 races; 10 times he finished on the podium; he led at least one lap in all but three events; and his tally of laps led (506 out of 1,335) was close to twice as many as his nearest rival. He started from the pole eight times and his lowest starting position was third (at Cleveland, Vancouver and Las Vegas), marking the first time in the series' history that one driver had started among the top three in every race.

The key to Bourdais' remarkable success lay in the relationship he had developed with the entire Newman/Haas organization, and especially with race engineer Craig Hampson. Both men are outwardly rather serious but each possesses a quick wit and a steely determination. Neither is willing to accept second best, even when the chips are down. Bourdais demonstrated that trait in sensational fashion at Denver, where a first-corner incident (with his teammate) relegated him to the back of the field. By Lap 80, he was in the lead and pulling away. His eventual margin of victory was over seven seconds. On that day in August it became abundantly clear that it was his destiny to win the championship.

SÉBASTIEN BOURDAIS

1

Sébastien Bourdais

Date of birth: February 28, 1979

Residence: Tampa, Florida

Team: Newman/Haas Racing

Equipment: Ford-Cosworth/Lola/Bridgestone

Champ Car starts in 2004: 14

Points ranking: 1st

Wins: 7; Poles: 8; Points: 369

Date of birth: November 4, 1976

Residence: Miami, Florida

Team: Newman/Haas Racing

Equipment: Ford-Cosworth/Lola/Bridgestone

Champ Car starts in 2004: 14

Points ranking: 2nd

Wins: 2; Poles: 1; Points: 341

2

BRUNO Junqueira etched his name in the record books following the 2004 season, but not for the reason he had anticipated: He became only the second driver in Champ Car history, dating to 1909, to finish as runner-up in three consecutive seasons, mirroring Johnny Rutherford in 1974-76. (Coincidentally, both men lost out in their quest for that elusive first title to three different drivers; JR was beaten by Bobby Unser, A.J. Foyt and Gordon Johncock in successive years, while Junqueira played second fiddle to Cristiano da Matta, Paul Tracy and, most recently, Sébastien Bourdais.) But perhaps the Brazilian can take heart from the fact that the Texan did finally achieve his goal – albeit four years later when he dominated proceedings with Jim Hall's revolutionary Chaparral 2K design.

Enough of the history. Junqueira began '04 in a positive frame of mind. He recognized teammate Bourdais and defending champion Tracy as his fiercest rivals, but began his title quest in the best possible manner, taking pole at Long Beach. He wasn't to know it at the time, but the tone for his season was set on a picture perfect Californian race day when "PT" executed a daring pass for the lead at the very first corner and never relinquished his advantage. Junqueira had to make do with second. It was the same story next time out in Monterrey, Mexico, only this time he was vanquished by Bourdais.

Junqueira said he wasn't concerned. He knew consistency would be a key to success and remained confident his time would come. He was even relatively content after finishing a lackluster sixth on the Milwaukee Mile, especially since he had seen Bourdais crash out in the early going. But after two more visits to the middle step of the podium, at Portland and Cleveland, the writing was on the wall: The "nearly man" had been soundly beaten by Bourdais on each occasion.

The 28-year-old's frustration boiled over following a clash between the pair at Road America, and it was clear there was little love lost between the teammates when they collided again at Denver – at the very first corner. Junqueira appeared to get the upper hand on that occasion, but it didn't last. By the end of the afternoon his rival was well in command.

A remarkable tally of seven second-place finishes says much for Junqueira's ability, but time will tell whether he has what it takes to achieve his ultimate goal.

BRUNO JUNQUEIRA

A.J. ALLMENDINGER

HE finished only sixth in the championship and failed to win either a race or a pole but rookie A.J. Allmendinger's performances in 2004 were truly exceptional, especially given his relative lack of experience. Consider that just three years earlier, the youngster from Hollister, California, was still driving karts... as a protégé of none other than '03 Champ Car titlist Paul Tracy. Since then his progress had been meteoric.

After winning a scholarship to drive in the Skip Barber Formula Dodge National Championship, Allmendinger finished a close second in the '01 points table. He scooped a Team USA Scholarship prize (with another Champ Car star, Jimmy Vasser, among his mentors), followed by the 2002 Barber Dodge Pro Series crown before earning the biggest break of his career when Carl Russo invited him to join his fledgling RuSPORT team to graduate into Toyota Atlantic. Nine poles and seven wins later he had another title in his pocket.

By now acknowledged as one of America's most talented open-wheel rising stars, Allmendinger's Champ Car debut was eagerly awaited. Yet the youngster was under no illusions. He knew the team faced a mighty challenge in stepping up into the Champ Car arena, and the arrival of veteran Michel Jourdain Jr. as a teammate merely three weeks before the start of the season was surely a mixed blessing. On the one hand, the Mexican's vast experience could prove invaluable; conversely, adding an extra car at the 11th hour put a huge extra strain on the organization.

As usual, Allmendinger took everything in stride. He had, after all, emerged from a modest background and had worked hard to create his own opportunities. So far as he was concerned, this latest hurdle was no different. The 22-year-old already had established an excellent rapport with his team in Toyota Atlantic, and he proved an equally quick study in his latest career enhancement. Eighth on the grid for his debut at Long Beach represented a very promising start. His first top-five finish came in arguably the most difficult race of the season, on the Milwaukee Mile oval, and his maiden podium appearance followed less than two months later on the unforgiving streets of Vancouver.

True, he made several mistakes during the year but he never shied away from responsibility and by the end of the season was a bona fide contender. Can he follow in the footsteps of Sébastien Bourdais by winning the overall crown just one year after claiming top rookie honors? Why not? For Allmendinger, the sky's the limit.

3

Date of birth: December 16, 1981

Residence: Denver, Colorado

Team: RuSPORT

Equipment: Ford-Cosworth/Lola/Bridgestone

Champ Car starts in 2004: 14

Points ranking: 6th

Wins: 0; Poles: 0; Points: 229

Date of birth: December 17, 1968

Residence: Las Vegas, Nevada

Team: Forsythe Championship Racing

Equipment: Ford-Cosworth/Lola/Bridgestone

Champ Car starts in 2004: 14

Points ranking: 4th

Wins: 2; Poles: 3; Points: 254

4

PAUL TRACY

VICTORY at Long Beach ensured the perfect way for Paul Tracy to begin the task of defending his long-awaited first Champ Car World Series crown. The sport's most charismatic – and enigmatic – star did what he does best, delivering a scintillating pass for the lead at the very first corner and controlling the remainder of the race to notch the 27th victory of his career. He wasn't to know it at the time but the year would bring precious few additional highlights.

It's hard to pinpoint what went wrong. The enforced withdrawal (due to tobacco legislation) of team owner Jerry Forsythe's long-time supporters, Player's, certainly ensured there were less resources at his disposal, but there was no lack of commitment from either Forsythe or his team. Tracy had the benefit of stability, too, with Todd Malloy remaining as race engineer and Kiwi Steve Moore as chief mechanic. There were no excuses. But for some reason the new-found consistency that had provided the launchpad for his '03 championship deserted him. And his propensity for off-track excursions increased dramatically – some would argue reverting to more usual levels for the previously incident-prone Canadian.

His troubles began as early as the second round in Monterrey, Mexico. "PT" was never happy with the handling of his car, but kept his head until tangling with fellow former champion Jimmy Vasser at the final corner. Tracy was lucky. He maintained his seventh position while Vasser fumed after ending his race against the barriers. Next time out in Milwaukee, Tracy pushed the envelope a little too hard while trying to pass teammate Patrick Carpentier, and on this occasion it was he who came off worst. He rebounded to finish on the podium at Portland then claimed the pole in Cleveland, only to be taken off by an over-zealous Alex Tagliani at the first corner. A week later in Toronto he earned not one but two drive-through penalties for initiating "avoidable" contact. Again he bounced back, speeding to a dominant victory in Vancouver.

It was that kind of year: extreme highs and extreme lows. But there were far too many of the latter to enable him to do any better than fourth in the final championship reckoning. Admittedly, not all were of his making (Cleveland, for example, and a rare mechanical failure on the parade lap in his adopted hometown of Las Vegas) but Tracy knows he must regain his consistency – and make fewer errors – if he is to win another series title.

PATRICK CARPENTIER

THERE was little to choose in 2004 between the two Forsythe Championship Racing teammates, Paul Tracy and Patrick Carpentier. In terms of points Carpentier emerged with a slender advantage, securing himself third in the final standings to match his personal best achieved in 2002. But in hard results, Tracy had more to crow about – two fine victories and three poles compared to one pole and one win for his Canadian countryman. Disappointments? Well, they were probably about equal in that department. Tracy's woes are detailed elsewhere. Carpentier, meanwhile, was unlucky to suffer a rare Ford-Cosworth engine failure while running well at Cleveland, ending his hopes of a fifth consecutive top-four finish to continue the strongest start he had ever made to a Champ Car season (having debuting in 1997). Indeed, prior to his arrival in Ohio, the 32-year-old trailed series leader Bruno Junqueira by just six points.

The blow-up put a dent in his championship aspirations, but much worse was to follow: He was punted off in Vancouver while running well in the early stages, and next time out at Road America he was again the innocent victim of someone else's accident. He rebounded to finish on the podium in front of his home crowd in Montreal and used the resulting boost in his confidence to win convincingly for the second straight year at Mazda Raceway Laguna Seca.

Carpentier kept the podium streak alive at Las Vegas, where he took the pole, and most likely would have offered a stronger challenge to the Newman/Haas pair had he not been hindered on the restarts by a gearbox glitch. Then came a big crash at Surfers Paradise after he elected not to make a pit stop to change a damaged front wing. Bad call. He was lucky to escape a high-speed accident without serious injury.

There's no doubt that Carpentier recovered most of his élan after having been comprehensively overshadowed (and demoralized) by Tracy in 2003. He had endured a difficult off-season, too, unsure whether he would be driving at all until Jerry Forsythe finally gave the green light just a few weeks prior to the first race. Under the circumstances (which included the fact that he did not have a spare car at his disposal for much of the year), third place in the championship represented a significant accomplishment. Then again, one can't help but wonder what Carpentier might be capable of achieving if he could consistently muster the same flair he displayed at Laguna Seca....

5

Date of birth: August 13, 1971

Residence: Las Vegas, Nevada

Team: Forsythe Championship Racing

Equipment: Ford-Cosworth/Lola/Bridgestone

Champ Car starts in 2004: 14

Points ranking: 3rd

Wins: 1; Poles: 1; Points: 266

Date of birth: December 1, 1975

Residence: Mexico City, Mexico

Team: Herdez Competition

Equipment: Ford-Cosworth/Lola/Bridgestone

Champ Car starts in 2004: 14

Points ranking: 5th

Wins: 0; Poles: 0; Points: 244

6

VOTED Bosch Most Improved Driver by his peers following an impressive sophomore Champ Car season in 2003, Mario Dominguez continued to make good progress with Keith Wiggins' Herdez Competition team. The amiable Mexican failed to win a race or a pole in '04 but it certainly wasn't for a lack of effort. Indeed, he came to be regarded as a legitimate front-runner, as exemplified by the fact he qualified among the top five in eight of the 14 races (compared to just once in 2003). A career-best fifth in the final points table was thoroughly well deserved.

Self-confidence has long been regarded as one of the foremost attributes in any race car driver, and there's no doubt that Dominguez has come a long way since his tentative first steps as a rookie in 2002. His relationship with the Herdez team played a crucial role in his development. Level-headed technical director Tom Brown helped Dominguez focus on what's important in terms of setting up the car, and he wasn't fazed by the departure of race engineer Brian Ma, with whom he had established a strong rapport during the '03 campaign. Instead he quickly built a similar bond with Ma's replacement, Michael Cannon, who brought a wealth of experience gleaned from six years with Player's/Forsythe Racing.

Dominguez began the year firmly believing he could mix it with the best in the Champ Car World Series, and he did just that, qualifying among the top six in each of the first four races. He finished fifth in the opener at Long Beach, following a lengthy battle with Patrick Carpentier, and could hardly wait to get to the next race in Monterrey for the first of the season's two visits to his homeland. He didn't disappoint. The 29-year-old thrilled a huge crowd by qualifying a career-best second, and while his enthusiasm got the better of him early in the race, resulting in a spin, he then mounted a sensational charge back through the field to finish third. Sure, his progress was aided by some timely full-course cautions, but let that not detract from a fine drive.

He was (unusually) eclipsed by team-mate Ryan Hunter-Reay in the next race at Milwaukee, but still ran as high as third in the early stages before losing valuable time when an air-gun malfunctioned. Cruelly, an identical problem in Montreal quite conceivably cost him a victory, since he had cleanly overtaken Bourdais and seemed to be set fair.

MARIO DOMINGUEZ

7

Date of birth: July 13, 1974

Residence: Miami, Florida & Barcelona, Spain

Team: Dale Coyne Racing

Equipment: Ford-Cosworth/Lola/Bridgestone

Champ Car starts in 2004: 14

Points ranking: 10th

Wins: 0; Poles: 0; Points: 199

ORIOL SERVIA

NO doubt about it, Oriol Servia was the revelation of the 2004 season. Well, perhaps that's not entirely fair – it was more a case of his *team* making a quantum leap rather than the driver. The likeable Spaniard, indeed, had displayed good form on numerous occasions since graduating at the beginning of the Y2K season as the reigning Indy Lights Champion. The same, quite frankly, could not be said for Dale Coyne Racing which had a solitary podium finish to its credit from a total of 248 Champ Car races since Coyne himself made his debut as a driver at Mid-Ohio in 1984.

Servia, however, had been left without a drive when Pat Patrick pulled out at the end of 2003. And yet he, like Coyne, had developed a real passion for the Champ Car World Series. So when an opportunity presented itself for the pair to join forces, Servia, to his immense credit, decided to take the plunge. Many other drivers with a similar level of experience might not have been so bold, perhaps fearful that joining Coyne might somehow jeopardize their reputation. But Servia – in common with ex-Formula 1 driver Roberto Moreno, who in 1996 secured Coyne's best-ever finish of third at Michigan – is not encumbered by a fragile ego. His reasoning was simple: He wanted to remain in Champ Car. Coyne had a car available. Go for it.

It wasn't just a stab in the dark. Servia had worked previously with race engineer David Watson (at the new and short-lived Sigma Autosport team in 2001), and they had gotten along well. He knew, too, that chief mechanic Andy Green had a solid pedigree in the sport. Together, they produced by far Coyne's most productive campaign.

It would be stretching the point to say that Servia was a frequent front-runner, but he certainly gave an extremely good account of himself and regularly humbled far more illustrious operations. His best finishes were a third at Laguna Seca and a fourth at Cleveland, although he was running ahead of second-place finisher Jimmy Vasser before being punted off by Alex Tagliani at Toronto and was unfortunate to be caught out by the scoring fiasco at Las Vegas. Servia barely put a scratch on the #11 yokeTV.com Lola all year long (which was just as well, since money, as ever, was excruciatingly tight) – at least until Surfers, and even then he bounced back well to earn his best qualifying position of the year in Mexico. Job well done.

JUSTIN WILSON

FOR years, Justin Wilson battled the odds as he attempted to carve a career for himself in Formula 1. There were two major obstacles in his way: First, as with so many other talented youngsters, he needed to source the funding; second, he had to overcome the perception that at six-foot-three-plus he was simply too tall to fit into a top-line modern-day open-wheel car.

Well, he made it to F1, thanks in large part to his successes in the developmental classes (he won titles in Formula Palmer Audi and Formula 3000) as well as astute management by ex-Formula 1 driver-turned-businessman Jonathan Palmer. His own refreshing honesty and no-nonsense approach also served him extremely well.

Wilson's initial opportunity in F1 came in 2003 with perennial backmarker Minardi. No matter; it was a start. A series of strong showings in uncompetitive machinery led to a late-season switch to Jaguar, which, with the benefit of hindsight, turned out to be a blind alley. By year's end, it was apparent that his F1 options were drying up. So he looked instead to reestablish his reputation in the Champ Car World Series.

A deal was eventually brokered for him to join Mi-Jack Conquest Racing – less than a month before the start of the season. There was time enough for just one test session, but Wilson squeezed his lanky frame into an ex-Team Green/Patrick Racing Lola and immediately applied himself to the task at hand. He was grateful for the chance to renew his working relationship with Conquest's team manager, Chris Mower, whose Nordic Racing team had guided him to the F3000 title in 2001, and quickly impressed the remainder of the team with his application and technical acumen.

The 25-year-old from Sheffield, England, finished a strong sixth on his debut at Long Beach, then set tongues a-wagging by qualifying third in Monterrey. Extreme tire wear (due to a less-than-optimal setup) caused him to slip to sixth again by the finish, but Wilson continued to show well. He took a magnificent second on the grid at Cleveland, only to be involved in a first-corner fracas, then was punted off again while running well in Toronto. Lady Luck clearly was not on his side. The team/driver combination's lack of experience saw Wilson struggle at Laguna Seca, but he rebounded with a solid drive on the Las Vegas oval and rounded out the year with a fine drive to fourth in Mexico City. Even though a podium finish eluded him and he ended up outside the top 10 in points, Wilson had made his mark.

Date of birth: July 31, 1978

Residence: Northampton, England

Team: Mi-Jack Conquest Racing

Equipment: Ford-Cosworth/Lola/Bridgestone

Champ Car starts in 2004: 14

Points ranking: 11th

Wins: 0; Poles: 0; Points: 188

8

ALEX TAGLIANI

THE highlight of Alex Tagliani's year was a long overdue maiden Champ Car win. It came, appropriately, at the scenic and challenging Road America – most drivers' favorite track and the scene of more than a few past heartbreaks for the enigmatic French-Canadian. Whimsically, given that he had come tantalizingly close to victory on numerous occasions during his previous 84 starts, only to be stricken by one calamity or another, his moment of triumph owed more than a little to good fortune. In this instance it was the series' capricious pit stop regulations which, for a change, played right into his hands. (Ironically, shortly afterward they were consigned to the history books.)

What Tagliani lacked most of all in 2004 was consistency. On his day he looked as good as anyone. On other occasions he was all but invisible. And from time to time he was neither, seemingly responsible for more than his fair share of scrapes.

He was involved in a long-running feud with "fellow" Canadian Paul Tracy, triggered when the reigning champion accused him of blatant blocking tactics at Portland when "Tag" already was a lap down to the leaders. The 31-year-old was penalized two championship points for ignoring both blue and black flags in that event, but his most conspicuous gaffe came next time out in Cleveland, where he leaped from fifth on the grid to take out both front row starters (Tracy, again, and Justin Wilson) at the notoriously hazardous Turn One. He promptly went some way toward making amends – to his team, at least – by overcoming another early spin and charging all the way back to third place by the checkered flag. Tagliani was in the wars again in Toronto, clashing this time with Oriol Servia.

Surprisingly, he was regularly handicapped by his poor form in qualifying. After earning five poles from his first four Champ Car seasons, only twice in '04 did he start from among the top five positions, which meant that he usually had much to do on race day... and might go some way toward explaining his propensity for desperate maneuvers. Even when he triumphed at Road America, Tagliani had started a lowly 13th.

With the weight of expectation lifted from his shoulders on that joyous August day in rural Wisconsin, most pundits expected him to reap the benefit, but surprisingly, his season tailed off dramatically and he slipped from a high-water mark of third in the points table to seventh.

9

Date of birth: October 18, 1972

Residence: Las Vegas, Nevada

Team: Rocketsports Racing

Equipment: Ford-Cosworth/Lola/Bridgestone

Champ Car starts in 2004: 14

Points ranking: 7th

Wins: 1; Poles: 0; Points: 218

Date of birth: November 20, 1965

Residence: Las Vegas, Nevada

Team: PKV Racing

Equipment: Ford-Cosworth/Lola/Bridgestone

Champ Car starts in 2004: 14

Points ranking: 8th

Wins: 0; Poles: 0; Points: 201

10

JIMMY VASSER

THE career of 1996 Champ Car title-holder Jimmy Vasser incorporated several new dimensions in 2004. Most visibly, looking toward the future, he took on additional responsibility by joining Dan Pettit and Kevin Kalkhoven as co-owner of the newly titled PKV Racing team. Also, at the age of 38, he unwittingly inherited the mantle of Champ Car racing's senior statesman (following Roberto Moreno's inability to find a ride), and assumed the unofficial responsibility of acting as one of the series' prime cheerleaders.

Vasser had made no secret of his passion for the Champ Car World Series, and in the tumultuous days following Bobby Rahal's decision to jump ship merely a month before the first race, he took it upon himself to try to ensure that Mexican star Michel Jourdain Jr. was able to continue his involvement.

In the meantime there had been quite a few changes within the PKV team during the off-season, the most important, of course, being the expansion to a two-car operation with the arrival of young Mexican Roberto Gonzalez. Vasser himself took a little time to get acquainted with his new surroundings, and with testing at a premium as Champ Car sought to reduce its teams' operating costs, qualifying proved to be his weakest link -- especially in the first half of the season. Indeed he didn't record a top-five start until the eighth round at Road America, where he took a fine third on the grid.

Misfortune also seemed to strike with inordinate frequency. JV was eliminated on the very first corner of the opening race in Long Beach, and next time out at Monterrey he was rudely punted off by Paul Tracy – ironically this time at the last corner – while disputing seventh place with the reigning champion. Fortunately, subsequent races proved rather more productive, and Vasser confirmed on several occasions that he was more than capable of producing the same kind of form that had earned him a total of 10 race wins over the years. He used his wealth of experience to excellent effect on the Milwaukee Mile, finishing fourth, enjoyed a solid run in Cleveland to take fifth and took full advantage of others' indiscretions in Toronto to place a season-high second.

He reached a milestone in Montreal, eclipsing Al Unser Jr.'s ironman record of 192 consecutive Champ Car starts, and while the results certainly were not as good as he had hoped for in 2004, there were more than enough signs that he could still cut it at the sport's highest level.

1
Forsythe
RACING.COM
INDECK
COSWORTH
BOSCH
Ford
BRIDGESTONE

3
Corona
INTER
PROTECCION
COSWORTH
BOSCH
Ford
USACELL
Pensamos en ti
BRIDGESTONE

INDECK
Forsythe
RACING.COM
Corona
Forsythe
RACING.COM

Corona
Forsythe
RACING TEAM
Corona
INDECK

MODEL STUDENT

by Gordon Kirby

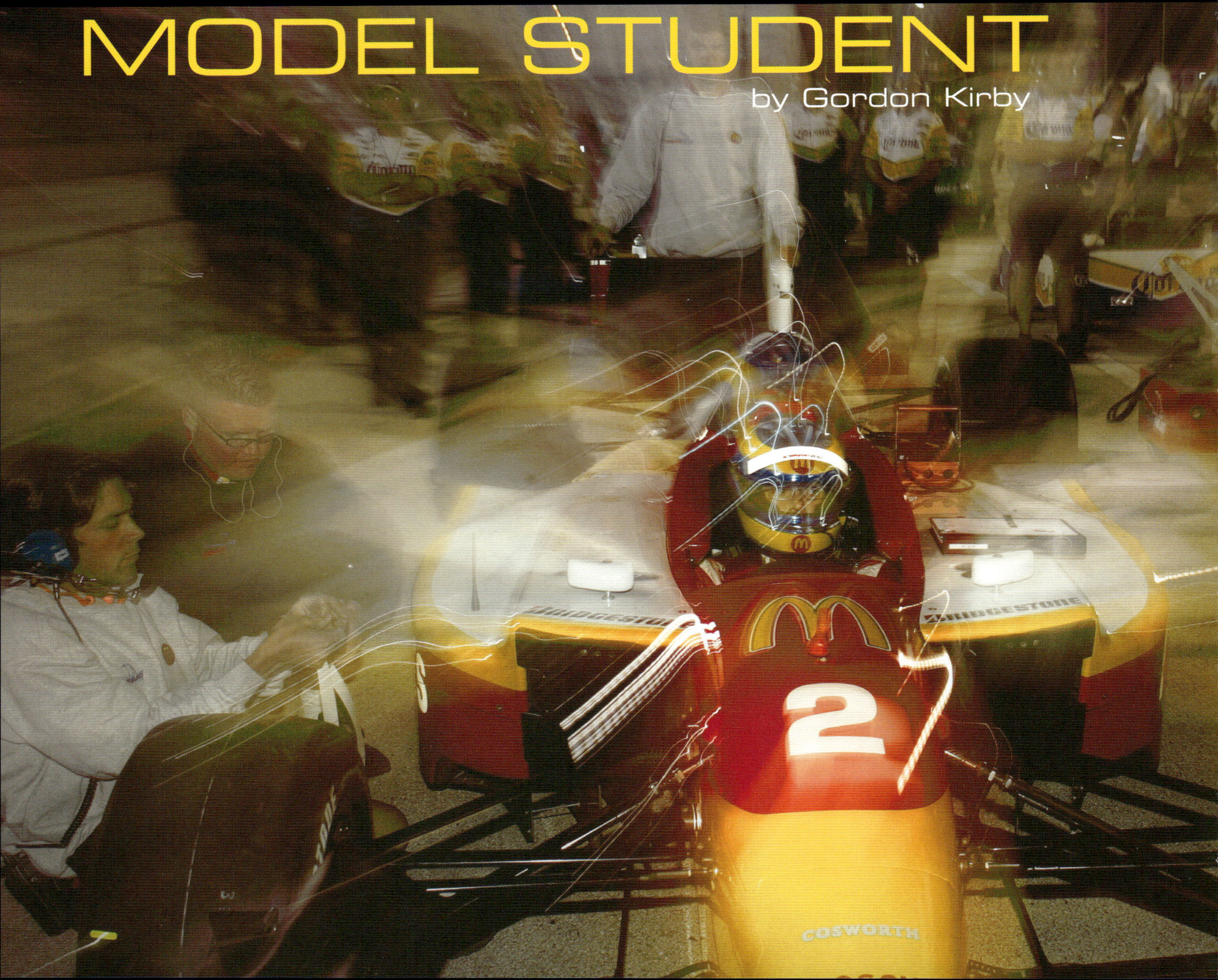

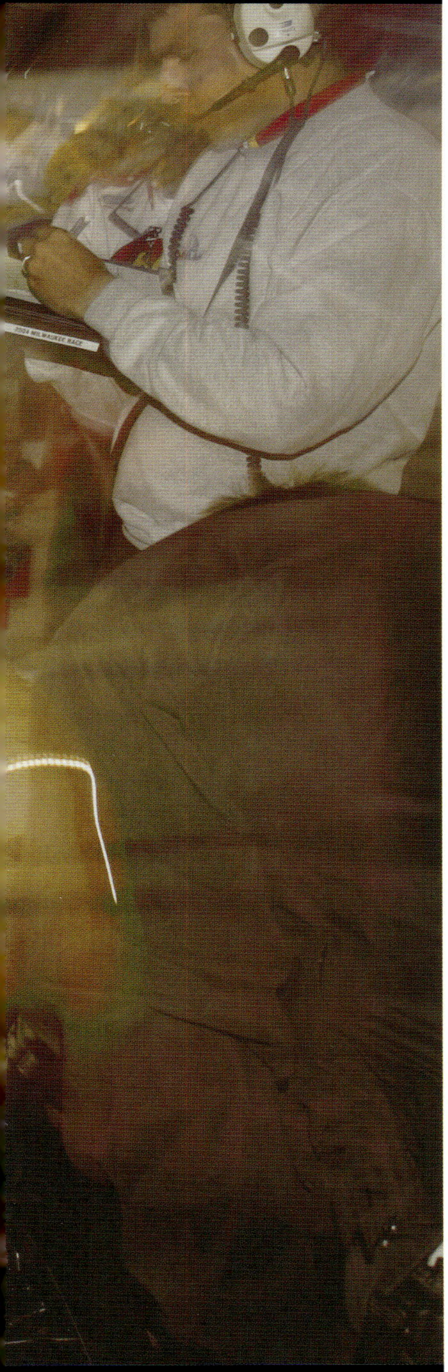

SÉBASTIEN Bourdais is intelligent, ambitious and exhibits an assiduous work ethic; the 25-year-old Frenchman also possesses a keen sense of humor, as evidenced by the fact he was immediately christened "Kermit" (the frog) by his Newman/Haas Racing teammates. Above all, though, he's *fast*, and since stepping into a Champ Car for the very first time in December 2002, the young Frenchman has made an indelible impression on the North American auto racing scene.

After winning the Jim Trueman Rookie of the Year Award, Bourdais quickly emerged as a title favorite in the 2004 Bridgestone Presents the Champ Car World Series Powered by Ford, which culminated in a tense duel with Newman/Haas teammate Bruno Junqueira. Bourdais looked untouchable during the summer, but a couple of untimely incidents kept Junqueira in the hunt right up to the season finale in Mexico City.

Bourdais was in irrepressible form south of the border, however, romping to his seventh victory from the 14-race season and wrapping up the crown in consummate style. It was the fifth title success since the partnership between movie legend Paul Newman and auto racing entrepreneur Carl Haas was formed prior to the 1983 season, but the first time their drivers had monopolized the top two positions in the final point standings.

"Overall it was just a fantastic season," Bourdais says. "We had some ups and downs, as you do every season, but it was really completely positive from day one. I cannot say it was easy in the second half of the season because we had some trouble. There was the incident with A.J. [Allmendinger] in Montreal and Paul [Tracy] in Laguna. We should have wrapped up the championship in Las Vegas but obviously we didn't, and the last few races were difficult [for me] because I've lost a few championships at the last race or even the last lap. I lost the F3000 championship at the last race [in 2002 to Tomas Enge, before ultimately being awarded the title after his rival was disqualified from one race], and I was thinking, sh*t, not again!"

No one seriously challenged his domination at the famed Autodromo Hermanos Rodriguez, although Bourdais came alarmingly close to negating all his (and the team's) fine work when a momentary lapse of concentration resulted in him spinning the #2 McDonald's Ford-Cosworth/Lola in Turn 14 at two-thirds distance. Mercifully, he was able to resume without losing his lead, but Bourdais was all too aware of how he had flirted with catastrophe.

"I insulted myself when I lost [control]," he recalls with a wry smile. "I was kind of surprised by Mario [Dominguez, who was directly ahead, almost a lap down] and by the shade on the racetrack. It got my attention for a fraction of a second and I lost it. It happened very fast and I jumped on the throttle going backwards and was fortunate not to hit anything. It could have been a disaster if I had hit something or stalled the engine. It would have been all over.

"After that I took it a bit easier and cruised around. I said to myself, 'That was stupid! You're trying to win this damn race when you don't even need to.' I guess it was a question of honor because you feel like you deserve the win and you really want it bad and you want to finish [the year] on a positive note. You know drivers! The ego is always there."

Such self-deprecation comes naturally to Bourdais, who remains one of the most humble and likeable characters in the paddock. And that's in spite of the fact that the young man from Le Mans already had established himself as one of the hottest properties in international automobile racing even before he crossed the Atlantic. He won the French Formula 3 Championship in 1999, at the age of 20, and three years later added the FIA International Formula 3000 crown (after Enge failed a drug test).

Bourdais was then invited by Renault's corporate and racing bosses to test a Formula 1 car at Jerez, Spain. He was immediately impressive, circulating within fractions of a second of the team's regular drivers Fernando Alonso and Jarno Trulli. He was substantially quicker than Telefonica Nissan World Series star Franck Montagny, too, but it was his fellow Frenchman who got the nod and was appointed as Renault's test driver for the 2003 season.

Days after his unofficial F1 debut, Bourdais gained his first taste of a Champ Car when he was invited to test for Newman/Haas Racing at Sebring, Florida. The team was looking for a replacement for departing champion Cristiano da Matta (who had signed for the Toyota Formula 1 team), and Bourdais was a convincing winner of the shoot-out, besting Brazilian F1 test driver Ricardo Zonta and Toyota Atlantic champion Jon Fogarty.

"He wasn't necessarily the very fastest," admits Haas, "but he was very consistent and the guy that was slightly faster had very little rapport with the engineers. But they were very impressed with Sébastien's comments and input about the car."

The engineers – indeed the entire team – also were struck by his professional approach and his dedication to the task, which had become abundantly clear the first time he made contact with the Lincolnshire, Illinois-based organization.

"The first thing that impressed me was [when] he came to the shop to do a seat-fitting a week or two before he did the test," recalls Newman/Haas Racing General Manager Brian Lisles. "He arrived from Europe at five or six in the evening and we were on a tight schedule because he had to go back to Europe to do some kind of function. So we needed to do the seat that evening, and he came in and we worked until about 10 or 11 o'clock.

"He was very straightforward. He knew exactly what he wanted and wouldn't compromise. But he wasn't difficult to work with. He knew what he wanted and we were able to get it done for him. He was very clear in his mind what he wanted and that's always a good start.

"When we tested him not only was he very quick out of the box but he told us all the things that we knew he should be saying about the car," continues Lisles, who had accumulated a wealth of experience in Formula 1 (with Ken Tyrrell's team) before joining Newman/Haas in 1989. "During the test we had him do short runs, long runs and pit stops. We put on cold tires, tried low pressures and looked for quick laps on his out-laps, and he was doing everything he should be doing. So for us, it was a pretty straightforward choice."

Lisles' impressions are echoed by Craig Hampson, who has served as Bourdais' race engineer the past two seasons. Given Bourdais' prior successes in Europe, Hampson was fully expecting his new charge to be fast during his initial mid-December test, but he was even more excited by the clarity of his technical feedback.

"That car had just won the championship with da Matta," he observes. "It had a championship-winning setup on it and he had an opinion on how to improve it. In our view that wasn't insulting, that was a very good quality.

"His enthusiasm and cerebral approach were very important factors [in his selection]. Also, for his age he has a lot of experience and that part of his resume really impressed us. It was very clear he was the guy. It didn't take long for us to decide. When we got home from that test I said, 'God, I hope we get this guy. It would be the

Above: The close ties between Bourdais and his crew were crucial to his success.
Michael Levitt/LAT

Far left: Longtime flagman Jim Swintal stepped out of Race Control to end the season with a flourish in Mexico City.
Dan Streck/LAT

Left: Ecstasy, and perhaps a touch of relief, as Bourdais savors his victory.
Dan Streck/LAT

Right: Bourdais will get to appreciate another of Swintal's talents, as his fine effort in Denver is captured on canvas.
Courtesy of Bridgestone

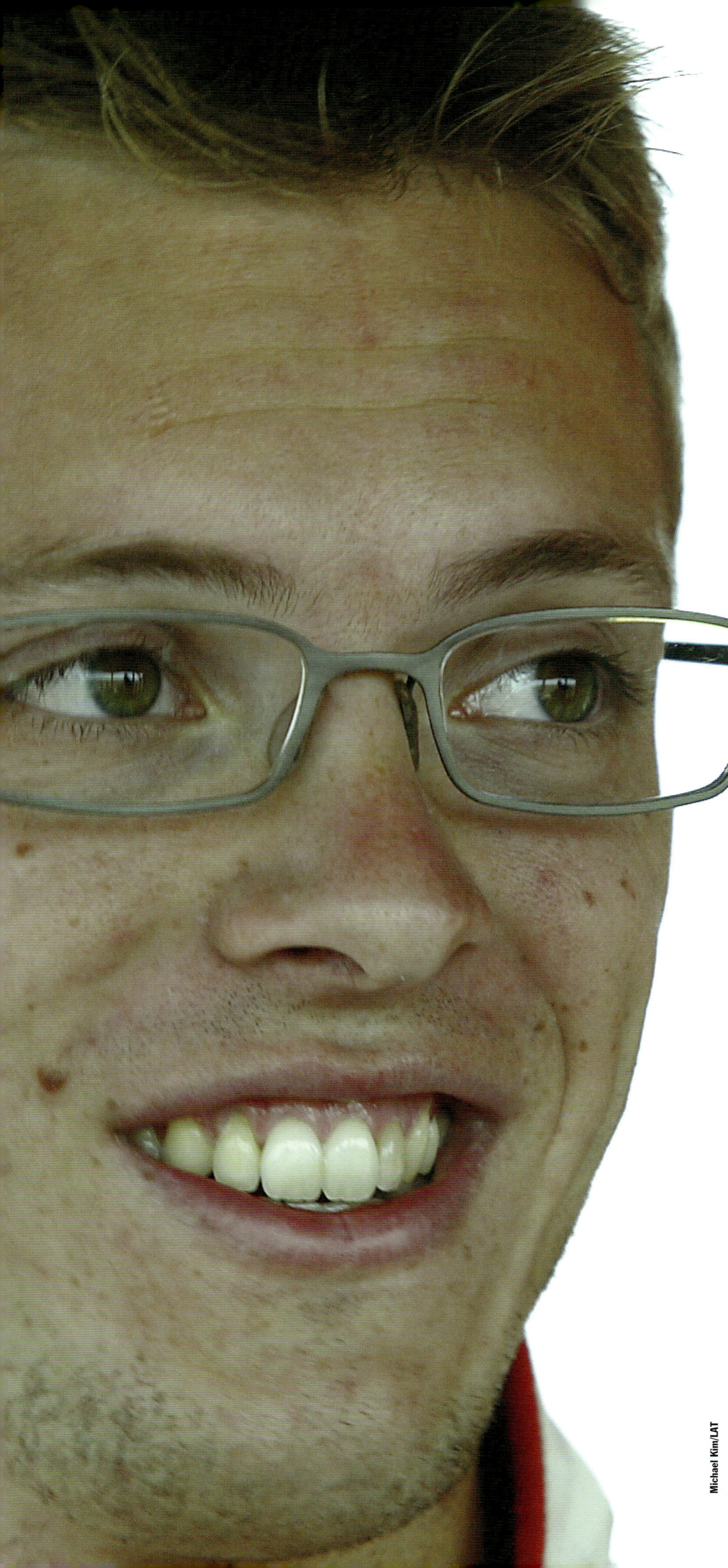

Michael Kim/LAT

greatest Christmas present I could get.' I figured Renault's F1 team would take him. I was shocked when they didn't, but it was a fantastic opportunity for this team."

Bourdais' breadth of experience appealed to all the Newman/Haas decision-makers. In addition to the usual European-style apprenticeship, graduating through karts and small-formula cars, he had raced regularly in the world-famous 24-hour sports car race in his hometown since 1999. He was also a part of the race-winning team in the 2002 Spa 24 Hours GT/touring car classic, driving a Chrysler Viper GTS-R.

"I think that's one of the reasons why he's so good," asserts Lisles, "because he has a huge amount of experience in dealing with different types of problems with different types of cars. As far as I'm concerned that was all just accelerated training that he'd been through.

"We didn't have to teach him anything about fuel economy because he'd driven at Le Mans for three or four years and fuel economy is everything at Le Mans. He knew exactly what he needed to do in order to do the fastest lap time on the minimum amount of fuel. So he brought a lot of experience with him which is fairly unusual for such a young driver. Usually it's a big thing to try to teach them and get them to understand how to save fuel."

There were several other aspects of the Champ Car World Series of which Bourdais had very little experience, however. Rolling starts weren't entirely new to him, but certainly he was more accustomed to the traditional standing starts that are the norm in European racing. Then there were all the intricacies of full-course cautions and their inherent complications, which frequently play a pivotal role in determining the outcome of Champ Car events.

"Most of the foibles of this series, which are different to European racing, come from the full-course yellows," says Lisles. "The reality in Champ Car racing is that you should never give up because opportunities always appear to allow you to recoup from an error. That probably took longer for him to learn than almost anything, but he's learned the lesson well."

Bourdais agrees there was much to digest when he lined up in St. Petersburg for the opening event of the 2003 season. He proved a quick study, although not everything went to plan. Far from it, in fact. History relates that he made a stunning debut, qualifying on the pole, only to be brought back to earth when, following a strategic miscue that dropped him out of the lead, he glanced the wall while trying a little too hard to make up the lost ground. The impact broke his car's suspension; he was done for the day. Next time out in Monterrey he again started from the pole. Just as in St. Pete, however, his early lead was negated by a couple of full-course cautions. Then, after missing an initial radio call to make a pit stop, he overstepped the mark on his way into the pits, collecting the barriers and again damaging his Lola's suspension.

Looking back, he accepts that he had to adapt his way of thinking to cope with the ebb-and-flow caused by the frequent yellow-flag interruptions.

"It was so different for me and it's difficult to accept that when you're leading a race and feel so strong that you can lose it because of the yellow flag and there's nothing you can do about it," he says. "But I've learned that, all in all, it balances itself out. Sometimes you don't win races you definitely deserve and other times you end up winning when maybe you really didn't deserve it."

Bourdais bounced back from his early mishaps and scored his first victory, at Brands Hatch in England, in only his fourth Champ Car start. He won again one week later on the majestic EuroSpeedway Lausitz superspeedway oval in Germany to complete an enormously satisfying sweep of the series' European swing. Another win at Cleveland and four additional top-three finishes were enough to secure an impressive fourth in the overall standings, and he easily won Rookie of the Year honors.

Bourdais therefore began the 2004 season as one of the firm favorites to take home the historic Vanderbilt Cup trophy. He made his mark early, winning the second round in Monterrey at a canter and maintaining his form throughout the summer to join Jacques Villeneuve and Alex Zanardi as the only drivers to win top rookie honors and the overall championship in successive seasons. (Juan Montoya, of course, grasped the overall spoils as a rookie in 1999, emulating Nigel Mansell's feat from 1993.)

Race engineer Hampson is not at all surprised by the level of success his charge has achieved in their two years together. Indeed, as he recognized from their first test, Bourdais is a perfect fit for Newman/Haas Racing.

"We view ourselves as an engineering-based, engineering-driven organization," he states. "We put a huge amount of effort into the engineering preparation going into a weekend and [compiling] a technical study of how we should set up the car. The changes we make to the car we do via science and engineering, not just pulling it out of thin air. So we need drivers who will work in that way. The driver has to believe in that philosophy and he also has to be very bright."

According to Hampson, Bourdais has much in common with the great Mario Andretti, around whom the Newman/Haas team was first assembled in 1983. Andretti went on to claim 18 race wins for NHR, as well as his fourth and final championship (in '84).

"This was Mario's team and it has developed somewhat in Mario's image," declares Hampson. "Mario developed the car. He would test and test and test, and think about how and why each [setup] change affected the car. Newman/Haas learned to operate in that style and Sébastien fits that style very well."

High praise indeed. General manager Lisles agrees, and reckons what stands Bourdais apart from the majority of his rivals is his overall focus.

"I would say his strength probably is in his ability to help us make the car better and to point out in the correct order what we need to look at," Lisles says. "As he gets experience he gets better at that because now he understands the influence of the track conditions on our cars.

"He's very clear, just as he was when he came to do his seat-fitting. He knows what he wants and when we give it to him there's never any second-guessing or changing his mind. He's the same in all the things he does. If he doesn't like it, he tells you, and when it's fixed he moves onto the next issue. That's probably his great strength.

"He's a very smooth driver," Lisles adds. "But equally, he's very aggressive in terms of getting the car right up on the limit and maybe even a little bit beyond it. You see that because he gets up to speed very quickly, and that's the only way you can do that. Even when he's going quickly and not trying to save fuel he's relatively fuel-efficient, which is a mark of a smooth driver. Nor does he damage the car."

Smoothness and consistency, of course, are important traits for any driver with championship aspirations, while a propensity for minimizing errors – and therefore keeping repair costs under control – is likely to be especially appreciated by those who pay the bills. Cigar-chomping team co-owner Carl Haas doesn't tend to say a great deal these days, but he has certainly been impressed by what he has seen over the past two years. And like everyone else, he was astonished by Bourdais' recovery drive in the 2004 Centrix Financial Grand Prix of Denver after a first-corner tangle with teammate Junqueira had relegated him to the back of the field.

"I guess I really can't say a lot more than look at the record," Haas says. "And if anybody had any doubts that he was quick, they should watch a replay of Denver. He didn't have necessarily the best brakes in the world, but he just went through the field."

Bourdais' drive that day will long be remembered, and for Paul Newman, Haas' cohort on the championship-winning team, it epitomized another important aspect of the Frenchman's temperament.

"Sébastien doesn't rattle," he observes. "Some guys get mad; Sébastien gets even. He gives good feedback, excellent in fact. He's very good on his in and out laps. He's consistent and he also has a certain panache. When he came from the back of the field to win in Denver, he turned the fast lap of the race on the second-last lap, just to let them know how much he had left. Now that's style!"

Such flair, coupled with the statistics that Bourdais has amassed during first two years in the Champ Car World Series – 10 race victories from just 32 starts, representing a strike rate of .31, and an even more remarkable 13 poles at .41 – already have established him among the sport's all-time greats. Since he began karting at the age of 12, however, his sights have been set on a career in Formula 1, and while that ambition presently remains unfulfilled, Bourdais realizes that his current position of prominence in the United States is to be envied.

"I feel really lucky and [driving in Champ Car has] changed my orientation," he says. "Formula 1 is still my goal but [here] I can drive a very good car for a great team in a very good series and do a professional job, and I'm very happy to be able to do this.

"I would like to get back to Europe and F1 because that's my country. But I feel kind of adopted here. I really feel welcome here. I'm buying a [house in Florida] with water access, something I really could not have anywhere in Europe. The quality of life here is great and I feel very fortunate for a lot of reasons. If I can continue to win races and fight for the championship, I couldn't ask for much more."

Whether or not Formula 1 remains his ultimate destiny, the foreseeable future will include the sight of Bourdais driving Newman/Haas Racing's McDonald's Lola. And judging by the success he has achieved in just two years, the Champ Car record books will continue to take a beating.

MY AMERICAN GRANDFATHER

BEST known, of course, as an Academy Award-winning actor, Paul Newman also has emerged as one of the most important figures in the sport of auto racing as a team owner, advocate and, even at the age of 80, an extremely good amateur racer. He's a noted philanthropist, too, running a series of summer camps at locations around the world catering to children with life-threatening illnesses.

Over the course of the past two seasons Newman has formed a particular bond with Sébastien Bourdais, especially following the Frenchman's summer '04 visit to a new "Hole in the Wall Camp" that had been established in his homeland.

"Sébastien was just incredible with those kids," Newman says. "They had a show where the kids did acts and sang. We were all walking back toward the manor house, and Sébastien had a kid on his shoulders and was holding two kids by the hand. It was very touching."

Not surprisingly, the sentiments are reciprocated, and Bourdais treasures the times they have spent together, chatting about a variety of topics and interests.

"It's very difficult to quantify Paul," Bourdais says. "In so many ways he's so extraordinary. He has so much energy and he's doing a lot of different things, for the kids and for his charities, and of course, he's really active in the racing world. He's so devoted to so many things. The clarity of mind he has is quite remarkable to me, and to involve himself in so many things. He has an exceptional background, he's done a lot of things and he uses it in the best way he can for what he really loves and believes in.

"I cannot remember one time where I didn't have fun being with him because he always laughs and makes jokes. Every time you're with him you're going to have a good time. I don't consider him my boss. He's a lot more than that. We've spent evenings together. We went to see a play and we had a wonderful time. And he loves [my girlfriend] Claire; and his wife, Joanne [Woodward], she's a great lady too.

"In so many ways I feel like he's my American grandfather. He's really inspiring. I just wish one thing, and that's to be in that good shape when I'm 80 years old, both physically and mentally."

He came to appreciate first-hand another of Newman's many qualities in January '05 when they co-drove a prototype sports car in the famed Rolex 24 Hours at Daytona, teaming up with another former Newman/Haas Racing Champ Car title-winner, Cristiano da Matta, and Newman's long-time racing partner, Michael Brockman. Bourdais was extremely impressed.

"I'm sure he could have done it professionally if he had discovered racing earlier in life," he says. "I think he definitely had the talent and more than that he's a perfectionist and he's definitely chasing that as hard as he can; and he has a true love of racing. With all that he could have been a great driver, which he already is for me. He's just a fantastic guy. He doesn't like to hear all these compliments, but sh*t, that's what he is."

Above: Heartfelt congratulations from Newman after yet another Bourdais win.
Leland Hill/LAT

Below: He might be well over three times Bourdais' age, but PLN is still fast.
Richard Dole/LAT

Bottom: Newman at the wheel of their Daytona Prototype in the Rolex 24 Hours.
Ricard Dole/LAT

DICK EIDSWICK

OUT OF THE ASHES

by John Oreovicz

IN late January 2004, the future of the Champ Car World Series hung, quite literally, in the balance, awaiting the outcome of a crucial bankruptcy hearing in an Indianapolis courtroom. When Judge Frank J. Otte cleared the way for Open Wheel Racing Series, LLC to take over the series' operations, the hard work began for OWRS partners Kevin Kalkhoven, Gerald R. Forsythe and Paul Gentilozzi and auto racing neophyte-turned-Champ Car World Series President Dick Eidswick. Less than three months later, the championship campaign began on schedule in California with the 30th annual Toyota Grand Prix of Long Beach.

His initial mission accomplished, Eidswick reflects on the twists and turns of a tumultuous season.

Q: *One year into the life of the "new" Champ Car, how do you assess the progress that has been made?*

Dick Eidswick: I'm very pleased with the results. What we did in the first year of the new Champ Car was put on 14 fabulous races that featured strong attendance and competition and produced a great champion in Sébastien Bourdais. The fans like what we do, and for 2005 we are introducing a much stronger television product so we're going to be able to take that show and make it available to more people – not just domestically but internationally as well.

From the business side, we have new relationships with McDonald's and Roshfrans, and America Online announced a new partnership at our promoters' meeting to put Champ Car branding on AOL subscriptions. It's going to be an interesting activation that will feature McDonald's and Ford Motor Company and our other partners.

Q: *Thirteen months ago, in the lead-up to the asset auction hearing in Indianapolis, a lot of people thought Champ Car had one foot in the grave...*

DE: We heard that a lot. But our "team" – the three owners – never entertained any ideas along that line. We knew that we had to get ready for the 2004 season; we knew it was going to happen. We just had to put the resources in place to get it done. We didn't waver in our commitment even through those darkest days and we were inundated with positive input from our fans.

The key that came from the court case was the importance of the promoters – the guys who put the races on. Promoter after promoter stood up in that courtroom and said, "This is an important sporting event in our country that means a lot to us. We really want to see it succeed and if it doesn't succeed, we're in deep trouble."

The teams, the fans, the sponsors – everybody stepped up and supported us. It wasn't just the three owners carrying the flag out front. We had a lot of help.

Q: *How difficult were the first couple of months?*

DE: The darkest days were between the media preview in Long Beach (March 8-9) and the first race, because we just had to scramble. But Michel Jourdain stepped up and made a commitment to the series and Newman/Haas made a strong commitment to the series. As the newcomer, it looked at first to me like we were at risk of losing them. But by the time the season got underway, they became our strongest supporters. Carl Haas, in his quiet way, did an important part, and Paul Newman was always there for us through all of our difficulties early on. You couldn't ask for a better spokesman or supporter of our series than Paul Newman.

Carl Russo had never run in Champ Car before, but he put up two cars and did very well and made some valuable contributions.

Q: *After a year of working with them, how do you characterize the three owners, Jerry Forsythe, Paul Gentilozzi and Kevin Kalkhoven?*

DE: Kevin has emerged as the visionary and a forceful factor in what we are doing, but Paul did a lot of the work at the beginning, almost at the neglect of his other businesses. He focused almost a full-time effort from late 2003, far beyond the start of the season, into working out what the new Champ Car wanted to be from an operational point of view. That was a huge contribution. He's gotten some criticism, but worked his fanny off to do all the right things, and we wouldn't be here without him.

Jerry was always there when we needed him. He ran three cars [in 2004] and he was a strong supporter across the board of everything we did. Although he was not as public in his expression of where we were going, on a private basis he was totally committed.

I think Kevin is a brilliant marketer. He thinks things through carefully and then he has a commitment to what he wants to do.

That commitment is highly focused and he wants very, very badly to succeed. That commitment is what I believe in and what got us to where we are.

All three of them know what their vision is and that makes life easier because we don't have to doubt where we are going. It's just a matter of how we get there.

Q: *How long have you had an association with Kevin?*

DE: I met Kevin in 1972 when we both worked for the same high-tech company called Compshare, which was an international computer time-share company – one of the leading edge companies trying to bring computing to what we now think of as internet computing, where you can share a computer from afar. We built that company up into a very strong competitor in the worldwide market. Then Kevin and I went our own way where we both ran different companies that were not related to each other. We didn't come back together in a business sense until Champ Car, but we have remained friends throughout.

Q: *Presumably, this company is unlike any other you have managed in your career. Can you touch on what you did prior to taking on this challenge?*

DE: It was certainly a big step for me, going from management of high-tech companies and investment companies, to running Champ Car in the racing environment that exists today. What is common is the technology companies that emerged in the past that I was involved with were faced with a lot of challenges, with conflicts and issues that had to be resolved. When I arrived here I saw an environment where people often wanted to go to court to solve problems and I think one of the things that I have been able to do in this company is to change that attitude to where we address our problems with our partners or whomever we are dealing with and resolve them without having to get a third party or lawyer involved.

What didn't carry forward is that auto racing is an entertainment business that has to do with the public, where I didn't have any experience, and it has to do with television. In fact, television is the most important single thing about the sport, and I had no experience with that. So I had to surround myself with people who did know to guide me and consult with me about what to do. In the racing business, those people didn't always agree with each other, but out of the input I got I think we came up with some good solid answers.

Q: *There are again only two ovals on the 2005 schedule. Will that number grow in the future? And will any of the traditional road courses dropped from the schedule in the last couple of years come back?*

DE: I think we want a couple of ovals to keep our hand in that type of racing, but most of the excitement comes from the city and road courses. With the road courses, it isn't a matter of the relationship, it's a matter of attracting the fans to those tracks so the promoter can afford to bring the race to the venue. If the promoter can't attract the crowds, they don't have enough revenue to support the event. We are working with Road America and Mazda Raceway Laguna Seca to try to find a way to be able to run a race, because of the rich tradition of those two venues. They can both attract huge numbers of fans, but they haven't been coming.

Q: *The cost of competing in the series has been reduced dramatically in the last couple of years, but some now criticize it as a spec formula. Will you open up the engine and chassis markets in the future?*

DE: We have discussed it, but it is the belief of the ownership of this series that we want to have racing that concentrates on the drivers and the driver skills. That's why we have such a variety of races – to test those drivers, no matter where they go. Having everyone run the same tires and the same engine gives the drivers an even playing field. In our racing, anyone can win. Some teams are stronger than others, but anyone can win, and we think that's a good thing. Our tendency is to continue along with that pattern.

Q: *It was widely assumed that your were hired as a temporary CEO. How long do you plan to work at this latest challenge?*

DE: It is a challenge and when I first came here, I was a stopgap solution to what needed to be done. They decided right at the end of '03 that CART was going to go into bankruptcy and they needed somebody to keep the company focused on putting on the 2004 season. The way it worked out, I continued through the season and then got hooked on the sport and on the company and the lofty goals that we have.

One of the great pleasures I had this year was getting to know the owners and getting to know the drivers. I've never seen such a cooperative group of people in my life. They don't always express themselves in the same way, but they all want the same thing, which is the success of the series.

So as far as I'm concerned, I'm here until the company is back to where it should be, to where it has the kind of fan support and TV ratings that it should have, and the economic performance for the teams and the promoters is where everyone can survive. Then I will feel that will be a worthwhile accomplishment.

Top: OWRS partners Kevin Kalkhoven and Paul Gentilozzi pose with Dick Eidswick at the 2004 Season Premiere at Long Beach.
Lesley Ann Miller/LAT

Above: Eidswick presented the Champ Car Nation's Cup trophy to Alex Tagliani, Paul Tracy and Patrick Carpentier in Australia.
Michael Levitt/LAT

Opposite: New to auto racing when he took the job, Eidswick is now a firm fan.
Lesley Ann Miller/LAT

JOHNSON CONTROLS
BOSCH
Saputo
Futaba
OMP

8
JOHNSON
ROCKETSPORTS
www.rocketsportsracing.com

A.J. ALLMENDINGER and JUSTIN WILSON

THE NEW KIDS ON THE BLOCK

by Gordon Kirby

AFTER winning successive Barber Dodge Pro Series and Toyota Atlantic Championships, A.J. Allmendinger lived up to his young phenom reputation in 2004. The 22-year-old Californian demonstrated quite plainly that there's substance behind the hype as he battled for Roshfrans Rookie of the Year honors with Formula 1 refugee Justin Wilson. Allmendinger not only won the title, he also finished an excellent sixth in the overall point standings.

Allmendinger thereby became the first American in 13 years to win the rookie-of-the-year title; the last to do so was Jeff Andretti back in 1991. In fact, Allmendinger is only the fourth American in the past 23 years to achieve the feat (the others being Bobby Rahal in 1982 and Eddie Cheever in 1990). Even Al Unser Jr. and Michael Andretti were eclipsed by foreign-born drivers in their debut campaigns. Unser was beaten in 1983 by Italian Teo Fabi while Andretti had to give best the following year to Colombian Roberto Guerrero. Of course, one of Champ Car racing's strengths for the past 20 years has been its international appeal, and that tradition clearly is set to continue well into the future.

Allmendinger is the real deal, clear-headed and a straight talker. Driving for the same RuSPORT team with which he had won the Toyota Atlantic crown in '03, he showed himself to be a quick study as he made the podium twice and was on the front row in Montreal.

It's hard to comprehend that only three years earlier he was driving karts, as a protégé of Paul Tracy, and it was entirely appropriate that when Allmendinger made the Champ Car podium for the first time, finishing third in Vancouver in July, race winner and former mentor Tracy was among the first to congratulate him.

"It was a great day for A.J. today," praised the Canadian. "And it's really a testament not to my karting team but to the whole ladder system."

It's fair to say that the RuSPORT operation was an equally exciting addition to the Champ Car World Series. The Colorado-based operation had served notice of its potential by dominating the 2003 Toyota Atlantic series, with Allmendinger claiming an impressive record of seven wins and nine poles.

Owner Carl Russo is a successful businessman who rallied and raced as an amateur for more than 20 years. Most recently, before starting RuSPORT in 2003, he competed in IMSA sports cars, Formula Ford 2000 and even Toyota Atlantic. In addition to his racing exploits, Russo is the president and CEO of Calix, a manufacturer of optical network transmission equipment. Prior to founding Calix he worked for Cisco Systems after selling his own business, Cerent, to Cisco.

His race team is based in Loveland, Colorado, and is run by retired sports car racer and ex-Barber Dodge managing director Jeremy Dale and Steve Wulff, also a retired racer as well as an engine builder and crew chief in a variety of series, including the IRL.

Russo originally planned to run a solitary Lola in 2004 for Allmendinger, but barely a month before the Long Beach season-opener an opportunity came his way to field a second entry for veteran Michel Jourdain Jr. It was, to say the least, an ambitious move for a new team, but Russo was fully aware of the enormity of the challenge that lay ahead.

"Prior to Long Beach my feeling was abject terror because we chose to take on something that was very difficult," he admits. "But the team did a wonderful job. The team is an outstanding family of folks who did a great job just to get to the grid at Long Beach. Our goal at Long Beach literally was just to participate, not to compete, not to contend and not to win.

"Somebody asked me on the way to the grid on Friday at Long Beach what my expectations were and I said I didn't have any. I said if we don't set the car on fire at every pit stop we will have had a good weekend. So that was the first step, just to participate."

As the season progressed the close-knit organization did a lot more than just participate, and indeed emerged as a real force to be reckoned with. Both drivers made their presence felt at the front of the field, with Allmendinger especially strong at Montreal, Mazda Raceway Laguna Seca and Mexico City.

Despite his outstanding performances in 2004, the youngster says making the final step up from a 240hp Toyota Atlantic car to a 750hp Champ Car was more demanding than he anticipated. "It's a huge difference," he admits. "It's just a different beast. There was so much more power than I was used to and so much more braking force. Your right foot is a big deal in these cars.

"What I've found is that in an Atlantic car you can get a good baseline setup and work with that all year. You definitely have different adjustments at each track but if you get a good baseline and good feel for an Atlantic car, you can work with that all year. But the Champ Car is completely different each weekend and what throws me off is that you need a different feeling in the car each weekend. Some tracks you need a lot of front grip, some tracks you need a lot of rear grip. Some tracks you need a good overall balance. So each weekend you've got to figure out what the car wants for this track."

Then there was the additional challenge of graduating into the Champ Car World Series with a new team: "It was tough to come into the series as a rookie driver and compete, but I think with a rookie team it was 10 times tougher because if we didn't put a good car on the track on Friday morning then we were fighting all weekend to get it there. We couldn't go back to last year's setup and notes. That made it tough, but I think overall, we did a very good job.

"I give the team the highest regards. A lot was put on the team because going into the season we barely had enough guys to do one car and then Michel (Jourdain) was added. There was a huge amount of work to be done and the guys in the team worked their butts off every night at the shop and at the track. They were probably the team that left the latest every night and got there the

Above: He's still a fun-loving kid at heart, but A.J. is all business at the race tracks.
Michael Levitt/LAT

Facing page: The RuSPORT Lola was hard to miss, and quickly became a force.
Phil Abbott/LAT

Above: "Hey, I won it," A.J. tells mentor Carl Russo after clinching the Roshfrans Rookie of the Year Award and $10,000.
MikeLevitt/LAT

Top: Learning the ropes. Allmendinger oversteps the mark a little in Toronto.
Michael Levitt/LAT

Top right: His first Champ Car podium came after a fine team effort in Vancouver.
Lesley Ann Miller/LAT

Bottom right: Allmendinger has emerged as one of America's brightest young stars.
Michael Levitt/LAT

Far right: Justin Wilson impressed with Mi-Jack Conquest Racing and will join A.J. at RuSPORT for the 2005 season.
Michael Kim/LAT

earliest. They've really done a great job.

"They could have made mistakes and they would have had an excuse for those mistakes, but they didn't. We didn't have many mechanical problems and we got all the laps we could during the weekend. From that standpoint I give them the highest regards."

Allmendinger also says he takes great confidence from the commitment made to him by Russo: "It's a big deal because there's not many drivers out there who can say that if they know they make a mistake they're not sure if they're going to be fired or not the next weekend. Carl shows so much confidence in me. If I make a mistake, he's tough. He'll tell me to fix it, but it's not like, if you don't fix it you're fired. He knows it's a learning curve for everybody. He knows how long it takes to come in here and be competitive. Carl has been great -- not just Carl, but the whole team. They show confidence in their drivers."

Allmendinger believes he learned some valuable lessons from mistakes he made in Cleveland and Toronto in July. Indeed, while he is sometimes described as cocky, and certainly has an unshakeable self confidence, one of Allmendinger's most appealing characteristics is a refreshing willingness to accept responsibility when he has dropped the ball.

"The thing I was least happy with in the first part of the year was me making too many mistakes that I'm not accustomed to making," he reflects. "I made too many mistakes that cost us better finishes. I had to go to work on that. I just needed to get through the first stint no matter what the car was like. Once we did that, then it's time to go racing. I learned that after a few races of making the same mistakes.

"At Cleveland we were running third and the car wasn't exactly right. We had it too low. It was bottoming, but we were still third early in the race, and I just made a mistake and lost it. It wasn't so much the spin that got me. It was the 10 laps after we pitted and put new tires on. I was just out of control. I was going off the track a lot and doing stuff that I usually don't do.

"Then in Toronto after getting spun during a yellow I started at the back and started panicking, trying to get around the guys, knowing that Sebastien [Bourdais] was coming up to lap everybody. Once again, I made a mistake and threw it away.

"You see how the race goes and realize that you could've finished second or third. So there were definitely a couple of top fives and maybe a podium or two that I threw away."

Despite the errors, Allmendinger made up an early deficit to Wilson in their battle for top rookie honors, and ended up with a substantial advantage. It was a fight he will cherish for years to come.

"It was great to be able to race with Justin for the rookie title," A.J. says. "He's an excellent driver and to battle with him meant I was doing something right."

Like all top-line drivers, Allmendinger recognizes the importance of physical and mental fitness. He works out on a regular basis and eats carefully but doesn't maintain a rigorously religious diet.

"I try to be on a 'bike or a stationary bike five or six times a week for at least one hour to an hour and a half a day," he says. "I also lift weights every other day.

"I don't have a specific diet, but I know what's good for me. I stay away from fast food. I eat a lot of chicken, pasta, salad and vegetables. I don't restrict myself by saying I can't go eat Mexican food, for example. I know what's good for me. My weak spot is candy. I like candy!

"Physically I feel great. I'm not tired during the races so I'm happy with that. Overall, it's been OK. As long as we keep making progress I'm going to be happy."

But what about his ultimate goal in racing? Many young drivers are totally focused on trying to make it to Formula 1. Allmendinger, however, insists that he will not cross the Pond at any price; for the time being he is more than happy where he is.

"First and foremost I want to win many races and championships in Champ Car," he emphasizes. "That's always been my goal and that's what I want to do. I love these cars and this series and with RuSPORT behind me I believe I can achieve my goals. Down the road, let's see about Formula 1. But I would only do it if it was with one of the top teams. Like I say, I believe racing Champ Cars with RuSPORT is where my career is for many years to come."

Which, of course, jives nicely with team owner Russo's own goals and dreams.

"I think we're very focused under our tent," he says. "We don't spend much time looking around at other people's tents. As long as we keep doing that, keep looking at what we did right and what we did wrong and improve so that our learning rate is the best in the paddock, it doesn't matter how far behind we are, we'll catch people. As long as we're getting better, I'm happy, because like a tic on a dog, we're not going away.

"We have a high goal which is to be the best open-wheel team in North America," Russo continues. "That's the goal and that doesn't mean next week or next year, but over the life cycle of what we're doing. And that's not judged by us or by the press, but judged by the fans and by the world.

"You just don't build that in a day or week or year. If we wanted to rush we would have been in the Champ Car paddock in 2003, but we're proud to be here now on the first phase of a long path."

RuSPORT made impressive strides during its rookie campaign, and all indications suggest that it will continue its upwardly mobile progress in 2005. Indeed, with the addition of Wilson to the driver strength, many pundits expect the team to offer a serious challenge to the might of Newman/Haas Racing.

"We've got two great drivers and a great team," Russo says. "In 2004 we achieved our goal of winning the Rookie of the Year award for A.J., and in '05 our goal is to try to win races and hopefully, if things goes well, we can even contend for the championship."

THE LONG AND THE SHORT OF IT

JUSTIN Wilson followed the well-trodden path from Formula 1 to Champ Cars in 2004, and quickly emerged as a very fast, smooth but aggressive driver. Right away it was clear that here was a major talent that had been classically short-changed by grand prix racing.

FIA International Formula 3000 Champion in 2001, Wilson graduated to F1 in 2003 with Minardi and then was hired by Jaguar. His best result for Jaguar was eighth in the United States GP, but at the end of the year his F1 adventure ground to a halt. He turned instead to the Champ Car World Series and signed with Eric Bachelart's small Mi-Jack Conquest team for 2004.

The lanky Englishman began strongly, finishing sixth in each of the first two races. He was unfortunate not to be able to capitalize on his front row start at Cleveland in July, when he was the innocent party in a first-corner accident, nor quite make the podium after qualifying third for the season finale in Mexico City. But there were plenty of highlights, especially his race-long battle in Portland with primary rookie rival Allmendinger.

"That's how I like it. I like to race hard but fair," Wilson says. "There's nothing more frustrating when you give a guy a little bit of room to either make the move happen or back out of it and he does something silly, and A.J. didn't do that. He was very good. You want to leave just enough room to either make the move happen or not. It's good for TV and it's good for us. I went and spoke to him afterwards and both of us enjoyed our race."

Wilson also quickly grew to appreciate the eclectic selection of race tracks on the Champ Car schedule, from the flat-out Las Vegas Motor Speedway oval to classic road courses and tight, city-center street tracks. And, like many European drivers accustomed to the cutthroat F1 paddock – memorably dubbed "The Piranha Club" by Eddie Jordan – he found the camaraderie among Champ Car drivers a revelation.

"I enjoy the whole scene," he says. "It's an unbelievably friendly atmosphere. It's very tough on track and yet we'll shake hands and ask each other how we're getting on off-track. In some ways it's a bit like kart racing when you're younger. In those days you go to the track and play with your mates beforehand and then you get in the driving seat and you don't give in. It's very competitive once the visor's down."

Wilson's performances with Mi-Jack Conquest Racing, allied to his no-nonsense approach, made him an obvious target for like-minded RuSPORT owner Carl Russo. And relatively early in the off-season, Russo confirmed that Wilson would drive alongside Allmendinger in 2005. The combination is expected to be extremely potent. Wilson, of course, was disappointed when his F1 opportunities dried up at the end of the 2003 season, but he has no regrets whatsoever about the decisions he has made since then.

"If I make a career racing Champ Cars and get to stay in America for years to come, then great," he affirms. "If I got an offer in three or five years to go back [to F1] then I'd look at it. If it was a good offer, I'd go. If it wasn't, I'd stay.

"I can say that I've done Formula 1. Obviously, it was a great experience, but I want to have a chance of winning races and you don't always have the chance in Formula 1, whereas in Champ Cars at least we're all racing similar cars. So if a good F1 opportunity came along at the right time I would seriously look at it, but I'm enjoying myself now and this opportunity with RuSPORT is really fantastic. Carl Russo is here for the long run and I'd love to build my career with his team. I couldn't have hoped for a better opportunity."

FORD-COSWORTH

BUILDING FOR THE FUTURE

by Gordon Kirby

WHEN it comes to high performance, Cosworth is one of the world's most renowned brands. It has been at the forefront of motor racing technology for close to a half-century. During that time it has forged a close relationship with Champ Car racing, and its willingness to develop a powerful, yet cost-effective power plant when the purse strings were in desperate need of being tightened has proven to be one of the most compelling reasons why the Champ Car World Series has emerged from the brink of oblivion.

Cosworth Engineering was founded in 1958 by Keith Duckworth and Mike Costin, two English engineers who already had considerable hands-on racing experience. After successfully building a series of modified four-cylinder Ford racing engines for a variety of applications, Costin and Duckworth were able to convince the Blue Oval to bankroll the Ford-Cosworth DFV (double four-valve) Formula 1 engine which achieved instant success in 1967 with Colin Chapman's Lotus team and Scotsman Jim Clark. Over the next 17 years the DFV won 155 world championship F1 races and 12 world championships, dominating the category like no other engine before or since. Subsequent-generation Ford-Cosworth F1 engines have added another 21 wins so that Ford-Cosworth's tally of 176 grand prix victories is second only to Ferrari.

Cosworth made its Champ Car debut in 1975 with a turbocharged version of the DFV. Developed and raced initially by the Vel's Parnelli Jones team as a challenger to the ubiquitous Offenhausers, the motor was dubbed the DFX. Al Unser scored the engine's first win in 1976 and the DFX went on to replicate the DFV's F1 success, winning 151 USAC and CART races between 1976 and 1989, and claiming nine consecutive CART championships from 1979-'87.

A brand new Ford-Cosworth Champ Car engine, the XB, was debuted by Newman/Haas Racing in 1992, this time with full Ford backing. The XB won 25 races and two championships (1993 and 1995) before being replaced in 1996 by the XD, which was a response to a new challenge from Honda. It turned substantially higher rpm and made more power. The XD won 16 Champ Car races through 1999 when it was supplanted by an even smaller, lighter, higher-revving engine, the XF. This engine was raced for three years and won 18 races before it was superseded in 2003 by the current XFE "spec" engine.

The XFE has proved to be a very successful exercise in cost control. The engine produces 750 horsepower and is designed to run 1,200 miles between rebuilds with a 12,000 rpm rev limit. Without any competing manufacturers, the move to the XFE also allowed Champ Car to enforce a workable ban on traction control, returning the art of throttle control to the drivers and improving the spectacle for the fans.

Development of the XFE was carried out primarily at Cosworth's home base in Northampton, England, although the rebuilding process for the pool of 100 engines is conducted at Cosworth's US headquarters in Torrance, California.

"Obviously, it was a huge task for us both in Cosworth Torrance and in the UK," says Ian Bisco, vice president of Cosworth Inc. "Getting all the necessary parts manufactured in the UK and getting those parts out to us in Torrance and for us to put together the engines and get them tested and distributed was a huge undertaking by everybody at Cosworth."

In its first season the XFE accumulated a grand total of 180,000 miles with only five failures. From 342 race starts in 2003 there was only one in-race engine failure, a rate of less than 0.3 percent! The engine proved equally reliable in 2004.

"There was a lot of skepticism about engines running 1,200 miles and there being parity between all the teams, but those fears are behind us now," declares Bisco. "The teams have realized the engines are very comparable, and that they maintain their performance all the way through to the end of their mileage."

Bisco is justifiably proud that Cosworth has been essential to Champ Car in developing what he believes is an ideal engine package for the times: "We've probably been involved in a wider variety of racing than any other company out there. We've got a very good knowledge base to draw from and I think in conceiving this program with Champ Car, with these rules and regulations, we had to dig deep from our racing roots to come up with the parameters and discuss those with Champ Car. I like to think that with the conditions in the market at the moment we've come up with the ideal answer."

Cosworth Racing was absorbed into the Ford Motor Company empire in 1998. Last fall, however, the company was put up for sale, along with the Jaguar Formula 1 team, and in November 2004 it was bought by Champ Car's two principal owners, Kevin Kalkhoven and Jerry Forsythe. The purchase demonstrated

Above: The XFE's electronic systems are complex but impressively reliable.
Michael Levitt/LAT

Left: Cosworth has carved an enviable reputation with its Champ Car motors.
Michael Levitt/LAT

Far left: Kalkhoven sees Cosworth as a critical element in Champ Car's future.
Lesley Ann Miller/LAT

Above: **There's precious little space in the engine bay, so packaging is crucial.**
Dan Boyd/LAT

Right: **Cylinder heads are assembled.**

Center right: **The main workshop at Cosworth's UK base in Northampton.**

Far right: **Cosworth employs the very latest computer-aided design systems.**
Photos courtesy of Cosworth

Kalkhoven and Forsythe's financial commitment to the business of racing as well as their willingness to adopt aggressive strategies when required.

Kalkhoven and Forsythe now own one of the world's most renowned race engine companies with an impressive record of success over many years across a broad reach of international automobile racing.

Cosworth will continue to support Ford's factory Focus World Rally Championship cars in 2005, and the company intends to develop a variant of the Ford Duratec alloy-block engine for a new Ford Focus 2006 rally car. Ironically, Cosworth also has designed and built an IRL engine that has been campaigned by its bitter production car rival, Chevrolet, the past two years. In addition to maintaining that association in 2005, for the final year of Chevy's IRL program, Cosworth will continue to supply Formula 1 engines to Red Bull Racing (formerly Jaguar) and Minardi.

"When Jerry and I first talked about the possibility of acquiring Cosworth it was something that filled us with a great deal of excitement, partly because we're both motor racing nuts and also because we're businessmen," relates Kalkhoven. "Cosworth is one of the great motorsports engineering companies in the world. Its legacy extends on both sides of the Atlantic to many, many victories and championships. When we started talking and thinking about it, we also began to realize the opportunities for the future. While Cosworth does have a significant heritage and legacy, what is equally important is where we take it from here.

"The first aspect of that is the Formula 1 side, and I'm delighted that the Red Bull team will be on the Formula 1 grid in 2005 with Cosworth engines, as will Minardi."

Another key reason behind Kalkhoven and Forsythe's purchase of Cosworth was to continue an uninterrupted supply of Cosworth XFE engines to the Champ Car World Series.

"CART – and subsequently Champ Car – has used Ford-Cosworth engines for many years and some of the great victories in the series have been scored with Cosworth engines," notes Kalkhoven. "The Cosworth engine we use today in the Champ Car World Series has proven to be an outstanding engine with significant horsepower. The engine has done everything that we asked of it, and for the foreseeable future we will continue to use the Cosworth XFE engine which has proved to be so reliable and so competitive in the past two years."

Kalkhoven and Forsythe also are taking a serious look at the possibility of Cosworth developing engines for Champ Car's ladder system formulae: "We are completely committed to Toyota for the 2005 Toyota Atlantic season," says Kalkhoven, "but we will examine the 2006 season and beyond and discuss the engines with a number of manufacturers. There are certainly some interesting opportunities out there."

Outside racing, Kalkhoven has some ambitious plans for Cosworth's Torrance facility: "We will extend the capabilities of Cosworth into the very fast-growing tuner car market. That g eneration of folks from 16 and above, typically ending at about 30, are dedicated, rabid fans of their motor cars and wish to continue to improve them. The Cosworth brand is a wonderful platform to be able to provide tuner accessories for these folks."

As a precursor to this initiative Cosworth released three performance kits for the Ford Focus at the SEMA show in the fall of 2004.

Meanwhile, NASCAR has powerfully demonstrated that the most important factor in ensuring a successful racing series is having the sanctioning body squarely in control – writing and enforcing sensible rules and enjoying good relationships with the manufacturers competing in its series. It's abundantly clear that if Champ Car is to achieve long-term success it must be effective in this key area where

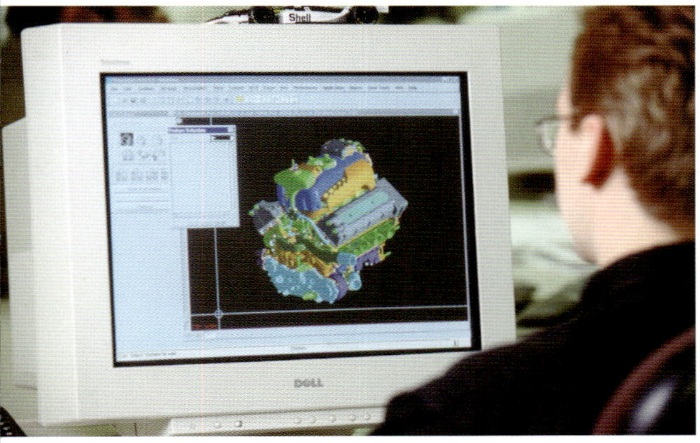

so many other sanctioning bodies have failed.

"Manufacturer support is by definition a two-edged sword," observes Kalkhoven. "The financial support that the manufacturers bring is obviously significant but the financial support when it disappears, as well we know in Champ Car, causes some significant heartburn. We lived through this and we've taken a very deliberate approach. We've worked with one manufacturer very successfully – our partners at Ford – in order to provide something that is increasingly important in motorsports which is the fact that it is entertainment. It's not just a purist form of racing.

"We have to provide entertainment for our fans, and that entertainment comes from not just seeing manufacturers compete with each other but seeing close and competitive racing where the driver is the determining factor – not the manufacturer or the amount of money they've spent. What we've achieved in Champ Car is a series where the driver is very much the king, where any driver – now that they all have very much the same package – can rise to the top, and where new teams can come in and rise to the top as we have seen with RuSPORT and A.J. Allmendinger."

Thus has Cosworth become an essential element in Champ Car racing's newfound stability.

"Cosworth is an icon of motorsports and we're thrilled to continue its development," says Kalkhoven. "We look forward to the next generation of Cosworth technology and we look forward to having Cosworth engines in the Bridgestone Presents the Champ Car World Series Powered by Ford for a long time to come, together with a very successful relationship with Ford."

Ford and Cosworth's marriage with Champ Car already has produced an effective, crowd-pleasing blend of technology and close competition. And thanks to Kalkhoven, Forsythe and the Cosworth engineers, the Champ Car World Series is looking toward the future with renewed vigor.

THE HEART OF THE MATTER

Dan Boyd/LAT

ONE of the most remarkable aspects of the Cosworth XFE engine project is the equality of performance across the pool of 100 engines. Indeed, regular dynamometer testing has shown that the variation in power output between engines is even less than anticipated.

"There was a 20-horsepower variation in the planning but we've come out within 10 horsepower on our dyno tests," notes Cosworth Inc. Vice President Ian Bisco, proudly. "All the engines we've run on the dyno that were mileaged-out were within the specified percentage parameters. Power loss was negligible, all within the tolerances specified."

Because of the much higher mileage achieved by the XFE in comparison to its predecessors, Bisco has not had to make any major changes or addition to his engine-building staff in Torrance, despite the fact he now has to service the entire field.

"Historically, we've always looked after about a third of the field and an engine that used to run around 400 miles [between rebuilds]," says Bisco. "What we've done is triple the life of an engine, so in terms of rebuilds per year and manpower to service the engines, no real change was needed. We ended up doing around 200 rebuilds a year, as we have in the past."

What has changed is the number of personnel required to support the program at the races. In 2002, says Bisco, only eight technicians were employed to oversee the five (sometimes six) Cosworth customers. Now, because the company is contractually bound to provide more spare engines and service three times as many cars, 16 people are needed, along with a second support truck to house the operation.

The administrative duties also have increased dramatically, especially in terms of keeping track of all the data and individual records of each engine. Furthermore, the ECUs (engine control units) are randomly passed out and collected on a daily basis by Champ Car officials, just like pop-off valves, to ensure fair play.

"The ECUs are locked and hard-coded so that nobody can do anything devious," explains Bisco. "Champ Car monitors the ECUs and distributes them. If there was a potential to get an electronic whiz to fiddle with the ECU, a team might have an advantage for the session that they have that particular ECU. But the next session, or race, that ECU is going to go to somebody else. So there's no advantage to doing that."

So far as the engine characteristics are concerned, the power band of the current XFE is a little narrower than it was a few years ago, requiring more gear-shifting. However, says Bisco, "the torque is probably up 25 percent on what it was in 2002. It's a very fat torque curve. The boost comes in at 7-8,000 rpm, and from 8,000 to 12,000 rpm it's a very flat torque curve. That really helps the cars get up to speed quicker, even without traction control. The good drivers are very good at modulating the power and sensing where the power is and making the most of it."

WESTERN UNION
sparco
WESTERN UNION

LOLA and CHAMP CAR

THE SECRETS TO LOLA'S SEARCH FOR SUCCESS

by Gordon Kirby

LOLA is arguably the world's most successful racing car manufacturer. The company has been in business for almost half a century and has catered to almost every category of racing outside stock cars.

Founded in 1956 by design genius Eric Broadley, Lola has manufactured a succession of important sports and formula cars of all kinds, helping spawn the iconic Ford GT40 back in the early '60s and providing the chassis for Honda's first successful Formula 1 foray in 1967 and '68. Lola also became a mainstay of American racing, competing in everything from SCCA formula and sports cars to Can-Am to Formula 5000 and, of course, Champ Cars.

Lola's first Champ Car raced successfully in 1966 in the hands of drivers such as Jackie Stewart and Graham Hill, and in 1978 Al Unser achieved the unique feat of winning three 500-mile races in one year, driving a Lola for Jim Hall's Chaparral team. Its first championship victory came in 1984, when Mario Andretti and Newman/Haas Racing scooped the top prize. Over the years Lola has established itself as the most successful and enduring brand in Champ Car racing with a total of 154 wins, and counting.

Going back to the mid-1960s Carl Haas was Lola's North American sales agent and distributor. Haas was the driving force behind Lola's long line of American successes, and his race team won titles in both F5000 (in partnership with Chaparral creator Jim Hall) and the Can-Am before moving into the Champ Car arena in 1983 in a new partnership with famed actor/racer Paul Newman.

Meanwhile, founder Broadley retained his interest in Formula 1, and a variety of unsuccessful cars were built and raced from 1983-'93. In 1997, Broadley tried to re-enter F1 with his own team. The consequences were disastrous. The project pushed Lola into bankruptcy, and after more than 40 years in business Broadley had to sell out.

Fortunately for the sport in general, Lola Cars, based in Huntingdon, England, an hour or so's drive northeast of London, was acquired by Irish-born entrepreneur Martin Birrane, who set about restoring the company's damaged reputation. A tough-minded businessman as well as a tremendous racing enthusiast and widely experienced amateur racer, Birrane also owns Mondello Park, Ireland's leading road circuit venue. Birrane's property sales business is based in London, trading and developing property all over the United Kingdom and Ireland, and in Spain.

Birrane recalls being faced with a dilemma after he had finalized the purchase of Lola in 1997 – and realized what a parlous state the company was in: "Was I going to just run it down? Or was I going to rebuild it back up to what it was in the past which was the biggest and the best racing car manufacturer in the world?

"I made the decision to do the second of those choices," he affirms.

So, where to start? Well, in spite of some negative suggestions from outside sources, Birrane quickly realized one of the cornerstones of his restructuring plan would be to rebuild his company's emphasis on Champ Car racing. The series had provided a strong platform in the past, and Birrane decided to focus much of his attention on regaining Lola's market share, which had been largely eclipsed by a rival British car constructor, Reynard.

"Champ Car was very important to me despite being told I shouldn't waste my money trying to get back in," Birrane says. "Remember there were four other manufacturers back then. There was not just Reynard who were dominating. There was Penske, Dan Gurney's Eagle and there was Swift which had Carl Haas behind it. There was serious competition; but there's nothing like a challenge and therefore I decided we were going to compete and beat the opposition. I knew we had to work at it."

With Haas having lost patience with the old Lola management and instead concluding a deal to run American-built Swift chassis in 1997, and with Reynard otherwise controlling the scene, Lola did not win a single Champ Car race for three years. But Birrane was determined to get Lola back in the winner's circle. A new Champ Car was designed for 1998 and campaigned by unheralded German rookie Arnd Meier. The following year Helio Castroneves served notice of progress with some stellar performances aboard Hogan Racing's B99/00, albeit stymied by wretched luck. By 2000 Birrane had been able to convince Haas to return to the Lola fold and in May of that year Michael Andretti and Newman/Haas Racing scored Lola's first Champ Car victory in three and half years at Twin Ring Motegi.

Lola went on to win seven races in 2000, then 10 in '01 and 16 in '02 as Cristiano da Matta took the championship for Newman/Haas. In 2003, Lola won 17 of the 18 races as Paul Tracy claimed the title with Jerry Forsythe's team, leaving the once-mighty Reynard concern – which had itself fallen into receivership in 2002 – with a solitary victory. The wheel had turned full circle. Lola was unbeaten in 2004 and looks likely to remain that way for some time to come. Birrane had achieved his goal of re-establishing Lola, but, as he correctly points out, had done so in a very damaged environment. Indeed both the economy and the overall state of open-wheel racing in America were in decline.

Left: **Martin Birrane (left) and Rupert Manwaring have combined to ensure a bright future for the historic Lola name.**
LAT Photographic

"Having got there we had what you could say was a Pyrrhic victory because no sooner had we got to be the dominant chassis, [than] things turned down," Birrane says. "Reynard went bust and a lot of people thought that was good news for us. But I knew it wasn't, because the economy was turning down and people would not be looking to do the same amount of development and improvements, so that our huge engineering resource would be underused.

"That was a very painful time for us because we didn't downsize in time and we lost money. Our accounts were blood red. It always takes too long to turn around. It's like turning the Queen Mary. When you know you want to make a change, it just takes forever and during that time you're bleeding because you have to pay your overheads and your staff. In the time it took to downsize, it cost us a lot of money."

Thankfully, over time, the outlook began to improve. Lola went from a workforce of 283 people three years ago to 180 people last year and back up to 243 employees in early 2005.

"A lot of these additions are in the non-core businesses," Birrane says. "Three years ago we had 50 engineers. That went down to 23 between six months and a year ago and we've built that back up again to probably 30. We lost a couple of names but we still had the core team and they remain with us, and we're not afraid to take on any project."

The managing director of Lola Cars International, Rupert Manwaring, has a wealth of experience in the sport, having managed the Lotus and Tyrrell Formula 1 teams during the 1980s and '90s, among other postings, and he makes the point that Birrane has made as big an investment as anyone in the Champ Car World Series.

"In 1998, Martin decided to invest a lot of money and resources in developing the car to beat Reynard," Manwaring says. "That was an expensive exercise and we rarely passed on the costs to the customers because [the marketplace] was so competitive. Eventually our cars got the upper hand and we were about to reap the rewards of all that investment. At that point CART unfortunately went into decline, but we had made that investment

THE
CONSTRUCTOR'S
CHAMPCAR

BIRRANE THE RACER

MARTIN Birrane started racing himself way back in 1966, and soon was driving American sedans such as Ford Fairlanes, Falcons and Mustangs in British saloon car races. He then got into long-distance racing with a variety of sports and GT cars. He tried his hand at Formula Atlantic one year and also ran Formula 5000 in the UK in 1974, driving the unique Brabham BT43 he had traded with Bernie Ecclestone for a Porsche Carrera.

In 1978 Birrane broke his back in a parachuting accident which kept him out of racing for a while, but otherwise he's raced every year. He's competed in 10 Le Mans 24-hour races, finishing three times and winning his class once in 1985 driving a BMW M1 Procar. In the early '90s he even did some NASCAR Winston Cup racing – as an entrant – in a Chevrolet he bought from Richard Childress.

Last year Birrane, who's 69, raced a historic Lola T212 sports car a few times and contested the Le Mans Classic with Murray Smith in a de Cadenet sports/racer. He plans to do half a dozen races this year and also wants to race a Formula 5000 car again.

"I'd love to do more racing," Birrane says. "I've still got my FIA grade B license so I could drive at Le Mans if I wanted. I could drive at any race except for Formula 1."

Birrane bought Mondello Park in his native Ireland 18 years ago. The track stages a dozen car race meetings each year, eight motorcycle races and eight rallycrosses, as well as hosting track days and car launches. "Two years ago we had 300 days of use. This year it's about 260 but still, that's going well," Birrane remarks.

In recent years Birrane has rebuilt and upgraded the previously rustic Mondello: "I decided to do the job properly from the paddock and new garages to hospitality suites and a new tower, to extending the track and making it a full 3.5 kilometers (2.2 miles). We did the lot and it's transformed it into a profitable venture.

We've turned it into a proper FIA grade 2 track. I have this problem: I need to fix things! I did that for auld lang syne. I wanted to get the track back in use for the Irish competitor."

Top: Birrane won his class at Le Mans in 1985, driving a distinctive BMW M1.
LAT Photographic

Right: The Irish-born entrepreneur has raced successfully in a variety of cars.
LAT Photographic

Left: Birrane is the proud recipient of the 2004 Champ Car Constructor's Championship – Lola's third in a row.
Michael Levitt/LAT

and it wasn't in our interest to walk away from the series.

"Obviously, the winter of 2003 was a terrible time for everybody. We didn't know whether to make cars, stockpile cars, or do nothing. In the end we chose the middle ground. We made a few cars and hoped that things would work out, which they did.

"We were delighted that the guys in OWRS (Open Wheel Racing Series) were able to take over and revive the series," Manwaring adds. "Business has obviously not been the best the last two years but we are really excited about the way things are going. There's a feeling of excitement inside the series that Champ Car racing has a big future, and hopefully we can continue to be a big part of it, which is obviously our plan."

Nevertheless, with all the Champ Car teams set to race Lolas in 2005, Manwaring admits his company will need to take a close look at the cost of producing cars in today's changing economic climate.

"We're still adjusting to the new situation where everyone is running Lolas," he says. "That's different for us and it means our philosophy is very different compared to when Martin reinvested so much money and resources to beat Reynard. We need to look very hard at our production costs and how we design the cars to get some cost out of it; and the teams need a more efficient car to run because the economic circumstances have changed. That's something we're very mindful of. I think over the next two years we're going to have to work really hard to make sure we are the chassis that the teams continue to choose.

"The interesting thing at the moment," emphasizes Manwaring, "is by not having car manufacturers competing it gives us a very stable platform. There's a downside because the teams aren't spending in development and new parts, but the important thing is we have a really stable and robust platform as a base for the promotion of the series."

Manwaring takes pleasure from watching his cars in action and is a big believer in the current chassis and engine formula: "I think the strength that Champ Car now has is it's got a very exciting car with a fantastic power unit," he enthuses. "I always make a point of going out on the circuit and watching the cars, and there is no doubt that there's enough performance and excitement in that package to give the fans what they want.

"One thing that's obvious is that these are real racing cars that need to be driven. They've got lots of power, they slide and drift, all of those things. That's the sort of thing that drivers are brought up on which may not be the case with other big formulas in America.

"I think the [Cosworth] engine [package] is fantastic," Manwaring adds. "I think it's just brilliant. The power is there and the sound too. It's great to listen to and watch, and it's unbelievably reliable. Champ Car has created a great engine formula that's really working well."

Lola's home base in Cambridgeshire, England, will be fully occupied in 2005, building an array of Formula Nippon, Formula 3, LMP2 prototype sports cars and the new A1GP cars, in addition to its Champ Car mainstay. Furthermore, Birrane has developed a strong agenda of engineering and consulting projects for his subsidiary business, Lola Group Holdings.

"The non-core businesses outside of racing are absolutely flying," he says. "Lola Group Holdings includes design for outside parties, and the composite business has gone into overdrive. We make composite parts for four Formula 1 teams. We also make composites for the ministry of defense and all kinds of military equipment for aircraft and helicopters. That business has really picked up. It went from about $5 million to $10 million turnover and we're expecting $20 million within the next 18 months. That side of the business is going well and the niche engineering is picking up."

Birrane, meanwhile, is keen to emphasize his long-term commitment to Champ Car racing: "I've got to know and like the people in Champ Car racing. They're our customers and I would have felt like I was letting them down if I closed Lola two or three years ago. It's a fact of life that we've been losing money on Champ Car. It's true to say, in fact, that only one year, 2001, did we actually make a profit. But if you're in something for the long-term – which was a decision I made in the first three months after I bought the company – then it's wrong to cut and run when things aren't going properly.

"My property business is very profitable and has been growing all along, and it makes it possible to do daft things like turning my hobby into a business and bearing with it until it comes to fruition," Birrane adds with a wry smile. "But I have no doubt that Lola will be seriously profitable in the next two years. I'm convinced I will get my investment back, and a return on that too."

PacifiCare
HERDEZ
McCORMICK
McDonald's

TEAM-BY-TEAM REVIEW

A total of nine different teams and 24 drivers contested the 2004 Bridgestone Presents the Champ Car World Series Powered by Ford. In the following pages, the Autocourse editors analyze what went right – and wrong – for each organization.

NEWMAN/HAAS RACING

Base: Lincolnshire, Illinois
Drivers: Sebastien Bourdais, Bruno Junqueira
Sponsors: McDonald's, PacifiCare
Engines: Ford-Cosworth XFE
Chassis: Lola
Tires: Bridgestone Potenza
Wins: 9 (Bourdais 7, Junqueira 2)
Poles: 9 (Bourdais 8, Junqueira 1)
Total points: 710
Bourdais 369 (1st), Junqueira 341 (2nd)

2 SÉBASTIEN BOURDAIS

Michael Levitt/LAT

6 BRUNO JUNQUEIRA

Michael Levitt/LAT

AFTER an off-season of turmoil for the Champ Car World Series, the most stable team in the paddock translated its solidarity into results as Newman/Haas Racing won nine races, nine pole positions and finished first and second in the final standings. Indeed when Sebastien Bourdais took the checkered flag in Mexico City ahead of teammate Bruno Junqueira to secure his first Vanderbilt Cup triumph, it represented the fifth championship title since actor/racer Paul Newman and racing entrepreneur Carl A. Haas combined forces in 1983. Perhaps more significantly it was the first time they had laid claim to the top two positions.

Newman/Haas' quest for the championship began in perfect style as Junqueira (PacifiCare Lola) and Bourdais (McDonald's Lola) shared the front row for the season opener at Long Beach. Even with the departure of long-serving senior engineer Peter Gibbons, both Craig Hampson (Bourdais) and Rocky Rocquelin (Junqueira) continued to be masters of their craft. The two race engineers provided the technical expertise that allowed the team to monopolize the front row of the starting grid four times in the 14 races and saw at least one Newman/Haas driver on the front row on 11 occasions. They were just as successful on race days, clinching no fewer than six one-two finishes – including the last three races in a row – and only three times failing to have at least one of its stars on the podium. Remarkable statistics.

The team's dedication was typified by its standard of preparation. Chief mechanics Pedro Campuzano (Bourdais) and Donny Hoevel (Junqueira) and their regular crews did a superb job in building and maintaining the cars as neither driver was sidelined with a mechanical failure during the season.

Newman/Haas Racing's intensity was epitomized perfectly under the lights in Las Vegas, where Bourdais and Junqueira staged a battle for the ages as the clock struck midnight. From Lap 83 through until the checkered flag on Lap 166, the duo monopolized the proceedings. Team orders, as usual, did not come into play as Junqueira and Bourdais battled side-by-side for the final 15 laps, never separated by more than two-tenths of a second, before the Frenchman edged out his Brazilian teammate by the sixth-closest margin of victory in Champ Car history, a scant 0.066 second.

Bourdais was very much the man to beat in 2004, eclipsing teammate Junqueira in every conceivable way and thoroughly vindicating the team's decision to hire him following an impressive test at the end of the 2002 season. "Sebastien was quick from the very beginning," noted team co-owner Paul Newman, "but more than that he gave really marvelous feedback to the crew. It was pretty quickly decided that he would drive for us if the pay was right. It was. And it's going to get better."

Above: **Newman/Haas employed a unique front wing mount for its Lolas.**
Phil Abbott/LAT

Right: **The obligatory champions photo: Newman, Junqueira, Bourdais and Haas.**

Left: **Bourdais and race engineer Craig Hampson developed a strong bond.**
Photographs: Mike Levitt/LAT

Far left: **A picture of concentration.**
Michael Kim/LAT

Bottom left: **Junqueira won at Montreal with the "alternate" Bridgestone tires.**
Phil Abbott/LAT

Below: **Bruno won also in Australia.**
Lesley Ann Miller/LAT

THE ULTIMATE ONE-TWO PUNCH

Winning a championship is no easy task. It takes an elusive combination of driving skill, strategy, mechanical reliability and of course a little bit of luck.

By claiming Newman/Haas Racing's fifth Champ Car title, Sebastien Bourdais joined an illustrious group comprising Mario and Michael Andretti, Nigel Mansell and Cristiano da Matta. Even so, the 2004 campaign created a new high-water mark for the Lincolnshire, Illinois-based operation as Bourdais and teammate Bruno Junqueira dominated the top two positions in the point standings. It was only the fifth time in the past 26 years that a team had achieved the feat. (Team Penske managed it on three occasions, in 1979, '81 and 94, while the most recent occurrence was in 1998 when Alex Zanardi and Jimmy Vasser finished first and second for Target/Chip Ganassi Racing.)

Auto racing, however, stands in stark contrast to most stick and ball sports; teammates compete against each other for wins and titles. Though Bourdais and Junqueira worked together for the majority of each weekend, sharing data to assist their engineers in optimizing the performance of their cars, once the green flag dropped it was each man for himself.

The benefit of their cooperation manifested itself right away as Newman/Haas Racing shared the front row of the grid at the season opener. Indeed, qualifying at Long Beach was a pointer for things to come, and it soon became apparent that the greatest obstacle to the championship for either Bourdais or Junqueira would most likely come from within their team's own ranks.

Much of the credit for Newman/Haas' success must go to general manager Brian Lisles, team manager John "TZ" Tzouanakis and the group they have put together, many of whom have been with the team for at least 10 years. Lisles, who joined the organization in 1989, and Tzouanakis, who has been with the team since its inception, kept everyone focused on their goals and displayed the leadership needed to make Newman/Haas the best team in 2004 while still allowing its two drivers to battle it out on the race track. It speaks volumes that neither car was forced to retire from a race with a mechanical problem all season.

FORSYTHE CHAMPIONSHIP RACING

Base: Indianapolis, Indiana
Drivers: Paul Tracy, Patrick Carpentier, Rodolfo Lavin
Sponsors: Indeck, Corona
Engines: Ford-Cosworth XFE
Chassis: Lola
Tires: Bridgestone Potenza
Wins: 3 (Tracy 2, Carpentier 1)
Poles: 4 (Tracy 3, Carpentier 1)
Total points: 676
Carpentier 266 (3rd), Tracy 254 (4th), Lavin 156 (14th)

PAUL TRACY
Michael Levitt/LAT

PATRICK CARPENTIER
Michael Levitt/LAT

RODOLFO LAVIN
Michael Levitt/LAT

ODDLY, despite coming off the most successful season in its history, Forsythe Championship Racing found itself clouded in uncertainty as the winter months unfolded. Paul Tracy, of course, would continue to lead the team as he sought to defend his hard-earned Champ Car World Series crown, but there was intense speculation as to whether or not long-time Forsythe driver Patrick Carpentier would remain with the organization – especially after it was announced that young Mexican Rodolfo Lavin would be joining the team with high-profile sponsorship from Corona.

The indecision was caused by a lack of sponsorship following the enforced withdrawal of its stalwart supporter, Player's Ltd., due to increasingly tight anti-tobacco legislation. Eventually, just a few weeks before the start of the season, Jerry Forsythe confirmed he would expand the team to include a third car, with Carpentier joining Tracy in their familiar blue-and-white color scheme (albeit now bearing allegiance to the team owner's Indeck group of companies, a proven leader in power generation technology).

FCR's Vice President of Operations Neil Micklewright and Team Manager Phil LePan suddenly were faced with the task of ramping up the operation, and they did so to remarkably good effect.

Tracy, indeed, won the opening race at Long Beach, and Carpentier also led a couple of laps on his way to a fourth-place finish. Ironically, given the earlier uncertainty, the French-Canadian went on to produce his best-ever start to a Champ Car campaign, adding another pair of fourths and a runner-up finish in Milwaukee to emerge as a genuine title challenger.

Carpentier's championship bid fizzled out in midseason following a rare engine failure at Cleveland and a couple of incidents, neither of which were his fault, but he bounced back to win convincingly at Mazda Raceway Laguna Seca -- for the second year in a row. He won the pole, too, at Las Vegas. His partnership with race engineer Eric Zeto and chief mechanic Jason Weatherford played a pivotal role in his successes, which culminated in an equal-career-best third in the final point standings.

Tracy's gifted race engineer Todd Malloy took on an additional responsibility in '04 – that of filling the void left by the "retirement" of noted aerodynamicist/engineer/guru Tony Cicale, who had come to be regarded as one of the few people in the paddock who could keep the feisty "PT" on an even keel. Whether coincidental or not, Tracy lacked the consistency – and patience – that he had displayed in his triumphant '03 campaign, and was involved in more than his fair share of incidents. He added another commanding victory in Vancouver and claimed three poles, but could do no better than fourth in the championship.

New recruit Lavin, meanwhile, benefited enormously from being able to draw on the experience of his teammates, and was guided impressively by race engineer Mike Pawlowski and chief mechanic Dave Stephens. Lavin showed a promising turn of pace on occasion, raising his profile enormously and making the most of his opportunity by claiming a career-best second on the grid in Vancouver and a well-earned runner-up finish at Road America.

FCR maintained its reputation as a top-tier team, claiming a total of 10 podium finishes during the year, including a streak of seven in a row – shared, remarkably, among all three drivers – which only ended when Tracy spun out of a potentially race-winning position at Surfers Paradise.

Right: Paul Tracy began his year with a commanding win at Long Beach.
Phil Abbott/LAT

Right: The 2003 series champion also triumphed on home soil in Vancouver.
Lesley Ann miller/LAT

Bottom left: The brain trust: Jerry Forsythe chats with Neil Micklewright.
Lesley Ann miller/LAT

Below: Carpentier once again proved to be a powerful force at Laguna Seca.
Phil Abbott/LAT

Below right: Acknowledging the cheers of the crowd after his win in California.
Lesley Ann Millert/LAT

Left: Jerry Forsythe prefers to stay out of the spotlight but has made a massive commitment to the Champ Car series.
Michael Levitt/LAT

Below: Rodolfo Lavin improved by leaps and bounds after joining Forsythe.
Dan Streck/LAT

STEPPING UP TO THE PLATE

Gaining respect represents one of life's greatest challenges, and on the race track it is especially difficult given the pressure-cooker environment and regular race-weekend opportunities for judgments to be made by fans and rivals alike.

Rodolfo Lavin, in particular, faced a difficult task when his long-time sponsor, Grupo Modelo S.A. de C.V., through its famed Corona beer brand, made it possible for him to join the reigning champion team, Forsythe Championship Racing, alongside acknowledged Champ Car stars Paul Tracy and Patrick Carpentier. After all, the 26-year-old from San Luis Potosi, Mexico, hadn't produced much in the way of results from a handful of seasons in Indy Lights and Toyota Atlantic, and his rookie Champ Car season in 2003 with Walker Racing netted merely three top-10 finishes.

Nevertheless, after his first few tests with the Forsythe team – which entailed a switch from Walker's unloved Reynard chassis to the ubiquitous Lola – Lavin began to turn some very respectable lap times. Both Tracy and Carpentier suggested prior to the season opener that Lavin might spring a surprise or two as the year progressed. They were right.

Lavin, indeed, posted the fifth fastest time in the opening practice session at Long Beach, and was third in Friday's brief pre-qualifying practice, outpacing Carpentier on each occasion. He slipped back in official qualifying but the die had been cast. Several times during the first half of the season he posted some creditable lap times, especially during practice. To his chagrin, however, qualifying was generally a different story. Until Vancouver, that is, when he posted the fastest time in final qualifying and ensured himself a front row starting position.

Michael Levitt/LAT

A spin early in the race cost him any hope of a strong finish, but at least he had made his mark for the first time.

"It was a great feeling to be up there starting on the front row," he recalled. "At the time I just felt that it would be the beginning of good results for me and the team. I have been working really, really hard for many, many years and I felt as if we were starting to get into a nice groove."

True to his word, Lavin rode that momentum into the next event at Road America where he took advantage of a timely full-course caution to finish a strong second – by far the best result of his career to date. He drove well, too, at Las Vegas Motor Speedway, guiding his #3 Corona Lola to a fourth-place finish, and received the ultimate accolade at the season-ending banquet in Mexico City when he was presented (above) with a healthy check from the Robert Bosch Corporation.

"It was amazing to accept the Bosch Most Improved Driver award," said Lavin. "That is a very special award because the drivers are the ones who vote for it. These guys know how hard it is out there on the track because they have experienced it. We did not achieve everything we wanted last year but we made really good progress. Mr. Jerry Forsythe has been great to me, giving me the great opportunity to win in his team."

HERDEZ COMPETITION

Base: Indianapolis, Indiana
Drivers: Mario Dominguez, Ryan Hunter-Reay
Sponsor: Grupo Herdez
Engines: Ford-Cosworth XFE
Chassis: Lola
Tires: Bridgestone Potenza
Wins: 1 (Hunter-Reay)
Poles: 1 (Hunter-Reay)
Total points: 443
Dominguez 244 **(5th), Hunter-Reay** 199 **(9th)**

KEITH Wiggins' Herdez Competition team hoped to significantly up its game in 2004 after winning a race in each of the two previous seasons. The evergreen Brazilian Roberto Moreno was replaced by American up-and-comer Ryan Hunter-Reay, fresh off a promising rookie campaign with American Spirit Team Johansson. Mario Dominguez, who earned wins for the team at Australia in 2002 and Miami in 2003, was counted on to maintain his rapid rate of maturation.

After expanding to two cars in 2003, Herdez worked to strengthen its technical base. Team manager Vince Kremer brought on board engineers Will Phillips (from Rocketsports) and Michael Cannon (from Forsythe Racing) to augment highly respected technical director Tom Brown, while crew chiefs remained Mark Mason (car #4) and Daryl Fox (car #55).

In the end, Herdez achieved a single victory, so at least it didn't lose any ground in that respect. But fifth (Dominguez) and ninth (Hunter-Reay) in the title chase was a somewhat disappointing result for the Indianapolis-based team.

The win, however, was especially memorable, as Hunter-Reay led every one of the 250 laps from the pole at the Milwaukee Mile. His best road race, by contrast, came at Road America, where he qualified on the front row and finished fourth.

If points were awarded for qualifying, the Floridian would have been looking good. His record of starting among the top 10 in every race was matched only by the Newman/Haas pair, Sebastien Bourdais and Bruno Junqueira. But his race results lacked consistency. In the final seven races, for example, he claimed a trio of top-five finishes, while his best result in the other four races was a lowly 13th.

"The team is the most professional organization I've ever been with and I learned a lot from them," noted Hunter-Reay. "We had our really high highs and low lows this year and it was frustrating from that point of view because we came right out of the box and won the third race of the season. But we struggled on street circuits with low speed grip, and obviously that was a big problem in the Champ Car series because we have a lot of races on street circuits."

Dominguez failed to score a victory but his season was highlighted by a podium finish at Monterrey after an early spin dropped him to the back of the field. Additional third-place finishes were achieved at Montreal and Surfers Paradise.

"Keith has done a great job of getting the right people for the right jobs and everyone worked together really well," said the Mexican. "It was a team effort from everybody and we progressed together. We've got more engineers, more experienced people and have developed the car. We had a much more competitive package."

Right: Dominguez didn't win a race but he continued his steady improvement.
Phil Abbott/LAT

Left: Enrique Hernandez-Pons Torres celebrates with RHR in Milwaukee.
Michael Levitt/LAT

Below: Mark Mason's boys are a blur servicing Hunter-Reay in Milwaukee.
Phil Sedgwick/LAT

Bottom left: A podium for Dominguez in Monterrey was cause for celebration.
Michael Levitt/LAT

SUPER MARIO

As a child, racing go-karts and growing up in Mexico City, the thought of competing in a Champ Car at the famed Autodromo Hermanos Rodriguez in his hometown was merely a dream for Mario Dominguez. After years of hard work and dedication, Dominguez made his fantasy a reality when he joined the Champ Car World Series with Herdez Competition in 2002. He then took the concept to a whole new level in 2003 and 2004 as the only native driver to have earned a podium finish in both Mexican events. The achievements boosted his popularity to a new level in his homeland.

Now recognized as one of Mexico's brightest sporting stars, "Super Mario" Dominguez has thrived on the emotions, pressure and passion he has experienced twice each year – at either end of the Champ Car season – racing in his native country. Such fervor has nurtured a fresh ambition too: "One of the goals in life that I am determine to achieve is definitely to win a Champ Car race in Mexico," he asserts. "The Mexican fans deserve it and I intend to give them their first victory in Mexico."

Dominguez enjoys exuberant support from his Mexican fans by virtue of the two victories and six additional podiums he has achieved during his three seasons in the Champ Car World Series. His popularity has been further bolstered by his fifth-place finish in the 2004 standings, and he relishes the responsibility of representing his country: "I can't really describe the feeling of being a Mexican driver racing at a Champ Car race in Mexico," he says. "It is unbelievable. We have the most passionate, loyal and energetic fans in the world and I am so proud to represent them. I am incredibly honored by their support."

Dominguez's support from Mexico is not limited to his fans; he has enjoyed loyal commercial patronage from Mexican corporations throughout his career.

"Without a doubt, I would not be where I am today without the incredible support and partnerships throughout my career from companies like Herdez, Del Valle, Televisa and Telcel," he acknowledges. "I feel great responsibility to succeed not only for myself, but also for my partners. They have supported my career, and through my results I help them grow their brands, especially in Mexico where fans are so brand-loyal. We have mutually rewarding relationships; they support me and I do my best to represent them on the podium. It is fantastic these companies support their native athletes."

RuSPORT

Base: Loveland, Colorado
Drivers: Michel Jourdain Jr., A.J. Allmendinger (R)
Sponsor: Gigante, BG Products, Red Bull, Western Union
Engines: Ford-Cosworth XFE
Chassis: Lola
Tires: Bridgestone Potenza
Wins: 0
Poles: 0 **Total points:** 414
Allmendinger 229 (6th), **Jourdain** 185 (12th)

Carl Russo, it seems, is never one to shy away from a challenge. After racing sporadically over the previous 25 years, during which time he concentrated on carving a spectacular career in the business world, he returned with a vengeance – and a long-term plan – in the 2002 Toyota Atlantic Championship. The results were nothing to write home about, but then Russo himself never really had any intention of pursuing a career as a driver. Instead, he was laying the groundwork for the future.

He returned in 2003 under a new banner, RuSPORT, and hired a couple of young guns to spearhead his operation. The rest, as they say, is history. A.J. Allmendinger romped to the championship while Aaron Justus (a former FF2000 champion who had started out as Russo's driver coach the previous season) backed him up admirably.

And so to 2004. The decision had been made to graduate into the Champ Car ranks, and most of the pieces already were in place. It's true that the majority of the crew had precious little Champ Car experience, but there was a wealth of racing knowledge from which to draw. Team president Jeremy Dale, a successful driver in his own right, had joined Russo after serving as managing director of the Barber Dodge Pro Series. Operations director Steve Wulff (whose PDR team had fielded Russo's Toyota Atlantic foray in '02) had been involved in the sport as a driver and/or a manager for over 25 years. Chief engineer David Brown had worked with many of the top names in Formula 1, including the Williams and McLaren teams and world champion drivers such as Ayrton Senna, Alain Prost, Nigel Mansell and Damon Hill.

Seasoned Champ Car specialists were soon added to the mix, especially after the last-minute decision was taken to field a second entry for Michel Jourdain Jr. Veteran chief mechanics Larry "LE" Ellert and Roy Wilkerson took responsibility for the Lolas of Allmendinger and Jourdain, respectively, while accomplished engineer/designer Bruce Ashmore was brought on board to oversee Jourdain's Gigante car.

The new blend worked extremely well. There were, understandably, a few hiccups in the early part of the year, but presentation right from the outset was top-class and the results soon followed.

Allmendinger thoroughly lived up to the expectations fostered by successive championship seasons in Barber Dodge and Toyota Atlantic, while Jourdain displayed his class by finishing an excellent third in just the new team's third race, at Milwaukee. He out-qualified the young charger only twice – at each of the two oval venues – but was usually considerably closer in the races. The amiable Mexican added a fine second-place run at Vancouver and a fourth at Laguna Seca, and only a series of wicked misfortunes kept him out of the top 10 in points at season's end.

Michael Levitt/LAT

Michael Levitt/LAT

Left: Carl Russo is a perfectionist. It shows in the presentation of his team.
Lesley Ann Miller/LAT

Right: Allmendinger lived up to all the hype, taking rookie-of-the-year honors.
Michael Kim/LAT

Below: Jourdain overcame long odds in '04 and was often stymied by misfortune.
Phil Abbott/LAT

Below right: Early days as Jourdain tests for RuSPORT at Sebring in March after being left high and dry by Bobby Rahal.
Dan Boyd/LAT

TAKING THE PLUNGE

After a record-breaking first year in the Toyota Atlantic Championship, culminating in the 2003 series crown and the top two positions in the rookie standings, RuSPORT team owner Carl Russo took a step back and evaluated the season's journey.

"When RuSPORT set out to compete in the Toyota Atlantic series, we really had laid out a two- to three-year plan for ourselves," he related. "We had realistic expectations. We wanted to be competitive and win races, then win the championship. Well, at the end of our first season, we felt that we had accomplished everything we wanted in just one year, instead of the two or three."

During the winter months, Russo and team president Jeremy Dale carefully examined the options and the learning curve RuSPORT had just traveled before electing to take the plunge directly into the Champ Car World Series.

"We decided that it was the right time for RuSPORT to step up and compete at the highest level," said Russo. "We believed in the viability of the Champ Car World Series and its fans, and we are convinced that it will ultimately provide the best return for our partners and the best competition for our drivers and crew."

Boldly, Russo and Dale moved the entire team up together with its *wunderkind* A.J. Allmendinger. For an organization that sets great store by its culture of solidarity and continuity, the move deemed unconventional by most made perfect sense.

A few more key personnel were added, including chief race engineer David Brown, whereupon RuSPORT set to work with the goal of providing Allmendinger with a competitive car for the Long Beach season-opener. Everybody within the team realized that another steep learning curve lay ahead – and it was about to get a lot steeper.

Less than a month before Long Beach, veteran driver Michel Jourdain Jr. found himself without a Champ Car ride following the abrupt withdrawal of Team Rahal. The personable and recently married Mexican longed to stay in the series he loved – and in which he had finished a career-best third in the 2003 title-chase -- but found all the available seats taken. In stepped Russo, making another unconventional move and adding a car at the last minute.

"We knew that taking on Michel at that point would stress us enormously," recalled Russo, "but that it would be worth it in the long run. Michel had proven that he could win races, so pairing his experience with A.J. and bringing that to the team was an opportunity too good to pass up."

The gamble paid off as RuSPORT collected 15 top-10 finishes and made four appearances on the podium during an impressive debut campaign. Furthermore, Allmendinger led the team into the history books by becoming only the second driver to claim Rookie of the Year honors with a first-year outfit (mirroring the achievement of Jeff Andretti and Bayside Motorsports in 1991.) Few in the Champ Car paddock were left in any doubt that RuSPORT was destined for great things in the coming years.

PKV RACING

Base: Indianapolis, Indiana
Drivers: Jimmy Vasser, Roberto Gonzalez (R)
Sponsors: Gulfstream, NII Holdings, Nextel
Engines: Ford-Cosworth XFE
Chassis: Lola
Tires: Bridgestone Potenza
Wins: 0
Poles: 0
Total points: 337
Vasser 201 (8th), Gonzalez 136 (15th)

Michael Levitt/LAT

Michael Levitt/LAT

CHANGE was the watchword for this Indianapolis-based team in between the 2003 and 2004 seasons. Even the name changed – from PK Racing to PKV Racing – to reflect the ownership additions of Dan Pettit and owner/driver Jimmy Vasser and the departure of the original "P," Craig Pollock.

Pettit, a longtime Silicon Valley associate of principal team owner Kevin Kalkhoven, served as the nominal team head so that Kalkhoven could devote his attention to Champ Car's pressing needs. Russell Cameron continued to run the team's race operations, with engineering headed up by Steve Challis.

PKV Racing expanded into a two-car operation for 2004 as Vasser was joined by Mexican rookie Roberto Gonzalez who had a pair of Champ Car starts to his name heading into the season. Gonzalez's presence allowed the team to attract backing from NII International, the holding company for much of wireless communication giant Nextel's international reach. Meanwhile, Kalkhoven used his strong connections with private jet builder Gulfstream to secure a sponsorship deal for Vasser's #12 Lola.

Gonzalez did a reasonable job, claiming five top-10 finishes highlighted by a seventh-place run at Cleveland. His best qualifying effort came on the Las Vegas oval where he gridded 10th, but a 15th-place finish in the championship was not enough for him to be renewed for 2005.

Vasser's best performances also came on the ovals. He qualified on the front row and finished fifth at Las Vegas, augmenting the fourth-place finish he had achieved at Milwaukee in June. Curiously, the team lacked performance in road racing trim, although Vasser claimed second place at Toronto and additional top-fives at Cleveland and Mexico City. Perhaps the biggest missed opportunity came at Road America where he qualified a promising third only to be involved in a first-lap incident with Ryan Hunter-Reay.

Additional changes made during the autumn underscored that PKV Racing was impatient to step up and begin challenging for race wins. Vasser called upon his old friend Jim McGee, first on a consultancy basis before he was named general manager in January. McGee (whose massive experience gained over more than 45 years in the sport includes involvement in 89 race victories and nine national championships) brought along some of his trusted colleagues, including team manager Steve Krisiloff. Capping the changes, 2002 Champ Car series champion Cristiano da Matta was nominated to drive the second car alongside Vasser for the 2005 season, ensuring one of the strongest line-ups in the paddock.

"Dan Pettit and myself have been working on the race team side, as Kevin obviously is very busy in many other aspects of the sport, and I think it took some time for us to realize where the team's deficiencies were," said Vasser. "I think the moves that we've made certainly have caught the eyes and the attention of our competitors."

McGee has targeted improvement to PKV's shock absorber and vehicle dynamics programs and says he wants to focus on reducing the weight of the team's Lola chassis.

Left: Kevin Kalkhoven is the guiding light behind both PKV and Champ Car.
Maria Grady/LAT

Right: Gonzalez never played a starring role but always performed respectably.
Phil Abbott/LAT

Top right: The new regime for '05 with veterans McGee and Krisiloff on board.
Dan Boyd/LAT

Below: The 1996 champion at work.
Phil Abbott/LAT

Below left: Vasser and Pettit (right) joined Kalkhoven in a reborn PKV team.
Lesley Ann Miller/LAT

Bottom right: Chief mechanic Don Oldenburg will oversee da Matta in '05.
Maria Grady/LAT

LOOKING TO THE FUTURE

JIMMY Vasser was painfully aware of all the upheavals that had transpired within the Champ Car World Series during the previous few years, but when it came to finalizing his plans for 2004, one of the most recognized names in all of open-wheel racing knew where his destiny lay.

"I had other opportunities but I felt a commitment to the series that had made my racing career," confirmed the 1996 series champion. "I have competed in several other series and driven other cars, but it is the Champ Car that gives me the most satisfaction from behind the wheel."

The only real question mark concerned his choice of team. For nine years after making his Champ Car debut in 1992, Vasser represented only two principal owners: Jim Hayhoe and Chip Ganassi. In the subsequent three campaigns, however, and due to circumstances beyond his control, he flitted from Ganassi to teams owned by Pat Patrick, Bobby Rahal and Stefan Johansson. But when he was offered an opportunity to join the newly reconstituted PKV Racing team – and take a stake in its ownership alongside Kevin Kalkhoven and Dan Pettit – Vasser had no hesitation in grasping the chance both to take more control of his own destiny and begin an investment for his future.

"I know I have more racing behind me than in front of me, but I also know that I love competition and racing," he said. "Becoming an owner provides me with an outlet for both of those loves when I decide to step out of the cockpit."

The native Californian (who now makes his home in Las Vegas) has etched his name among the top 30 in almost every statistical category in the Champ Car record books and is widely regarded as being one of the most personable and respected drivers in the paddock. And with a total of 218 starts to his name at the culmination of the 2004 season, including a record-breaking streak of 197 races in a row, Vasser has a solid grasp on his priorities.

"Right now I am concentrating on my driving – trying to win races and helping the PKV Racing team achieve its goal of winning a championship," he said. "To be honest, at this stage I am more focused on racing than running the team. Besides, the other two owners are a lot more qualified than I am to run the business.

"However, I am very aware of what is going on with the team. I keep up with our marketing plans and have input into the personnel, structure and organizational decisions. I have been on successful teams during my career and I know what it takes to have a winning team. Having a successful team has never been because of any special parts on the car. The teams that do well are the ones that have great chemistry and handle themselves professionally."

Following the post-season decision to hire 2002 title-winner Cristiano da Matta and take on the vastly experienced Jim McGee as general manager, there seems little doubt that PKV is set to join the ranks of race winners in 2005.

ROCKETSPORTS

Base: **East Lansing, Michigan**

Drivers: **Alex Tagliani, Nelson Philippe (R), Memo Gidley, Guy Smith (R)**

Sponsors: **Johnson Controls, LeasePlan**

Engines: **Ford-Cosworth XFE**

Chassis: **Lola**

Tires: **Bridgestone Potenza**

Wins: **1 (Tagliani)**

Poles: **0**

Total points: **329**

Tagliani 218 (7th), Smith 53 (18th), Philippe 43 (*of 89* - 16th), Gidley 15 (21st)

Michael Levitt/LAT

Michael Levitt/LAT

Lesley Ann Miller/LAT

Michael Levitt/LAT

FOR a fledgling race team it is often said that the sophomore season poses even more challenges than the rookie campaign. Especially so when the decision is made to double the workload.

Such was the task facing Rocketsports Racing in 2004 as team owner Paul Gentilozzi expanded his operation to enter a second Lola for teenager Nelson Philippe alongside acknowledged team leader Alex Tagliani. The primary duties fell on the capable shoulders of team manager Phil Howard, since Gentilozzi himself remained focused on his various business interests – including his part-ownership of the Champ Car World Series through his partnership with Open Wheel Racing Series principals Kevin Kalkhoven and Jerry Forsythe – plus his own hugely successful racing exploits (Gentilozzi ultimately captured his record-equaling fourth Trans-Am Championship crown).

Under the circumstances, Rocketsports can be proud of its accomplishments. Sure, there were some growing pains, especially in relation to the second car, but the team assuredly made some forward strides, highlighted by its maiden victory at Road America. The win came in Tagliani's 85th career start and brought welcome relief following a series of heartbreaking near-misses in the past.

The remainder of Tagliani's season was blighted by inconsistency and various scrapes either with his rivals or officialdom (or both!), but, as ever, he never failed to give 100 percent. Expert preparation from veteran chief mechanic Tom Howatt and the crew ensured his only non-finish of the year came at Surfers Paradise, where he crashed following contact with Justin Wilson. The efforts of newly recruited race engineer Brian Ma saw Tagliani reach a high of third in the point standings after Road America, and even though he slipped to seventh by season's end, it still represented a solid improvement over his 10th-place finish in 2003.

The #17 car saw three different occupants as the season unfolded, which certainly kept chief mechanic Ed Daood on his toes. With just one season of racing under his belt, in the Barber Dodge Pro Series, 17-year-old Philippe was always likely to struggle at this level. The Frenchman abruptly left the team after a handful of outings, despite having claimed a couple of top-10 finishes.

After an absence of more than two years from the Champ Car scene, Memo Gidley stepped in for the Molson Indy Toronto at ludicrously short notice, and two weeks later showed (once again) that he was thoroughly deserving of a full-time opportunity by qualifying a sensational fifth in Vancouver. Sadly, money talked and he didn't have any, so the gifted American's services were dispensed with after just two races.

His place in the #17 car was taken by Briton Guy Smith, commencing at Road America. As with Gidley the 2003 Le Mans 24 Hours winner had spent a long time away from the open-wheel ranks – four and a half years in his case. Still, he showed flashes of form on occasion and performed particularly well at Las Vegas, running comfortably among the main pack until his engine let go

Above: **Philippe drove in just six races.**
Michael Levitt/LAT

Left: **The drought is broken -- Tagliani is congratulated on a job well done.**
Leland Hill/LAT

Right: **Paul Gentilozzi is a hard task master and a proven winner at all levels.**
Maria Grady/LAT

Bottom right: **The win at Road America was well deserved for Tags and Rocketsports.**
Michael Kim/LAT

Below: Gidley stepped in for two races at zero notice and performed admirably.

Below centre: Same car, different driver; Smith contested the final seven events.

Photographs: Michael Levitt/LAT

CHAMP CAR'S MR. FIX-IT

Creating a Champ Car team out of nothing is no easy task, as several ambitious wannabe car owners have found out to their chagrin in the past. One man who knows all – or at least most – of the pitfalls, however, is expatriate Englishman Phil Howard, (pictured below) who toward the end of the 2002 season was hired by Paul Gentilozzi to establish a Champ Car arm of Rocketsports Racing's hugely successful Trans-Am/sports car organization.

"The most important thing in building a team is to have an understanding owner," declares Howard. "Paul (Gentilozzi) was willing to spend money to get the right people and the right equipment in place."

Location, he soon discovered, is another crucial factor. Establishing a Champ Car team in Indianapolis, for example, is relatively straightforward, since most of the elements are close at hand – especially in terms of personnel. Rocketsports, however, is based in East Lansing, Michigan, and Howard had to use all of his guile and connections to lure some of the sport's most accomplished technicians away from their familiar environment.

Michael Levitt/LAT

Starting from scratch was nothing new for Howard. He had been through the same process with Della Penna Motorsports in the middle 1990s, and again with Tom Wieringa's Sigma Autosport operation which debuted in 2001. Sigma claimed a couple of top-five finishes in its maiden season with Oriol Servia, and notched its first podium with Max Papis at Long Beach just over one year later.

Results came just as quickly at Rocketsports as Alex Tagliani earned two pole positions and three podium finishes during its rookie campaign. Then came the decision to expand to a two-car operation for 2004.

"Adding the second car wasn't as big of a challenge," reckons Howard. "We knew well in advance that we were going to expand so we were able to work and make sure we had everything in place. It was much harder starting the team in 2003 when we had only 30 days to put a car on the grid with no resources to start with."

All the hard work was rewarded at the challenging Road America track in rural Elkhart Lake, Wisconsin, in August when Tagliani – and Rocketsports Racing – ascended to the top step of a Champ Car podium for the first time. It had taken only 26 races for Howard to lead the team to victory.

"The win was very pleasing," he says. "Paul is so very passionate about racing; it was great for him to succeed on another level in the sport."

The next step for Rocketsports Racing will be to become recognized as a genuine championship contender, which will necessarily include regular trips to victory circle.

DALE COYNE RACING

Base: **Plainfield, Illinois**

Drivers: **Oriol Servia, Tarso Marques, Gaston Mazzacane (R), Jarek Janis (R)**

Sponsors: **yokeTV.com, American Medical Response**

Engines: **Ford-Cosworth XFE**

Chassis: **Lola**

Tires: **Bridgestone Potenza**

Wins: **0**

Poles: **0**

Total points: **284**

Servia 199 (10th), Mazzacane 73 (17th), Marques 9 (22nd), Janis 3 (24th)

ORIOL SERVIA

Michael Levitt/LAT

TARSO MARQUES

Michael Levitt/LAT

GASTON MAZZACANE

Michael Levitt/LAT

JAREK JANIS

Lesley Ann Miller/LAT

DALE Coyne Racing made a substantial leap forward in 2004. After attracting sponsorship from American Medical Response and yokeTV.com, Champ Car racing's perennial underdog team transformed one of its two cars – for the very first time – into a veritable top-five challenger.

The cash infusion enabled Coyne to seek at least one seasoned professional driver, rather than having to rely, as usual, upon two paying customers. And when Oriol Servia became available, Coyne saw an opportunity to move forward.

"Oriol's always had a great attitude and it was a feather in our cap to have someone like him on board," said Coyne.

Now the pressure was on the team to perform. Vastly experienced English race engineer David Watson, who had worked previously with Servia at the short-lived Sigma team, was enlisted to handle setup duties on the #11 yokeTV.com car, and Scotsman Andy Green, another veteran on the circuit, came on board to oversee the mechanical issues. The results weren't long in coming. Incredibly, though, after Servia qualified ninth for the second race in Monterrey, it was only the fourth time in over 400 starts that a DCR entry had started among the top 10! And to put the icing on the cake, teammate Tarso Marques started 10th that same afternoon in Mexico.

Some of Servia's pit stops left a little to be desired in early-season races, but not for long. Green's crew worked hard to overcome the initial shortcomings, and by mid-season was a match for just about anyone on pit lane. Indeed, at Surfers Paradise the yellow-and-black #11 Lola spent less time on pit road than any other finisher.

Servia finished a strong fourth at Cleveland – only the second time a Coyne car had attained such lofty status in 20 years at this level – and went one better at Mazda Raceway Laguna Seca, claiming a podium spot to match the third-place finish achieved by Roberto Moreno at Michigan in 1996.

The team's second car, meanwhile, was rarely competitive. Marques showed some promise in the first two races, albeit with absolutely no luck, whereupon the gifted Brazilian was replaced by another F1 refugee, Gaston Mazzacane. The jovial Argentine made his debut at the daunting Milwaukee Mile (of all places!), and not surprisingly found the wall. Arguably, he never really recovered his confidence. After qualifying no better than 16th in 10 attempts, he opted to withdraw from the final two races, purportedly to concentrate on securing the finance to ensure a more productive effort in 2005.

Czech Jaroslav "Jarek" Janis didn't have a lot of fun in the Orlando Ledesma-tended #19 AMR car at Surfers Paradise and bowed out of his commitment to finish off the season in Mexico, whereupon Marques was invited to return. Once again he showed a good turn of speed, but finished a disappointed 18th after being involved in an early incident.

Mike Levitt/LAT

RAISING THE BAR

Dale Coyne (above) has been a regular on the Champ Car circuit since 1984, initially as a part-time owner/driver and since 1991 exclusively as a car owner. His passion for the series has remained undimmed, despite spending most of the intervening two decades toward the back of the field, continually searching for that elusive corporate support that would enable him to raise his team's game.

"Finding sponsors is tough on two fronts," he says. "First of all, in the economic times we are in right now, all motor sports are having to work very hard to get sponsors, and when you look at Champ Car specifically it gets doubly hard. That is beginning to change, but in the past when there was a lot of uncertainty about the future of the series, a lot of potential sponsors were being very cautious. Now, with the new series owners and the consistent TV package, it should get a little easier because finally we can give a sponsor the value they are looking for."

For 2004, Coyne's hard work behind the scenes finally began to pay off as he introduced two new sponsors to the sport. The inflow of funding enabled him to have more autonomy over his choice of drivers, and brought dramatically improved results thanks to the yeoman efforts of Oriol Servia in the #11 car.

"We are very proud to have brought in American Medical Response (AMR) and yokeTV.com as sponsors of the team," he asserts. "Every team and driver is chasing sponsors, whether they are in Champ Car, Formula 1 or even NASCAR. Drivers chase sponsors, too, and sometimes are able to bring them to a team. Some people call it ride-buying but who cares? It helps the team and the sport when new partners are brought in. We have relied on that in the past but this year our team has turned the corner and now we are able to be more selective in whom we put in the cockpit of our cars."

The process of signing up a sponsor frequently is a long drawn-out process, as Coyne (in common with every other team owner) will readily testify. However, he has found that one of the most effective means of transforming a spark of interest into a concrete commitment is by inviting a potential supporter to experience a Champ Car event in person.

"We brought American Medical Response to the Denver race two years ago," he reveals. "They are based in the Denver area; they came out to the event and we talked about what we could do for them, and we were also able to show them what we could provide. It was a great experience and they saw a lot of parallels between our team and their ambulance crews. They saw things like the teamwork and the brotherhood that went into making the team successful and were impressed by that."

Of course, the procurement of sponsors is no guarantee of success. But in the case of Dale Coyne Racing, at least it has served to level the playing field somewhat in comparison to the remainder of the Champ Car teams.

Above: Dale Coyne's team grew with Servia's experience and commitment.
Michael Kim/LAT

Far left: For the amiable Spaniard, third in Monterey felt almost like a victory.
Lesley Ann Miller/LAT

Left: Gaston Mazzacane drove most of the season in Coyne's #19 AMR Lola.
Michael Levitt/LAT

Right: If only Marques could secure the funding for a full Champ Car season...
Phil Abbott/LAT

MI-JACK CONQUEST RACING

Base: Indianapolis, Indiana
Drivers: Alex Sperafico (R), Justin Wilson (R), Nelson Philippe (R)
Sponsors: Mi-Jack, LeasePlan
Engines: Ford-Cosworth XFE
Chassis: Lola & Reynard
Tires: Bridgestone Potenza
Wins: 0
Poles: 0
Total points: 281
Wilson 188 (11th), Philippe 46 (*of 89* - 16th), Sperafico 47 (19th)

ERIC Bachelart's Mi-Jack Conquest Racing team began the 2004 season with high expectations. Formula 1 convert Justin Wilson provided an exciting addition to the ambitious team as it embarked on its second season in the Champ Car World Series, and after fielding a satellite operation for former champion Emerson Fittipaldi in 2003, this time a pair of cars were run from beneath the same awning. Brazilian rookie Alex Sperafico was signed up to pilot the second car.

Team manager Chris Mower (whose Nordic Racing team had guided Wilson to the F3000 title in 2001) paired his fellow Briton with race engineer Don Bricker, and the pair struck up an immediate rapport. Wilson finished a strong sixth at Long Beach, then repeated the feat at Monterrey after qualifying an excellent third. He struggled on the Milwaukee oval (where his team elected to run a Reynard rather than risk damaging its solitary Lola), but rebounded to start fourth in Portland and secure his first top-five result.

The momentum was carried into the next race at Cleveland, where Rich Howard's crew helped Wilson earn second on the grid. Unfortunately, he was unable to take advantage of his best starting spot of the year as the #34 Mi-Jack Lola more resembled a pinball than a race car at the always treacherous Turn One. Contact with Alex Tagliani and then polesitter Paul Tracy forced both front row qualifiers out of the race.

Though the Cleveland result sent the team into something of a summer slump (reaching a nadir at Laguna Seca where Wilson was never happy with his car's handling despite switching between a variety of differential options), Wilson rebounded to finish the season with three consecutive top-10 finishes, including a new best result of fourth in the Mexico City finale.

Pairing two rookies in such a competitive environment as the Champ Car World Series was always likely to provide a difficult challenge, and the unfortunate Sperafico was further handicapped by having to rely on the unloved Reynard chassis. After eight unconvincing appearances, he bowed to the inevitable and was replaced by ex-Rocketsports charge Nelson Philippe, who, at the tender age of 16, had undertaken his very first Champ Car test under Bachelart's tutelage the previous fall.

The young Frenchman impressed race engineer Adam Schaechter right away with his technical feedback, and at last gave chief mechanic Martin Bates and the crew something to smile about. The procurement of an ex-Team Rahal Lola also assisted progress. Philippe responded by claiming consecutive top-10 finishes at Las Vegas and Surfers Paradise, giving rise to renewed optimism heading into the off-season.

Michael Levitt/LAT

Michael Levitt/LAT

Dan Streck/LAT

Above right: Nelson Philippe found his Champ Car feet after struggling early in the year with Rocketsports Racing.
Dan Streck/LAT

Right: Alex Sperafico tried hard but was always likely to struggle in his Reynard.
Michael Kim/LAT

Bottom left: After adjusting the shocks, Wilson qualified second in Cleveland.
Michael Kim/LAT

Below: The lanky Englishman revived his career and put Conquest on the map.
Michael Levitt/LAT

THE OTHER SIDE OF THE FENCE

Mi-Jack Conquest Racing team owner Eric Bachelart (pictured below) was born in Brussels, Belgium, but has been an integral part of the North American auto racing scene for the past 15 seasons. During that time he has witnessed the sport from two entirely different vantage points – from inside the cockpit as a driver and along the pit wall as a team owner.

Bachelart graduated through the open-wheel ranks in Europe, but when his career hit a crossroads and he realized his chances of making it to his ultimate goal of Formula 1 were slim at best, he (like many others before and since) set his sights instead on a career in Champ Car racing.

After two years in Indy Lights, culminating in the 1991 championship title with Landford Racing, he stepped up to Champ Cars in 1992 with Dale Coyne Racing, competing in 13 of the 16 races and scoring the team's best finish of seventh at the difficult Belle Isle circuit in Detroit. He also took second in the Rookie of the Year standings. Then he ran out of funding.

Bachelart returned in 1995, rejoining the Coyne operation to make 11 starts and matching his previous best finish of seventh at Long Beach; but the writing was on the wall.

In 1996, realizing his career had stalled, he shifted his focus from driving to team ownership. He launched Conquest Racing the following year, contesting the fiercely competitive Indy Lights category with French rookie Christophe Tinseau. Despite starting from scratch, Conquest earned a podium finish in its rookie campaign.

For Bachelart, the transition from driving a car to owning a team was relatively seamless, and he soon found that many of the lessons he had learned inside the car were standing him in good stead in his latest endeavor.

"Hiring the best people you can and allowing yourself to learn from them is a key to success in almost any kind of business," he says. "That's true as a driver, trying to get the best mechanics and engineers to get the most of a race car; and it's true of a race team, trying to get the most performance out of the organization as a whole."

Conquest Racing switched its focus to the IRL in 2001 (guiding another Frenchman, Laurent Redon, to Rookie of the Year honors), before returning to its road racing roots and joining the Champ Car World Series in 2003. Bachelart has made the most of his transition from driver to team owner, and claims that the excitement level is just as intense.

"Running a team is not quite the same as strapping myself into the car, naturally, but yes, the moments leading up to a race start are still very exciting for me," he says with a broad smile. "It's also a bit different, because when you're a driver, all you have to do is drive and take care of yourself. Now, I'm responsible for nearly 30 people, so the ramifications of what happens on the track affect more people than when I was just driving, and so that brings its own intensity to the races for me."

Michael Levitt/LAT

WALKER RACING

Base: Indianapolis, Indiana
Drivers: Mario Haberfeld, David Besnard (R), Michael Valiante (R)
Sponsors: Cummins, Wright Patton Shakespeare, Wildlife Conservation Network, Wasteco
Engines: Ford-Cosworth XFE
Chassis: Reynard
Tires: Bridgestone Potenza
Wins: 0
Poles: 0
Total points: 182
Haberfeld 157 (13th), Besnard 18 (20th), Valiante 7 (23rd)

WHILE one team after another ditched its Reynard chassis in favor Lolas over a period of several years, Walker Racing remained as the last bastion for the chassis constructor that had won seven consecutive Champ Car titles from 1995-2001. In fact, Derrick Walker had taken over the lame-duck Reynard program when the British manufacturer went into receivership in 2002, intending to update it and keep it competitive with the latest Lolas. But Champ Car technical officials steadfastly refused to allow aerodynamic modifications to the Reynard, relegating it to midfield status at best.

Walker's 2003 drivers Darren Manning and Rodolfo Lavin had moved on, so his Indianapolis-based team ran a singleton entry for second-year Champ Car driver Mario Haberfeld in 2004. A second car was added for the two season-ending races. Australian David Besnard took advantage of a late full-course caution to finish seventh at Surfers Paradise, while promising Canadian Michael Valiante graduated from the Toyota Atlantic Championship to make his Champ Car debut for Walker at Mexico City. Valiante, too, acquitted himself extremely well.

Rob Edwards continued as team manager, with Brendon Cleave in charge of race engineering duties and Les Channen as chief mechanic, and together they always maintained an upbeat atmosphere within the tight-knit group, despite its obvious chassis deficiency.

"Because we had the Reynard we worked a lot harder on some of the things we can control, like race strategy and overall strategy for the weekend," noted Edwards. "The group did a very good job and next year we hope to capitalize on some of the things we did very well."

Indeed the #5 Cummins crew "won" the unofficial pit stop competition (for the least time spent on pit road) in five of the season's 14 races.

Haberfeld's calm and thoroughly professional demeanor was an asset to Walker Racing and the Brazilian generally maximized the potential of his car. The season was highlighted by a fourth-place finish at Toronto, which he said was "almost like a victory for us."

"I rate Mario very highly," declared Walker. "He is very focused, a very smooth and precise driver who is serious about his driving craft. He spends a lot of time analyzing the data. He has tremendous patience and dedication to the job and I think he brings out the best in our group. He's completely capable of opening his computer and analyzing the data himself, as well as with the team, so he's a very complete individual in the driver/engineer relationship."

For 2005, Walker plans to run two drivers – in Lolas. "In some respects we regret giving up on the Reynard," Walker said. "It provided a good package price-wise, but without some rule modifications we are forced to face reality and make the necessary change. The Lola progressively got further ahead of the Reynard this year and there were more Lolas running, so it made a difficult job even harder. But on the positive side, the team stayed focused on the job, morale has remained high and the team has closed ranks."

Michael Levitt/LAT

Michael Levitt/LAT

Michael Levitt/LAT

Above right: Haberfeld retained his focus during a difficult year with the Reynard.

Right: Besnard drove well at Surfers, in his first open-wheel race since 1998.
Photographs: Lesley Ann Miller/LAT

Bottom right: Haberfeld always tried his best, netting a fine fourth in Toronto.
Michael Levitt/LAT

Left: Valiante was very impressive, and a little unfortunate, on his debut in Mexico.
Dan Streck/LAT

Bottom left: After one final year with the Reynards, Walker is set to switch to Lolas.
Michael Levitt/LAT

THE FINAL FRONTIER

As one of only two teams to run a Reynard chassis in 2004, Walker Racing faced a major challenge in trying to remain competitive in the intensely fought Champ Car World Series. Derrick Walker had purchased all Reynard's assets when the British manufacturer went out of business in 2002, but with precious little funding for development and no leeway allowed by Champ Car's technical department, his team was always behind the eight-ball.

"Given that development of the Reynard was frozen in 2002, it was at a strong disadvantage," declares Walker Racing Team Manager Rob Edwards (pictured below). "The Lola chassis had two extra years of development, and when you start so far behind it is incredibly difficult if not impossible to dig out of that hole."

Though development of the Reynard chassis was not permitted, Edwards – perhaps surprisingly – isn't convinced that looser regulations would have made much difference.

"For us, opening the rule book to try and help the Reynard wouldn't have done any good," he says. "What you always need is more budget, and even if there were rule changes we still would not have had the budget to implement the new bits needed. The reason we were running the Reynard in the first place was due to our limited budget."

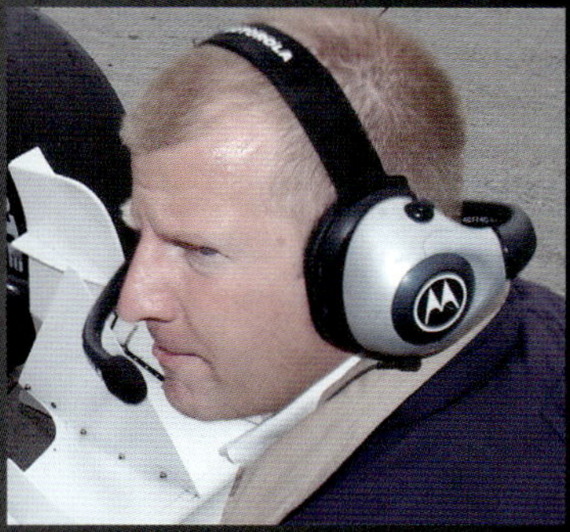

LAT Photographic

The financial shortfall also precluded Walker Racing from fielding a teammate to Mario Haberfeld (for all except the final couple of races), compounding his predicament, although perhaps that wasn't as much of a handicap as might have been thought.

"Running two cars is always an advantage over running just one," says Edwards, "but in the situation we were in, it wasn't as much of an issue. We had run the Reynard for years before so we had a strong collection of data and combining that with Mario's previous experience in the Reynard [with Mi-Jack Conquest Racing in 2003], we weren't lacking. On a scale of one to 10, with 10 being the most difficult, the lack of development was a nine, and only running one car was about a two."

Walker's decision to turn his back on the Reynard project in favor of running a pair of newly acquired Lolas in 2005 will leave the Champ Car World Series with a solitary chassis supplier. From a purist's perspective, the lack of competition is regrettable. But from a practical standpoint, Edwards believes the series in general will benefit.

"With my engineering background, having more than one type of chassis on the grid makes it more technically challenging," says the Briton, "but in the situation Champ Car is [in], I think it is better to have only one chassis. There is a very limited number of fans who care about the chassis we are running; the fans definitely identify more with the drivers and teams."

LOLA

Production base: Huntingdon, England; U.S. base: Indianapolis, Indiana

Number of cars built in 2004: 4

Wins: 14 (Bourdais 7, Junqueira 2, Tracy 2, Hunter-Reay 1, Carpentier 1, Tagliani 1)

Poles: 14 (Bourdais 8, Tracy 3, Junqueira 1, Hunter-Reay 1, Carpentier 1)

Laps led: 1,335 (100 percent)

AFTER running into dire financial straits in the late 1990s following an ill-conceived foray into Formula 1, Lola Cars International has undergone a remarkable renaissance during the past few years under the leadership of Irish businessman Martin Birrane. Nowhere has this been more apparent than in the Champ Car arena, where the historic British constructor has assumed a seemingly impregnable position of pre-eminence while its competition has either departed altogether (Penske, Swift, Eagle) or withered on the vine (Reynard).

Indeed, in 2004 Lola enjoyed a virtual monopoly of the chassis market, initially supplying all but two of the 18 regular entrants and tightening its stranglehold still further when Eric Bachelart laid his hands on an ex-Team Rahal B01/00 for Nelson Philippe prior to the Molson Indy Montreal. Not surprisingly, Lola's numerical dominance was mirrored in the results sheets, and after narrowly failing to complete a whitewash the previous year, it won all 14 races en route to its third successive drivers' and constructors' titles.

From a competitive standpoint, therefore, it could hardly have asked for more. On the flip side of the coin, while the rules-freeze instituted in 2002 successfully curbed escalating development costs – and contributed to Champ Car's overall financial viability – it also translated into a stagnant order book at Lola's factory in England. Very few of its customers required new chassis; some, indeed, relied on updated cars that had been campaigned as long ago as the 2000 season. Oriol Servia's #11 Dale Coyne Racing entry was one such, while Sebastien Bourdais employed a 2001 example to devastating effect. As in the previous year, just four new cars were delivered in 2004, three to the first-year RuSPORT squad and the other to Forsythe Championship Racing.

Having virtually fallen off the radar in 1997-98, Lola has unequivocally re-established itself and looks set to equip the entire Champ Car grid in 2005. It's a position the company has fully merited, but not one it takes for granted.

"It's a new situation for us and we're still adjusting to it," says managing director Rupert Manwaring. "It means our philosophy is very different compared to when Martin reinvested so much money to beat Reynard. We need to look very hard at our production costs, and the teams need a more efficient car to run because the economic circumstances have changed. That's something we're very mindful of. I think over the next few years we're going to have to work really hard to make sure we are the chassis that the teams continue to choose."

REYNARD

U.S. base: Indianapolis, Indiana

Number of cars built in 2004: 0

Wins: 0

Poles: 0

Laps led: 0

THE "battle" between the two chassis manufacturers in the 2004 Champ Car World Series was truly a David vs. Goliath contest – albeit without the miraculous outcome. Two years after the company had fallen into receivership, Reynard was reduced to a brace of entries for the majority of the season, neither of them blessed with anything resembling a front-running budget. It therefore came as no surprise that Lola monopolized the silverware while the best Reynard could muster was a single fourth-place finish, courtesy of Mario Haberfeld at Toronto. It was the first time the once-mighty British marque had endured a winless campaign in its 11-year history in the series.

Haberfeld and his Walker Racing team carried the Reynard standard almost single-handedly, since Alex Sperafico never looked likely to make much of an impact for Mi-Jack Conquest Racing. Two-thirds of the way through the season, Sperafico was benched, and later team owner Eric Bachelart procured a Lola for new recruit Nelson Philippe, leaving Haberfeld as the lone representative until Derrick Walker fielded one-off entries in the final two events at Surfers Paradise and Mexico City.

The personable Brazilian could usually be counted on to wring the maximum from the long-in-the-tooth chassis and finished half the races among the top 10. At Road America he looked on course for at least fifth place until a moment of over-enthusiasm soon after a late restart relegated him to 11th.

The Reynard's main Achilles heel, as before, was a lack of downforce in comparison to the Lola, which had benefited from several update packages since the advent of the initial "chassis freeze." Walker, who had purchased the assets of Reynard North America in '02 in the hope of sustaining it as a cost-effective alternative to the more prolific Lolas, had tirelessly lobbied Champ Car technical officials to allow corresponding aerodynamic modifications to the Reynard, but in vain. With some reluctance, he finally decided to give up the unequal struggle and switch allegiance to Lola for 2005, bringing down the curtain on Reynard's illustrious motorsport history.

TIRES

BRIDGESTONE

Production bases: **Akron, Ohio; Tokyo, Japan**

Wins: **14 (Bourdais 7, Junqueira 2, Tracy 2, Hunter-Reay 1, Carpentier 1, Tagliani 1)**

Poles: **14 (Bourdais 8, Tracy 3, Junqueira 1, Hunter-Reay 1, Carpentier 1)**

BRIDGESTONE/Firestone North American Tire, LLC continued to derive valuable media exposure from its role as the presenting sponsor of the Champ Car World Series. Its latest breed of Potenza racing radials, meanwhile, performed virtually flawlessly throughout the season, displaying the usual high standards of consistency, durability and reliability.

But what really sparked heightened interest in Bridgestone's activities in 2004 was the injection of a new strategic variable into the racing through its development of an "option" tire, whose softer rubber compound afforded more grip than the regular Potenza and therefore faster lap times. Introduced on a trial basis at the season-opening Toyota Grand Prix of Long Beach, the initiative was designed to foster overtaking opportunities by creating a noticeable performance differential between the two specifications of tire, each of which drivers would be required to use in the course of a race.

"The object is to have some cars on the standard spec Potenza and others on the option spec at the same time," explained Al Speyer, executive director of Bridgestone Motorsport.

The experiment proved inconclusive at Long Beach, where it transpired that the two compounds were too similar to make passing appreciably easier. But the Bridgestone technicians in Akron, Ohio made a number of refinements in time for the next appearance of the stickier tires (now more appropriately renamed "alternates") at Portland in June, to great effect. In the race's closing stages, second-placed Bruno Junqueira used a set of alternates to home in on primary-shod teammate Sebastien Bourdais, setting up a grandstand finish.

The alternate tires were used on three subsequent occasions, at Montreal, Laguna Seca and Mexico City, and further subtle tweaks ensured that they became increasingly popular with the drivers as the year progressed.

"Bridgestone brought an excellent alternate tire that not only was much faster but also very, very consistent," praised Bourdais following the season finale. "But they always give us great tires and I think we had only one puncture all season, which is remarkable considering what they go through."

The Frenchman's comments were echoed by his rivals up and down the pit lane. The new format proved a hit with the fans, too, especially once Bridgestone increased the visual differentiation between the two types of tire. By Montreal the alternates featured vivid red sidewalls that made them easily distinguishable from the standard sets and earned them the nickname "red stripes".

Above: **The Bridgestone Potenzas were consistent, durable and problem-free.**
Michael Levitt/LAT

Left: **The ingenious red-stripe "alternate" tires added a new dimension to the races.**
Lesley Ann Miller/LAT

Below: **The Ford-Cosworth XFE.**
Photo courtesy of: Cosworth

ENGINES

FORD-COSWORTH

Production bases: **Northampton, England; Torrance, California**

Wins: **14 (Bourdais 7, Junqueira 2, Tracy 2, Hunter-Reay 1, Carpentier 1, Tagliani 1)**

Poles: **14 (Bourdais 8, Tracy 3, Junqueira 1, Hunter-Reay 1, Carpentier 1)**

THE "spec" Ford-Cosworth engine formula adopted by the Champ Car World Series in 2003 had been so effective in meeting its key objectives that precious little tinkering was required over the winter. The re-engineered XFE power plant developed by Cosworth had proved powerful yet ultra-reliable, while a standardized electronic control unit had mercifully allowed traction control to be banished. Above all, the new package had transformed the economics of competing for the teams by slashing the annual cost of an engine lease from over $4 million to $1.25 million.

Heading into 2004, then, both Champ Car and Cosworth naturally were inclined to heed the adage, "If it ain't broke, don't fix it." But in an effort to spice up the racing they added one significant new element to the mix: the snappily-named "push-to-pass" device. Activated via a button on the steering wheel, this provided a temporary surge of boost worth an additional 300 revs and 50 horsepower, equating to an extra 2-3 mph of straightline speed. It could not be used indiscriminately, however, since drivers would be limited to a pre-determined allocation per race (usually 60 seconds).

"It's definitely going to make for some passing," reckoned Ryan Hunter-Reay prior to the Long Beach season-opener. "But it's also going to take some thinking on the part of the driver to figure out a game plan. It will really keep everyone on their toes."

Hunter-Reay's comments proved prophetic. Drivers soon learned that push-to-pass could be used defensively as well as offensively, while those who depleted their full supply in the early laps found themselves vulnerable on late-race restarts. Overtaking was still far from easy, but the consensus was that the innovative feature made an important contribution to improving the show.

Meanwhile the XFE remained a paragon of longevity and reliability. As a matter of course it completed 1,200 miles between rebuilds, and there were but a handful of failures during the grueling 14-race season – a testament to the continued hard work and dedication of Cosworth's engineers in both Northampton, England and Torrance, California.

Any potential turbulence from Ford's decision to put Cosworth Racing on the market in the fall was swiftly deflected by the news that the engine specialist had been acquired by OWRS principals Kevin Kalkhoven and Jerry Forsythe. It was a move that suggested that Cosworth will remain the linchpin of Champ Car's brave new world for the foreseeable future.

CANADIAN
CANADIAN LIGHT
HERDEZ
SecureHorizons
McDonald

2004 BRIDGESTONE PRESENTS THE CHAMP CAR WORLD SERIES POWERED BY FORD

FACTS & FIGURES

Position	Driver	Team/Car/Engine	Tires	Long Beach	Monterrey	Milwaukee	Portland	Cleveland	Toronto	Vancouver	Road America	Denver	Montreal	Laguna Seca	Las Vegas	Surfers Paradise	Mexico City	Points total
1	Sébastien Bourdais (F)	McDonald's Newman/Haas Racing Ford-Cosworth/Lola B01/00	BS	3^{f}	$1^{pf\dagger}$	18	$1^{p\dagger}$	$1^{\dagger}$	$1^{pf\dagger}$	5^{+}	3^{p+}	1^{pf+}	$15^{pf\dagger}$	8^{p+}	$1^{\dagger}$	2	$1^{pf\dagger}$	369
2	Bruno Junqueira (BR)	PacifiCare Newman/Haas Racing Ford-Cosworth/Lola B02/00	BS	2^{p+}	2^{+}	6	2^{f}	2^{f}	18	4	15^{f}	3^{+}	1^{+}	2	2^{f+}	1^{f+}	2	341
3	Patrick Carpentier (CDN)	Indeck Forsythe Championship Racing Ford-Cosworth/Lola B02/00	BS	4^{+}	4^{+}	2	4^{m}	16	3	16	14	9	2	$1^{\dagger}$	3^{p+}	16^{+}	6	266
4	Paul Tracy (CDN)	Indeck Forsythe Championship Racing Ford-Cosworth/Lola B02/00	BS	$1^{\dagger}$	7	17	3^{+}	17^{p}	5^{+}	$1^{pf\dagger}$	$12^{\dagger}$	$2^{\dagger}$	4	10^{+}	18	$4^{p\dagger}$	10	254
5	Mario Dominguez (MEX)	Herdez Competition Ford-Cosworth/Lola B02/00	BS	5	3^{+}	8	17	-	-	-	-	-	3^{+}	11^{f}	-	-	-	
		Herdez Competition Ford-Cosworth/Lola B03/00	BS	-	-	-	-	8	17	6^{+}	5	4	-	-	7	3	8^{m}	244
6	*A.J. Allmendinger (USA)	BG Products/Red Bull RuSPORT Ford-Cosworth/Lola B03/00	BS	12	17	5^{m}	6	6	11	3	-	-	-	-	-	-	-	
		BG Products/Red Bull RuSPORT Ford-Cosworth/Lola B04/00	BS	-	-	-	-	-	-	-	13	5	-	-	-	-	-	
		Western Union RuSPORT Ford-Cosworth/Lola B04/00	BS	-	-	-	-	-	-	-	-	-	5^{+}	15	-	6^{+}	3	
		Western Union RuSPORT Ford-Cosworth/Lola B03/00	BS	-	-	-	-	-	-	-	-	-	-	-	6	-	-	229
7	Alex Tagliani (CDN)	Johnson Controls Rocketsports Racing Ford-Cosworth/Lola B02/00	BS	8	5^{+m}	13	7•	3	7	7	$1^{\dagger m}$	10	7	6^{+}	16^{+}•	19	11	218
8	Jimmy Vasser (USA)	Gulfstream PKV Racing Ford-Cosworth/Lola B02/00	BS	16	12	4	8	5	2^{+}	10	8	17	8	17	5	12	5	201
9	Ryan Hunter-Reay (USA)	Herdez Competition Ford-Cosworth/Lola B03/00	BS	7	8	$1^{pf\dagger}$	-	-	-	-	4	16	18	5	13	-	-	
		Herdez Competition Ford-Cosworth/Lola B01/00	BS	-	-	-	12	11	8	8	-	-	-	-	-	5	19	199
10	Oriol Servia (E)	yokeTV.com Dale Coyne Racing Ford-Cosworth/Lola B2K/00	BS	15	14	7	11	4^{+m}	9	12	6	6	9	3^{m}	12^{+}	13	7	199
11	*Justin Wilson (GB)	Mi-Jack Conquest Racing Ford-Cosworth/Lola B02/00	BS	6^{m}	6^{+}	-	5	18	12	14	7	7	14	18	8^{m}	8	4	
		Mi-Jack Conquest Racing Ford-Cosworth/Reynard 02I	BS	-	-	11	-	-	-	-	-	-	-	-	-	-	-	188
12	Michel Jourdain Jr. (MEX)	Gigante RuSPORT Ford-Cosworth/Lola B04/00	BS	11	11	3	14	15^{+}	15	2^{+m}	9	14	6^{m}	4^{+}	11	17	9	185
13	Mario Haberfeld (BR)	Cummins Walker Racing Ford-Cosworth/Reynard 01I	BS	9	-	-	-	-	-	-	-	-	13	7	14	14	15	
		Cummins Walker Racing Ford-Cosworth/Reynard 02I	BS	-	15	10	9	14	4^{m}	9	11	8	-	-	-	-	-	157
14	Rodolfo Lavin (MEX)	Corona Forsythe Championship Racing Ford-Cosworth/Lola B03/00	BS	10	-	9	-	-	14	15	-	-	11	12	-	15	13	
		Corona Forsythe Championship Racing Ford-Cosworth/Lola B02/00	BS	-	13	-	18	9	-	-	2^{+}	11	-	-	4	-	-	156
15	*Roberto Gonzalez (MEX)	NII Holdings PKV Racing Ford-Cosworth/Lola B02/00	BS	14	-	12	10	7	-	-	-	-	-	14	10	-	-	
		Nextel PKV Racing Ford-Cosworth/Lola B02/00	BS	-	9	-	-	-	13	13	16	12^{m}	10	-	-	11	12	136
16	*Nelson Philippe (F)	LeasePlan Rocketsports Racing Ford-Cosworth/Lola B01/00	BS	13	10	-	-	-	-	-	-	-	-	-	-	-	-	
		LeasePlan Rocketsports Racing Ford-Cosworth/Lola B02/00	BS	-	-	14	15	10	-	-	-	-	-	-	-	-	-	
		LeasePlan Mi-Jack Conquest Racing Ford-Cosworth/Reynard 02I	BS	-	-	-	-	-	-	-	-	13	-	-	-	-	-	
		LeasePlan Mi-Jack Conquest Racing Ford-Cosworth/Lola B01/00	BS	-	-	-	-	-	-	-	-	-	17	16	9	10	16	89
17	*Gaston Mazzacane (RA)	American Medical Response Dale Coyne Ford-Cosworth/Lola B01/00	BS	-	-	16	-	-	-	-	-	-	-	-	-	-	-	
		American Medical Response Dale Coyne Ford-Cosworth/Lola B02/00	BS	-	-	-	13	12	6	NS	18	15	12	13	15	-	-	73
18	*Guy Smith (GB)	Rocketsports Racing Ford-Cosworth/Lola B02/00	BS	-	-	-	-	-	-	-	10	18	16	9	17	9	17	53
19	*Alex Sperafico (BR)	Mi-Jack Conquest Racing Ford-Cosworth/Reynard 02I	BS	17	16	15	16	13	10	17	17	-	-	-	-	-	-	47
20	*David Besnard (AUS)	Wright Patton Shakespeare Walker Ford-Cosworth/Reynard 02I	BS	-	-	-	-	-	-	-	-	-	-	-	-	7^{m}	-	18
21	Memo Gidley (USA)	LeasePlan Rocketsports Racing Ford-Cosworth/Lola B02/00	BS	-	-	-	-	-	16	11	-	-	-	-	-	-	-	15
22	Tarso Marques (BR)	American Medical Response Dale Coyne Ford-Cosworth/Lola B01/00	BS	18	18	-	-	-	-	-	-	-	-	-	-	-	18	9
23	*Michael Valiante (CDN)	Wildlife Conservation Network Walker Ford-Cosworth/Reynard 02I	BS	-	-	-	-	-	-	-	-	-	-	-	-	-	14	7
24	*Jaroslav "Jarek" Janis (CZ)	American Medical Response Dale Coyne Ford-Cosworth/Lola B02/00	BS	-	-	-	-	-	-	-	-	-	-	-	-	18	-	3

•Tagliani was penalized two championship points following the Portland race for violating Champ Car Rule 2.8.5.
•Tagliani led the race at Las Vegas but did not earn a bonus championship point, per the stewards' ruling.

Black type indicates car still running at finish * rookie p pole position f fastest lap † led most laps + lap leader m most improved positions NS did not start

Left: Bourdais leads into Turn One at Toronto, with Tracy slotting into second ahead of Junqueira and Dominguez who collide moments later and crash heavily.
Phil Abbott/LAT

Champ Car Nation's Cup

1	Canada	380
2	France	358
3	Brazil	352
4	United States	310
5	Mexico	295
6	Spain (Catalonia)	195
7	England	195
8	Argentina	73
9	Australia	17
10	Czech Republic	3

Constructor's Championship

1	Lola	462
2	Reynard	168

ROSHFRANS Rookie of the Year

1	A.J. Allmendinger	229
2	Justin Wilson	188
3	Roberto Gonzalez	136
4	Nelson Philippe	89
5	Gaston Mazzacane	73
6	Guy Smith	53
7	Alex Sperafico	47
8	David Besnard	18
9	Michael Valiante	7
10	Jarek Janis	3

2004
BRIDGESTONE PRESENTS THE CHAMP CAR WORLD SERIES POWERED BY FORD

Michael Kim/LAT

LONG BEACH

NEW RULES GET FIRST ROAD TEST

CHAMP CAR'S new competition rules got their litmus test at Long Beach, including the keenly awaited push-to-pass feature added to the turbocharged Cosworth XFE engines, which allowed drivers an extra 50 horsepower – literally at their fingertips.

The points system underwent its first overhaul in nearly 20 years as Champ Car looked to promote action throughout the field, paying points all the way through 20th place, ensuring that every starter in the 18-car field would earn at least three points. Additionally, points were awarded for every driver that led a lap, for the driver setting the fastest lap and the driver who gained the most positions from the grid order.

The push-to-pass mechanism was the X factor in the weekend as it was set up to allow each driver 60 seconds of added boost. Champ Car and Cosworth electronic engineers designed the mechanism to increase the boost at the push of the button on the steering wheel, and the extra power would be available until the driver cracked the throttle, meaning that the feature would primarily be used on the two long straightaways on the 1.968-mile circuit.

Paul Tracy had a different idea however, and it was one that would eventually become commonplace on the Champ Car trail. Tracy jumped on the button at the drop of the green flag, catching front-row starters Sebastien Bourdais and Bruno Junqueira napping. The move allowed Tracy to rocket past the Newman/Haas duo from the third spot and take the lead into the first turn. It would be as close as anyone got all day as Tracy led 78 of the 81 laps for his fourth Long Beach win.

"I used the button right on the line to pick up more speed," Tracy said. "Bruno braked earlier than I expected and I had so much momentum, my car started to slide but by the time we got to the first turn I had the lead."

The new points system meant that Tracy left Long Beach with only a three-point lead instead of what would have been a four-point advantage under the old system, while the award for fastest lap kept everyone charging hard as each of the 13 cars that finished the race posted their quickest times on Lap 65 or later.

Right: 2003 Champ Paul Tracy celebrates his fourth win on the Long Beach streets.

Left and below: Tracy out duels Bruno Junqueira with the new push-to-pass button at the start to take the lead heading into Turn One.

Photographs: Michael Levitt/LAT

QUALIFYING

Sitting in his car on Saturday afternoon, watching a wet track rapidly drying as the sand slipped through the qualifying hourglass, Bruno Junqueira (PacifiCare Ford-Cosworth/Lola) was secure in the knowledge that he would start the following day's season-opening race on the front row. He earned that security by leading the first round of qualifying. Nevertheless, Junqueira had to sit back and watch the track dry – and the lap times of his pursuers tumble – as he and his Newman/Haas team debated when to allow the provisional polesitter to join the fray.

Eventually the margin between the field and Junqueira's Friday time of 1m 08.913s narrowed enough to force Junqueira onto the track. But a spate of late-session red flags kept the pack at bay as Junqueira's first-round effort held up for the Brazilian's eighth career Champ Car pole, ahead of teammate Sébastien Bourdais.

The Frenchman had only one shot to vault to the second spot and made good on the chance, using his final lap around the 1.968-mile street course to displace defending Long Beach winner Paul Tracy (Indeck Lola) from the second position.

Tracy had held the fastest time of the day, carding his top effort of 1m 10.196s nine minutes into the session, and appeared to have caught a break when Forsythe Championship Racing teammate Patrick Carpentier brought out a red flag with a trip into the tire wall at Turn Nine. But the vaunted Champ Car Safety Team got the situation fixed in time for the field to complete one more green flag lap, and Bourdais used it to his advantage as he ripped past the timing line with the checkered flag in the air, displacing Tracy and securing a front row starting position.

Tracy fell back to third on a day where very little else changed at the top of the order from the first round of qualifying. Alex Tagliani joined Tracy in the second row, ahead of an all-Herdez affair, with Mario Dominguez equaling a career-best with a fifth-place run ahead of his new teammate Ryan Hunter-Reay.

Carpentier forfeited his fastest lap of Saturday's session as penance for causing a red flag, but his Friday time was good enough to maintain seventh spot, alongside top rookie A.J. Allmendinger who made an impressive debut for the RuSPORT organization.

PAUL Tracy began his defense of the Bridgestone Presents The Champ Car World Series Powered by Ford title in the best possible style by taking victory in the 30th Anniversary Toyota Grand Prix of Long Beach.

Tracy employed the same aggressive approach that had made him the series' most successful active driver, stamping his authority on the race from outset by making a daring out-braking maneuver on Bruno Junqueira at the first corner. The Canadian yielded the lead only briefly en route to scoring his 27th career victory and fourth in the streets of Long Beach.

"It's a great way to start the season, and for us to come out of here with the championship lead is a big lift for us," said Tracy, after leading 78 of the 81 laps. "The team is really working well together and it was important for all of us to come here and run well right out of the box. The car was so good all day that we didn't really have to push very hard to be fast."

Junqueira never allowed Tracy any room to relax, but neither did he ever get close enough to make a serious bid for the lead. On two occasions Junqueira whittled a three-second-plus deficit down to under one second, but each time Tracy was equal to the challenge.

"I feel that the PacifiCare car was very good this whole weekend," said Junqueira. "I knew that Paul was going to be pushing at the start, and he was able to get around me in Turn One. We were on a different pit strategy which caused us to pit earlier than everyone else that was running up front. That kind of hurt us, but we were catching [Tracy]. I am happy to be on the podium, but I am a little disappointed because I feel that we had the car to win."

Without a doubt, the deciding moment had come right away at the drop of the green flag. After the first attempt at a start had been waved off due to improper alignment of the field, Tracy lost no time in making his presence felt. He took maximum advantage of the extra horsepower given by the use of the new push-to-pass button on the Ford-Cosworth XFE engine, pulled alongside Junqueira on the blast down Shoreline Drive, braked as late as he dared, then saved a lurid slide to take the lead at the apex of the first turn.

"I got off the line cleanly without any wheelspin," related Tracy. "It was very important to do that so I could get the best from the push-to-pass button. I used it at the [start] line and kept it on all the way down to the braking zone. I came close to the wall on the inside and slid into Turn One. I was able to keep it under control and get a lead and maintain it."

Even Junqueira was impressed: "Tracy braked really late in Turn One and went sideways. I thought he would lose it, but he didn't. That's Tracy. He's a great driver. It's really difficult to hold a guy when he drives hard like that."

Alex Tagliani, who started fourth for Rocketsports Racing, followed his fellow Canadian's lead by shuffling Sebastien Bourdais (McDonald's Lola) down to fourth place at the first turn, followed by Ryan Hunter-Reay (Herdez Lola) and yet another Canadian, Patrick Carpentier (Indeck Lola), who managed to get the better of the second Herdez car of Mario Dominguez.

A little farther back, however, there was a midfield melee which ended the day for Jimmy Vasser (Gulfstream/PKV Racing Lola), Alex Sperafico (Mi-Jack Conquest Racing Reynard) and Tarso Marques (American Medical Response/Dale Coyne Racing Lola). Rookies A.J. Allmendinger (RuSPORT Lola) and Nelson Philippe (LeasePlan/Rocketsports Lola) also were involved. Both were able to rejoin, although Allmendinger's high hopes following a strong qualifying performance were wiped out as he lost two laps before being restarted.

Surprisingly, this turned out to be the only incident of the day, and after a relatively brief full-course caution, Tracy set about trying to hammer home his advantage. He built a cushion of over two seconds inside the first 11 laps, but then Junqueira responded, turning a couple of quick laps to reduce the margin by half.

Tagliani couldn't hold onto the leading pair but still managed to retain third place ahead of Bourdais, Hunter-Reay, Carpentier and Dominguez as the first round of pit stops approached.

Junqueira caused something of a surprise by bringing his PacifiCare Lola onto pit lane for the first time after just 25 laps. Hunter-Reay was the next of the leaders to stop, a full three laps later, while Bourdais took on his first service after 29 laps. Tracy, meanwhile, was able to cement his advantage by waiting until lap 30, as did Tagliani and Dominguez.

Junqueira's ploy appeared to have backfired, as he trailed Tracy by more than five seconds once everyone was back up to speed. Tagliani still clung onto third place, while a gamble by Dominguez's crew, who elected not to fill their car's fuel tank to the brim, enabled him to vault all the way to fourth for the second stint of the 81-lap race.

Dominguez used the dual benefits of a lighter car (due to less fuel) and the softer Bridgestone "option" tires to post a charge during the middle of the race, turning a string of fast laps – quicker than anyone else at that stage – to edge clear of Bourdais and bring himself onto the tail of Tagliani by Lap 41. Catching and passing, however, proved altogether different tasks, and pretty soon the Mexican found Bourdais once again looming large in his mirrors.

Junqueira, too, was on a charge, closing to within 1.2 seconds of race leader Tracy by Lap 41. But Tracy responded, keeping his rival at bay and even edging away a little. The gap between them was up to 2.8 seconds by the time Junqueira made his second and final pit stop after 52 laps.

As had been the case earlier in the afternoon, the second round of pit activity saw some more shuffling of the order. Tracy, who stopped after 58 laps, resumed with a healthy margin over Junqueira, but the unfortunate Tagliani lost a lot of time due to a problem changing the right-rear wheel on his Johnson Controls Lola. Tagliani fell back to eighth place.

"We had a good race strategy and speed, which is most important," he reflected. "We had a good race but some bad luck, but this is only the start and we'll be in the hunt for podium finishes and great results all season."

Bourdais was the immediate beneficiary, rising to third place, while Dominguez's early final pit stop saw him fall into a battle for fourth with Carpentier, who stretched his middle stint longer than anyone else and duly led for a couple of laps. The tactic enabled Carpentier to earn a valuable championship bonus point under the new-for-2004 regulations, before ceding the advantage again to teammate Tracy, who romped home to the victory, well clear of Junqueira.

Bourdais set the fastest lap of the race in the closing stages as he closed onto the tail of his Newman/Haas Racing teammate.

"Consistency is the key to winning the championship this season," noted the canny Frenchman, "and to finish in P3 is a pretty good start to the season. I started on pole for the opener in St. Pete last year and hardly left with any points. This is a much better start to the season."

Carpentier and Dominguez battled hard for fourth place, and were separated by just over a half-second at the finish.

"We showed everyone we have a good package and I can't wait to go for it again next month at a home race for me in Mexico," said a delighted Dominguez.

Sixth place was taken by Justin Wilson (Mi-Jack Conquest Racing Lola) after a strong Champ Car debut. The Briton earned the extra point for making up the most positions during the race, climbing from 11th to sixth, and was also the highest-placed rookie.

Hunter-Reay struggled with inconsistent handling, especially in the middle of the race, and wound up seventh ahead of Tagliani and Mario Haberfeld (Cummins/Walker Racing Reynard), who earned his 12th top-10 finish in his 19th Champ Car start. Rodolfo Lavin (Corona Lola) rounded out the top 10 in his first start with the Forsythe Championship Racing team, which had expanded to three cars for 2004.

Jeremy Shaw

Above: Justin Wilson makes a solid Champ Car debut by finishing in sixth.
Leland Hill/LAT

Far left: Bruno Junqueira on the curbing on his way to 2004's first pole position.
Tom Anderson

Left center: Mario Haberfeld pilots one of the few Reynard's campaigning in '04.
Michael Kim/LAT

Below left: Ryan Hunter-Reay looks for engineer Will Phillips to improve his car.
Lesley Ann Miller/LAT

Below: Champ Car's Billy Kamphausen awaits Paul Tracy in the winner's circle.
Leland Hill/LAT

Right: **Tom Cruise is the most famous backseat driver to have enjoyed a ride in the awesome Champ Car two-seater.**
Mike Levitt/LAT

Bottom right: **"Is this man safe?" asks Cruise of "Supersub" Roberto Moreno.**
Lesley Ann Miller/LATLAT

Top: **California girls are all smiles as they tour the pit lane prior to the start.**
Lesley Ann Miller/LAT

Above: **Patrick Carpentier handles the hairpin on his way to fourth place.**
Michael Kim/LAT

Right: **Youngster Nelson Philippe takes time with team owner Paul Gentilozzi.**
Maria Grady/LAT

Below: **The Herdez crew refuels Mario Dominguez's Lola (left) as rookie A.J. Allmendinger returns after his service.**
Lesley Ann Miller/LAT

RIDE OF A LIFETIME

AFTER making its debut in the hands of defending series champion Paul Tracy during the Pro/Celebrity Media Day in Long Beach and then being taken for a spin around Times Square in New York City by Ryan Hunter-Reay for a new series of television spots to be aired on Spike TV, the Champ Car two-seater made its public bow at the Toyota Grand Prix of Long Beach. PKV Racing owner/driver Jimmy Vasser and former Champ Car competitor Roberto Moreno shared the driving duties during Pace Car lap sessions on Saturday and Sunday, delivering VIPs, high-profile celebrities and lucky members of the media the thrill ride of a lifetime.

First, Moreno took John Lassiter, the head of Pixar Studios and a longtime Champ Car fan, for a spin. During the morning session on Sunday, 1996 series champion Vasser gave actor and model Antonio Sabato Jr. a taste of the action. Then rumors started circulating that an even bigger celebrity was going to be in the car right before the race. Someone who might have played a driver in a movie...

At the last moment, after the guessing was done and with the two-seater still standing empty in pit lane, a golf cart appeared and out jumped Moreno with...Tom Cruise! The pair wore matching red, white and blue Champ Car race suits. Cruise looked revved up to go, but admitted that even his experience with stock cars during the filming of Days of Thunder had probably not prepared him for what to expect of the all-carbon Reynard chassis, powered by the same turbocharged 750hp Ford-Cosworth XFE engine and Bridgestone Potenza racing slicks as a regular Champ Car.

The two-seater – which was created in late 1999 by the PacWest team but had lain dormant aside from one brief shakedown test at Putnam Park, near Indianapolis, in early 2000 -- also featured a "panic button" for the passenger to let the driver know in case the ride was more than they could handle.

PKV Racing owner Kevin Kalkhoven was on hand to offer a few last words of advice. He also pointed out the infamous panic button to Cruise, who responded with a smile: "Roberto can bury the car four feet into a concrete wall and I won't be pushing that button!"

With that, they put on their helmets and jumped into the car for two laps at speed. How fast did Moreno reach with his celebrity passenger?

"175 mph," the former Champ Car race winner said with a grin. "And, no, Tom Cruise never pushed the panic button."

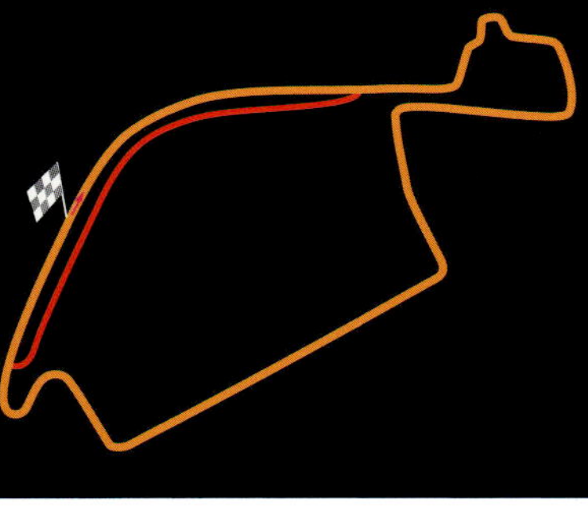

ROUND 1

TOYOTA

GRAND PRIX OF LONG BEACH

LONG BEACH STREET CIRCUIT, CALIFORNIA

APRIL 18, 81 laps of 1.968 miles – 159.408 miles

Pl.	Driver (Nat.)	No.	Team Sponsors Engine/Car	Tires	Q Speed	Q Time	Q Pos.	Laps	Time/Status	Ave.(mph)	Pts.
1	Paul Tracy (CDN)	1	Indeck Forsythe Championship Racing Ford-Cosworth/Lola B02/00	BS	102.447	1m 09.156s	3	81	1h 44m 12.348s	91.785	32
2	Bruno Junqueira (BR)	6	PacifiCare Newman/Haas Racing Ford-Cosworth/Lola B02/00	BS	102.808	1m 08.913s	1	81	1h 44m 18.029s	91.701	29
3	Sébastien Bourdais (F)	2	McDonald's Newman/Haas Racing Ford-Cosworth/Lola B01/00	BS	101.501	1m 09.800s	2	81	1h 44m 18.723s	91.691	27
4	Patrick Carpentier (CDN)	7	Indeck Forsythe Championship Racing Ford-Cosworth/Lola B02/00	BS	101.603	1m 09.730s	7	81	1h 44m 29.149s	91.539	24
5	Mario Dominguez (MEX)	55	Herdez Competition Ford-Cosworth/Lola B02/00	BS	102.001	1m 09.458s	5	81	1h 44m 29.875s	91.528	21
6	*Justin Wilson (GB)	34	Mi-Jack Conquest Racing Ford-Cosworth/Lola B02/00	BS	101.035	1m 10.122s	11	81	1h 44m 48.993s	91.250	20
7	Ryan Hunter-Reay (USA)	4	Herdez Competition Ford-Cosworth/Lola B03/00	BS	101.774	1m 09.613s	6	81	1h 44m 51.274s	91.217	17
8	Alex Tagliani (CDN)	8	Johnson Controls Rocketsports Racing Ford-Cosworth/Lola B02/00	BS	102.013	1m 09.450s	4	81	1h 45m 12.926s	90.904	15
9	Mario Haberfeld (BR)	5	Cummins Walker Racing Ford-Cosworth/Reynard 01I	BS	99.803	1m 10.988s	14	80	Running		13
10	Rodolfo Lavin (MEX)	3	Corona Forsythe Championship Racing Ford-Cosworth/Lola B03/00	BS	101.279	1m 09.953s	9	80	Running		11
11	Michel Jourdain Jr. (MEX)	9	Gigante RuSPORT Ford-Cosworth/Lola B04/00	BS	100.277	1m 10.652s	13	80	Running		10
12	*A.J. Allmendinger (USA)	10	BG Products/Red Bull RuSPORT Ford-Cosworth/Lola B03/00	BS	101.349	1m 09.905s	8	79	Running		9
13	*Nelson Philippe (F)	17	LeasePlan Rocketsports Racing Ford-Cosworth/Lola B01/00	BS	99.401	1m 11.275s	16	78	Running		8
14	*Roberto Gonzalez (MEX)	21	NII Holdings PKV Racing Ford-Cosworth/Lola B02/00	BS	99.373	1m 11.295s	17	76	Gearbox		7
15	Oriol Servia (E)	11	yokeTV.com Dale Coyne Racing Ford-Cosworth/Lola B2K/00	BS	100.818	1m 10.273s	12	14	Engine		6
16	Jimmy Vasser (USA)	12	Gulfstream PKV Racing Ford-Cosworth/Lola B02/00	BS	101.131	1m 10.056s	10	1	Accident		5
17	*Alex Sperafico (BR)	14	Mi-Jack Conquest Racing Ford-Cosworth/Reynard 02I	BS	99.453	1m 11.238s	15	1	Accident		4
18	Tarso Marques (BR)	19	American Medical Response Dale Coyne Ford-Cosworth/Lola B01/00	BS	92.239	1m 16.809s	18	1	Accident		3

*Denotes Rookie Driver

Caution flags: Lap 1, yellow start; laps 2-5, multi-car accident/Allmendinger, Vasser, Sperafico, Marques & Philippe. **Total:** Two for 5 laps.

Lap leaders: Bruno Junqueira, 1 (1 lap); Paul Tracy, 2-58 (57 laps); Patrick Carpentier, 59-60 (2 laps); Tracy, 61-81 (21 laps). **Totals:** Tracy, 78 laps; Carpentier, 2 laps; Junqueira, 1 lap.

Fastest race lap: Sébastien Bourdais, 1m 09.729s, 101.605 mph on lap 71.

Championship positions: 1 Tracy, 32; 2 Junqueira, 29; 3 Bourdais, 27; 4 Carpentier, 24; 5 Dominguez, 21; 6 Wilson, 20; 7 Hunter-Reay, 17; 8 Tagliani, 15; 9 Haberfeld, 13; 10 Lavin, 11; 11 Jourdain Jr., 10; 12 Allmendinger, 9; 13 Philippe, 8; 14 Gonzalez, 7; 15 Servia, 6; 16 Vasser, 5; 17 Sperafico, 4; 18 Marques, 3.

LONG BEACH SNIPPETS

Maria Grady/LAT

• The glamorous Toyota Grand Prix of Long Beach never fails to attract a host of celebrities. Among those sighted on race day were Sir Paul McCartney and his wife Heather Mills (above), who were guests of Newman/Haas Racing co-owner and fellow A-lister Paul Newman.

• Previously unheralded Mexican Rodolfo Lavin turned some heads in his first outing with Forsythe Championship Racing. Lavin generally languished toward the back of the pack during his rookie campaign in 2003, but he was fifth fastest in the opening practice on Friday and third quickest in the brief pre-qualifying warmup -- each time ahead of teammate Patrick Carpentier. "We're very pleased," said crew chief Dave Stephens. "He's doing a good job."

• Paul Tracy's 27th victory moved him into a tie for eighth in the all-time Champ Car records with Johnny Rutherford. A.J. Foyt remained easily the most successful driver in history with 67 wins, followed by Mario Andretti on 52. Tracy, incidentally, ran Forsythe Championship Racing's Lola B02/00 chassis 07 – the very same car he took to victory in 2003 at Long Beach, as well as Monterrey, Vancouver and Mid-Ohio during his championship year.

• Carpentier made a steady start to the weekend, which perhaps was hardly surprising given that his deal to run a third Forsythe Championship Racing entry was concluded relatively late in the off-season. Carpentier, incidentally, reverted to his original helmet design following the tobacco legislation-enforced withdrawal of previous principal sponsor, Player's. He eventually qualified seventh, and even after a quick spin in the warmup, which tweaked his Indeck Lola's rear wing, he pronounced himself content: "I think we've got a good race car," he said. "I'm pretty happy." The Canadian went on to finish a strong fourth.

• RuSPORT's performance in its first-ever Champ Car race was especially creditable, given that it had made the decision to field a second car (for Michel Jourdain Jr.) less than a month before the first race. The team duly arrived in Long Beach with no backup car either for the Mexican or its young American rising star, A.J. Allmendinger, who also made an impressive debut. "A.J.'s been very sensible, very mature," said RuSPORT Team President Jeremy Dale after the reigning Toyota Atlantic champion had qualified eighth. "He knows we only have two cars here, not four, and that he'll learn a lot if he finishes every session in one piece and does as many laps [in the race] as he can."

• The Newman/Haas and Rocketsports teams found themselves unexpectedly busy following the Sunday morning warmup session, after Sébastien Bourdais and Alex Tagliani were involved in separate incidents. Bourdais' McDonald's Lola sustained fairly substantial damage after running over the remnants of a broken driveshaft from Tarso Marques' car on the front straightaway. The car's carbonfiber undertray needed to be patched, and a bent right-front lower wishbone was replaced, along with the nose-wings. Tagliani's car required similar "surgery" after he had spun into the tire wall at Turn Eight.

• Bruno Junqueira produced some prescient words after finishing second to Paul Tracy – and ahead of Newman/Haas teammate Sébastien Bourdais -- in the opening race of the season: "I think it's going to be a great year," said the Brazilian. "I think there's going to be a big fight between me, Tracy and Sébastien. I believe that there's going to be other drivers that are going to be fast, as well. But for sure, you will have to be consistent to win the championship With Tracy and Sébastien, and some of the other guys, you have to concentrate all the time if you are going to do well."

• Tarso Marques (below) received a late call-up from Dale Coyne to drive his #19 American Medical Response Lola, but was beset by a multitude of problems. Marques, incidentally, had gained his first experience of a Champ Car in 1999, when he tested impressively for Coyne – and then was plucked away by Marlboro Team Penske. The likeable Brazilian was an impressive 10th fastest in the first practice session, but crashed early in provisional qualifying. Saturday's final session lasted just one lap due to clutch failure, and his warmup session was curtailed early when a driveshaft broke. Sadly, Marques' race was over almost before it had begun, as he was unable to avoid being involved in the fracas at Turn One.

Michael Levitt/LAT

Dan Streck/LAT

MONTERREY

BRIDGESTONE PRESENTS THE CHAMP CAR WORLD SERIES POWERED BY FORD • ROUND 2

MARIO'S MONTEREY MOMENT

THE abrupt departure of Adrian Fernandez from the Champ Car World Series in the spring of 2004 unexpectedly left some Mexican Champ Car fans in need of a new hero. Nine-year veteran Michel Jourdain Jr. still carried the banner and neophytes Rodolfo Lavin and Roberto Gonzalez had shown promise, but it was Mario Dominguez who stepped into the void when the series visited Monterrey's Fundidora Park.

Dan Streck/LAT

Dominguez made a huge splash in 2003 with a Miami victory, and outshone race winner Paul Tracy in the Mexico City season finale after taking the final spot on the podium, leading to perhaps the first time in series history that the third-place finisher got his own victory lap. His next trip to his home country was equally as impressive as he put together a sterling weekend, scoring his first Champ Car front-row start and coming home with a second consecutive Mexico podium.

Dominguez posted a pair of track-record laps in Saturday qualifying to threaten for the pole, but Sébastien Bourdais bumped him to the outside of the front row where he would stay after a red flag brought out by Gonzalez denied Dominguez a final shot at the pole.

The qualifying effort nearly went for naught on race day, however, as he spun on the second lap and dropped from second to 18th. Undaunted, the Herdez squad quickly developed a strategy that would get the hard-charging Mexican back to the sharp end of the field.

He pitted nine laps ahead of the leaders on his first stop allowing him to turn fast laps on a clear track as the rest of the field made their visits to the pit lane. Dominguez led briefly before his second pit visit, and then when the smoke had cleared after the second round of stops, Dominguez found himself in third, where he would finish after holding off Patrick Carpentier for the final 15 laps.

"I can't say enough about my team," said a jubilant Dominguez. "We had a good start and then I just lost it on the cold tires. My engineer told me that they were working up a strategy and that I should drive as hard as I could. I did and it was just unbelievable."

Above: Dominguez spins on lap 2, but recovers to finish third in his homeland.
Phil Abbott/LAT

Left: Hard work by the Herdez crew helps lift Dominguez to the podium.

Main photo: Newman/Haas teammates Bourdais and Junqueira lead the field on the opening lap at Fundidora Park.
Photographs: Mike Levitt/LAT

QUALIFYING

A controversial two days of qualifying ended with a thrilling final period on Saturday afternoon as Sébastien Bourdais and local hero Mario Dominguez traded fast laps midway through the 35-minute session like a pair of welterweights throwing punches. The winners of the last two Jim Trueman Rookie of the Year Awards swapped the top spot four times in a span of three minutes.

The flurry was halted when Roberto Gonzalez spun and crashed his #21 Nextel Lola near the pit entrance. Bourdais was atop the speed sheets when the green flag waved with 11 minutes to run in the 35-minute session, but once again there was a red-flag interruption, this time with just two minutes remaining when Nelson Philippe's Lease-Plan entry ground to a halt. Bourdais could breathe a sigh of relief as no one had approached his time, leaving him to snare the pole in Monterrey for the second consecutive campaign.

"This track is suiting me very well," said the Frenchman after posting a new track record at 1m 13.915s. "Bridgestone has brought a great tire and we have made some improvements to the car. That's why we are one second faster than last year."

Dominguez settled for second, earning the best grid placing of his three-year Champ Car career. His previous best starting spot was a fifth at Elkhart Lake.

"This is a fantastic result for my team, my sponsors and all of the great fans in Mexico," declared Dominguez. "I am very happy but I can't help but wonder what would have happened if the final red flag had not happened."

Rookie Justin Wilson (#34 Mi-Jack Lola) was the only driver to make a major move in the final minutes after the Gonzalez crash, vaulting to third on the grid ahead of Bruno Junqueira, who admitted he failed to put a representative lap together in his PacifiCare Lola, and the two Indeck/Forsythe Championship Racing Lolas of Patrick Carpentier and Paul Tracy. All of the top six bested the previous qualifying record of 1m 14.938s, set by Bourdais in 2003.

Above: Paul Tracy ponders his race prospects after qualifying in sixth.
Michael Levitt/LAT

SÉBASTIEN Bourdais had some unfinished business to take care of going into the Tecate Telmex Grand Prix of Monterrey. One year earlier, Bourdais had qualified fastest at the 2.104-mile road course set within Fundidora Park, but ended his day out of the money after a miscommunication triggered a chain of events that left him 16th. This time around, the Newman/Haas Racing pilot again took the green flag from the pole position and hardly turned a wheel wrong all day as he stormed to the fourth win of his Champ Car career on a glorious 92-degree day.

Bourdais led 43 laps, set a new fastest race lap record in his McDonald's Ford-Cosworth/Lola and outdistanced his teammate Bruno Junqueira's PacifiCare Lola by 3.852 seconds to vault into the series points lead. Coming on the heels of a strong third-place finish in Long Beach, the result enabled Bourdais to take another step toward erasing the memory of the opening two races of the 2003 season, when he earned two poles and yet failed to notch even a top-10 finish.

"Well, it's much better to be leading the championship than having two bad results to start with," said the 25-year-old Frenchman. "But, you know, it's still a long way to go. It's just going to be all about consistency and if we are in the top five consistently through the season, I think both Bruno and I should be fighting each other for the lead at the end."

Fastest in qualifying on both Friday and Saturday, Bourdais was clearly the favorite for top honors on race day. But after wearing out a right-rear Bridgestone tire after just a few laps in the final warmup, held in hot, humid conditions, Bourdais knew it would not be an easy task to translate his obvious pace into a race victory. After emergency consultation with race engineer Craig Hampson, the decision was made to seek a solution by altering his car's setup.

"It was the most dramatic changes I've ever done to a car between the warmup and the race," noted Bourdais. "We shifted the weight and made about three big changes. It was a big gamble and I was very worried. We ran the front [anti-roll] bar full stiff through the first stint and I came in a little early just to check the tires and make sure we were OK."

Despite his initial concerns, Bourdais led the 18-car field through a clean start as Mexican hero Mario Dominguez gave chase with the #55 Herdez Competition Lola. Dominguez fought gamely through the first lap before bringing forth a collective gasp from the expectant crowd as he spun in Turn Two and fell to the back of the pack, triggering the first full-course caution of the day.

Indeed, the early stages were peppered with minor incidents which ensured three more interruptions inside the first 21 laps. Next to run into difficulty was 17-year-old Frenchman Nelson Philippe – by far the youngest driver in Champ Car history – who, after starting 17th in the LeasePlan/Rocketsports Racing Lola, was up to 13th before spinning off at Turn 10. A little later Tarso Marques lost control of Dale Coyne's American Medical Response Lola in Turn Six. He had been running confidently in ninth place at the time. The Brazilian, too, required a tow-start by the Champ Car Safety Truck. Unfortunately, his day went from bad to worse when the tow rope somehow became entangled in his Lola's suspension, which promptly broke, so Marques became the afternoon's first official retirement.

After a half-dozen more laps of green-flag racing, Philippe was involved in his second adventure of the day, this time making contact with the Nextel/PKV Racing Lola of Mexican driver Roberto Gonzalez. Mario Haberfeld's Cummins/Walker Racing Reynard also was caught up in the melee. All three were able to rejoin.

The order at the front of the field, meanwhile, had remained unchanged. Bourdais still led from teammate Junqueira and the impressive Justin Wilson, who had qualified an excellent fourth in Eric Bachelart's Mi-Jack Conquest Racing Lola and, like Junqueira, had taken advantage of Dominguez's earlier miscue to

Far left: Mario Dominguez brings the Mexican crowd to its feet, as the Herdez driver earns a podium in his native land.
Phil Abbott/LAT

Left: Sébastien Bourdais raises just one of the many pole flags he would win in 2004.
Michael Levitt/LAT

Below: Justin Wilson continued to shine, holding off Tracy en route to another sixth.

Below: Alex Tagliani improved 10 spots on his way to a top-five finish for Rocketsports.
Photographs: Paul Abbott/LAT

THE BEST LAID PLANS...

LOOKING for a way to spice up Champ Car qualifying sessions and force teams to spend their time on the track instead of on Pit Lane, series officials introduced dramatic changes for Friday and Saturday qualifying in Monterrey. But the drama on the track brought on by the changes paled in comparison to the drama going on in the team haulers.

The idea was to split the field into two groups on Friday, with each group having just 15 minutes to run their best time. The five fastest drivers in each session then went into another 15-minute session where the single point for qualifying was up for grabs. The Friday leader, however, would only be guaranteed a spot in the final qualifying shootout on Saturday -- not the front-row starting position that the rules had guaranteed in the past.

Saturday's final session would be vastly different as well, with all 18 cars on track for a 30-minute session, whereupon the 10 fastest (or nine quickest plus the Friday leader) would be allowed seven laps each to determine the polesitter.

"We believe this format will provide intense, hard-fought action for our fans and create drama during both days of qualifying." said Vice President of Operations John Lopes.

The drama reached a fever pitch after provisional qualifying, however, as the Newman/Haas Racing duo led the crescendo of calls for a change. NHR's Sébastien Bourdais led the first session while teammate Bruno Junqueira paced the second, posting the day's best time of 1m 15.834s. But in the final session -- for which the earlier times did not count – Bourdais won the championship point by leading the session with a time of 1m 15.978s -- slower than the one Junqueira posted 15 minutes earlier.

The drivers let their feelings be known immediately after the session, leading to a change for Saturday's final round of qualifying.

"We came into Monterrey with a special procedure tailored to provide excitement for the fans," Lopes said. "After review and consultation with the teams, we felt our Friday qualifying did not achieve the intended result. Therefore, we will revert back to the original procedure."

Top: **Roberto Gonzalez locks his brakes, trying a little *too* hard for his home crowd.**

Above right: **Patrick Carpentier shows why he belongs in the car with his second consecutive top-four finish.**
Photographs Michael Levitt/LAT

move into the top three.

Wilson, though, was one of several contenders to struggle with excessive rear tire wear, and the Englishman was having to work increasingly hard to stay ahead of Long Beach winner Paul Tracy (#1 Indeck Lola). Jimmy Vasser held down a strong sixth in his Gulfstream/PKV Racing entry, followed by a charging Alex Tagliani, who qualified a disappointing 15th his Johnson Controls/Rocketsports Lola but by Lap 19 had worked his way past Oriol Servia's yokeTV.com Lola and into sixth place. Tagliani nipped ahead of Vasser almost immediately after the next full-course caution, then leapfrogged both Wilson and Tracy in Turn One, when Wilson's increasingly wayward machine finally got the better of him.

"The car was bouncing and sliding all over the place," recounted the Briton. "It was a real hassle. I guess Paul [Tracy] had a similar problem because he couldn't get by me. But a few others drove past like I was standing still...which I was!"

Bourdais' aforementioned slightly conservative strategy saw him become the first of the leaders to make their first scheduled pit stop, after 26 laps. Worse, a fumbled wheel nut cost him valuable extra seconds, and after Junqueira's crew executed a perfect pit stop one lap later, the Brazilian was able to rejoin ahead of the Frenchman.

The impressive Tagliani took over the point after the Newman/Haas cars had pulled onto pit lane, and the Canadian quickly built up a gap over the still-battling Wilson and Tracy before pitting himself after 30 laps.

Tagliani, Tracy and Ryan Hunter-Reay (#4 Herdez Lola) were the last of the leaders to take on service for the first time, but instead of the lead reverting to the Newman/Haas duo, it was Patrick Carpentier (#7 Indeck/Forsythe Championship Racing Lola) who suddenly found himself out in front. The French-Canadian had made his first pit stop shortly before the previous full-course caution, and was able to regain much of the time lost while everyone circulated slowly behind the pace car.

Dominguez, too, profited mightily from the propitiously timed caution, emerging in second place ahead of fellow Mexican Rodolfo Lavin in Jerry Forsythe's Corona Lola and Alex Sperafico (Mi-Jack Reynard). Junqueira and Bourdais followed in fourth and fifth, but quickly overhauled Sperafico and soon were hot on the heels of Lavin.

As expected, the second and final round of pit stops proved crucial. Dominguez and Carpentier needed to take on rather more fuel than those following the same strategy as Junqueira & Co., and so when the stops were completed – with Bourdais managing to complete one more lap than his teammate – the Frenchman was back out in front, followed by Junqueira, Dominguez and Carpentier. Bourdais then turned a sequence of stunningly quick laps – more than a half-second better than anyone else could manage – to open out an appreciable lead which he had no trouble in maintaining until the finish, despite the torrid conditions.

"It was one of the toughest races I've had for sure, along with Cleveland last year," reflected an exhausted Bourdais. "I pushed so hard I was really dehydrated at the end of the race. I could hardly walk when I got out of the car after the race."

Junqueira, meanwhile, was content with second place: "It was a great result, finishing 1-2 on the podium with Sébastien. It was a good race. Everyone had different pit strategies, which made it interesting and a bit of a challenge."

Dominguez chased gamely in third, merely 1.4 seconds adrift of Junqueira at the checkered flag after a fine effort in front of his home crowd.

"I am so happy," said Dominguez. "I was really worried after my spin but the Herdez team, I don't know how they got me back on the podium but it is a big result for us. To have a race like this and come back to run third in front of our Mexican fans makes me very excited."

Carpentier finished fourth for the second race in a row, while an excellent effort by Tagliani was rewarded with fifth. The Rocketsports Racing pilot also earned bonus championship points for leading the race and for gaining the most positions.

Wilson and Tracy overcame their handling woes to finish sixth and seventh.

Jeremy Shaw

ROUND 2

TECATE/TELMEX GRAND PRIX OF MONTERREY

PARQUE FUNDIDORA, NUEVO LEON, MEXICO

MAY 23, 72 laps of 2.104 miles – 151.488 miles

Place	Driver (Nat.)	No.	Sponsor(s) Team Engine/Car	Tires	Q Speed	Q Time	Q Pos	Laps	Time/Status	Ave. (mph)	Pts
1	Sébastien Bourdais (F)	2	McDonald's Newman/Haas Racing Ford-Cosworth/Lola B01/00	BS	102.474	1m 13.915s	1	72	1h 45m 01.498s	86.544	35
2	Bruno Junqueira (BR)	6	PacifiCare Newman/Haas Racing Ford-Cosworth/Lola B02/00	BS	101.800	1m 14.405s	4	72	1h 45m 05.350s	86.491	28
3	Mario Dominguez (MEX)	55	Herdez Competition Ford-Cosworth/Lola B02/00	BS	101.885	1m 14.343s	2	72	1h 45m 06.707s	86.473	26
4	Patrick Carpentier (CDN)	7	Indeck Forsythe Championship Racing Ford-Cosworth/Lola B02/00	BS	101.499	1m 14.625s	5	72	1h 45m 07.617s	86.460	24
5	Alex Tagliani (CDN)	8	Johnson Controls Rocketsports Racing Ford-Cosworth/Lola B02/00	BS	99.528	1m 16.103s	15	72	1h 45m 11.398s	86.408	23
6	*Justin Wilson (GB)	34	Mi-Jack Conquest Racing Ford-Cosworth/Lola B02/00	BS	101.869	1m 14.354s	3	72	1h 45m 12.866s	86.388	20
7	Paul Tracy (CDN)	1	Indeck Forsythe Championship Racing Ford-Cosworth/Lola B02/00	BS	101.366	1m 14.723s	6	72	1h 45m 18.545s	86.311	17
8	Ryan Hunter-Reay (USA)	4	Herdez Competition Ford-Cosworth/Lola B03/00	BS	100.636	1m 15.265s	8	72	1h 45m 23.749s	86.239	15
9	*Roberto Gonzalez (MEX)	21	NII Holdings PKV Racing Ford-Cosworth/Lola B02/00	BS	99.938	1m 15.791s	12	72	1h 45m 28.262s	86.178	13
10	*Nelson Philippe (F)	17	LeasePlan Rocketsports Racing Ford-Cosworth/Lola B01/00	BS	98.125	1m 17.191s	17	72	1h 45m 29.423s	86.162	11
11	Michel Jourdain Jr. (MEX)	9	Gigante RuSPORT Ford-Cosworth/Lola B04/00	BS	99.920	1m 15.805s	13	72	1h 45m 30.695s	86.145	10
12	Jimmy Vasser (USA)	12	Gulfstream PKV Racing Ford-Cosworth/Lola B02/00	BS	100.746	1m 15.183s	7	71	Spun		9
13	Rodolfo Lavin (MEX)	3	Corona Forsythe Championship Racing Ford-Cosworth/Lola B02/00	BS	99.537	1m 16.096s	14	70	Running		8
14	Oriol Servia (E)	11	yokeTV.com Dale Coyne Racing Ford-Cosworth/Lola B2K/00	BS	100.463	1m 15.395s	9	70	Running		7
15	Mario Haberfeld (BR)	5	Cummins Walker Racing Ford-Cosworth/Reynard 02I	BS	98.765	1m 16.691s	16	62	Accident		6
16	*Alex Sperafico (BR)	14	Mi-Jack Conquest Racing Ford-Cosworth/Reynard 02I	BS	97.437	1m 17.736s	18	46	Accident		5
17	*A.J. Allmendinger (USA)	10	BG Products/Red Bull RuSPORT Ford-Cosworth/Lola B03/00	BS	100.094	1m 15.673s	11	24	Fire		4
18	Tarso Marques (BR)	19	American Medical Response Dale Coyne Ford-Cosworth/Lola B01/00	BS	100.214	1m 15.582s	10	11	Accident		3

*Denotes Rookie Driver

Caution flags: Laps 2-3, Dominguez spun/stalled; laps 6-7, Philippe spun/stalled; laps 12-15, Marques spun/stalled; laps 21-23, Philippe & Gonzalez spun/Philippe stalled; laps 41-44, Servia spun/stalled; laps 63-64, accident/Lavin & Haberfeld, Lavin stalled. Total: Six for 17 laps.

Lap leaders: Sébastien Bourdais, 1-25 (25 laps); Bruno Junqueira, 26 (1 lap); Alex Tagliani, 27-30 (4 laps); Patrick Carpentier, 31-46 (16 laps); Mario Dominguez, 47 (1 lap); Junqueira, 48-51 (4 laps); Bourdais, 52 (1 lap); Tagliani, 53-54 (2 laps); Justin Wilson, 55 (1 lap); Bourdais, 56-72 (17 laps). Totals: Bourdais, 43 laps; Carpentier, 16 laps; Tagliani, 6 laps; Junqueira, 5 laps; Wilson, 1 lap, Dominguez, 1 lap.

Fastest race lap: Sébastien Bourdais, 1m 15.021s, 100.964 mph on lap 57 (new record).

Championship positions: 1 Bourdais, 62; 2 Junqueira, 57; 3 Tracy, 49; 4 Carpentier, 48; 5 Dominguez, 47; 6 Wilson, 40; 7 Tagliani, 38; 8 Hunter-Reay, 32; 9 Gonzalez & Jourdain Jr., 20; 11 Haberfeld, Philippe & Lavin, 19; 14 Vasser, 14; 15 Allmendinger & Servia, 13; 17 Sperafico, 9; 18 Marques, 6.

MONTERREY SNIPPETS

• Oriol Servia (above) qualified Dale Coyne Racing's yokeTV.com Lola a solid ninth – one position ahead of underrated teammate Tarso Marques. It was the first time since Gualter Salles took a magnificent fourth on the grid at Long Beach in 1998 that a Coyne car had started among the top 10 in a Champ Car race, and the first time ever that both of the veteran's entries had started within the top five rows. (In fact, the only other previous top-10 efforts for Coyne, who founded his team in 1984, had come at the final two races in 1997, when Michel Jourdain Jr. was eighth in qualifying at Laguna Seca, then fifth in the very next race at Fontana.) Sadly, both drivers were out of luck on race day. Marques was involved in a bizarre accident as the Safety Truck attempted to restart him following a spin, while Servia rose as high as sixth before spinning off and losing a lap.

• Sébastien Bourdais earned his sixth career pole in just his 20th Champ Car start, making him the first driver since Juan Pablo Montoya in 1999 to score six poles in his first 20 events. Bourdais also gave Newman/Haas Racing its third win in the four-year history of the Monterrey event. (Cristiano da Matta won the inaugural race in 2001, then repeated the feat in 2002.) The team's joy was compounded by Bruno Junqueira finishing second.

• Mario Haberfeld and his wife Ana (Aninha to be precise) virtually had to tear themselves away from their home in Key Biscayne, Florida, in order to make the trip to Monterrey. That wasn't due of any lack of enthusiasm for the task at hand, you understand. Instead it was because they had recently acquired a new member of the household – an adorable Bichon Frise dog by the name of Vida ("life" in Portuguese). "It was either that or a baby," joked Ana. Vida was left in the capable hands of close friends Christian and Andrea Fittipaldi while the Haberfelds journeyed to Mexico.

• While most drivers had merely completed one, or at most two tests during the month since the Long Beach season opener, Bruno Junqueira also had been busily preparing for the Newman/Haas team's one-off outing at the Indianapolis 500. And despite the fact Junqueira once again was forced out of the limelight by teammate Sébastien Bourdais in Monterrey, his experienced chief mechanic, Donny Hoevel, was impressed by the Brazilian's upbeat approach: "The guy's actually got a very good attitude. Maybe doing all these laps at The Speedway is doing him some good."

• Alex Tagliani battled a mysterious steering problem during the two days of practice and qualifying and lined up a disappointed 15th on the grid. Happily, the cause was finally determined (human error having ensured an incorrect camber setting), and Tagliani found his Johnson Controls/Rocketsports Racing Lola far more manageable in the race morning warmup, during which he set the fourth fastest time. His confidence restored, Tagliani immediately began picking off the cars ahead of him. By Lap 27 he even found himself in the lead, and eventually finished fifth. "The team gave me a great car and we worked together to develop a good strategy," said Tagliani. "We communicated throughout the race to make it happen and we gained enough positions for an excellent finish."

• Long Beach winner Paul Tracy had a weekend to forget. The defending series champion was never happy with the handling of his car – "It had no grip all weekend," he lamented – and was fortunate to finish as high as seventh. At least he fared better than fellow Las Vegas resident Jimmy Vasser, who was clearly faster in the closing stages but whose attempt to make an outside pass on the very last corner ended when he was punted into a spin. "PT completed screwed up," railed Vasser, who clambered out of his stricken Gulfstream car within sight of the finish line, falling from a potential seventh to 12th. "He should be the one out, not me."

• The Sunday crowd of 94,514 bettered the 2003 race-day crowd at Fundidora Park. The three-day total was 183,311, giving Champ Car a total attendance of over 350,000 fans after two events in 2004.

Photographs: Michael Levitt/LAT

BRIDGESTONE PRESENTS THE CHAMP CAR WORLD SERIES POWERED BY FORD • ROUND 3

MILWAUKEE

Inset left: Champagne sprays on the podium as Patrick Carpentier and Michel Jourdain toast Ryan Hunter-Reay's victory.
Michael Levitt/LAT

Main photograph: Hunter-Reay led from flag-to-flag to capture his second career win and his first for the Herdez team.
Michael Kim/LAT

RYAN'S BIG NIGHT

THE mood around the Herdez Competition shop was upbeat as the team headed to Milwaukee for the first oval race of the Champ Car season. Coming off a strong performance in Monterrey, and with one of the sport's top oval-track gurus in its corner, the squad expected similar results at the Milwaukee Mile.

Herdez Technical Director Tom Brown had accumulated a mass of experience during his 20 years on the Champ Car trail, and on a moonlit night in early June, if there was a man poised to tap into that know-how, it was rising American star Ryan Hunter-Reay.

Hunter-Reay was blindingly quick right out of the box, finishing first or second in each of the four on-track sessions leading up to race day, including a polewinning performance that gave the team and its young driver their first-ever Champ Car poles.

Race night was no different as RHR took command from the drop of the green flag and trounced the 18-car field en route to his second career victory. He led each of the 250 laps on the night, setting a record for most laps led in a single event.

"We had a great car, the crew gave me perfect pit stops and I did my part in the race," Hunter-Reay said. "I was concerned with traffic but I had a very strong car under me. Even so, I couldn't relax for a second out there. What a great day for our team."

Hunter-Reay put half the field a lap in arrears by Lap 32, and by Lap 61 only oval-track ace and Milwaukee record-holder Patrick Carpentier and 2003 Milwaukee winner Michel Jourdain Jr. remained on the lead lap. No one would ever get any closer.

"It was a perfect weekend for Ryan," concluded Herdez Managing Director Keith Wiggins. "The car was perfect all weekend and he made full use of it. This is a testament to the whole team."

QUALIFYING

During the previous two seasons, the Herdez Competition squad had been expanding into uncharted territory, with Mario Dominguez taking its (and his) first Champ Car victory in Australia in 2002 and then teaming with Roberto Moreno to add its first 1-2 finish a year later in Miami. The team continued that upward trend on a beautiful Friday night in the suburbs of Milwaukee as second-year driver Ryan Hunter-Reay scored the maiden pole of his Champ Car career and the first in the history of Herdez Competition. Hunter-Reay claimed the honor with a lap of 20.509 seconds (181.150 mph) to become the 165th driver in the all-time history of Champ Car racing to win a series pole.

Hunter-Reay was fast right out of the box on the Milwaukee Mile oval, leading Thursday night's practice and pacing Friday afternoon's run as well. He earned the final spot in the single-car qualifying order by virtue of being fastest in the earlier practice sessions, and turned a time on his first lap that was good enough for the pole. Cementing his superiority, the young American stayed in the throttle and dropped his time even lower on his second lap.

"We knew what we had to do going into qualifying and we were able to accomplish it," said Hunter-Reay matter-of-factly. "I have great expectations with my new team and I am so happy to put the Herdez car on the pole."

Hunter-Reay's effort relegated points leader Sébastien Bourdais to the outside of the front row for Saturday night's 250-lap race. The Frenchman earned his third front-row placing in as many races and his ninth in just 21 Champ Car starts – a solid effort given the fact he had crashed during a recent test and had been uncompetitive at Milwaukee during his rookie season.

"This result was a lot better than I expected and the car was good," said Bourdais.

Track record holder Patrick Carpentier put himself in a strong position to score his first Milwaukee victory, grabbing third on the starting grid with his Indeck Lola. Carpentier had finished on the podium twice in the previous four years including a third-place run in 2003.

Mario Dominguez made it two Herdez cars in the top four. The Mexican maintained his show of strength in qualifying this season, starting in the first two rows for the second race in succession despite never having qualified better than fifth previously.

THE 2003 Champ Car race at the Milwaukee Mile resulted in what was labeled a dominant performance by veteran Michel Jourdain Jr., who led all except 16 laps; but series sophomore Ryan Hunter-Reay came up with a new definition of the term in the 2004 edition, watched by an enthusiastic Saturday-night crowd.

Hunter-Reay set off from the pole as night fell on the historic speedway and immediately stamped his authority on the Time Warner Cable Road Runner 250 Presented by U.S. Bank. The Herdez Competition driver went on to become the first Champ Car driver in 12 seasons to lead every inch of an oval event, pacing a new single-race record 250 laps.

"What a day!" exclaimed the American. "It was a tough battle with all the traffic, I couldn't relax one second. It was a great team effort. We stayed sharp all night long, had excellent pit stops and a great car setup. It is a terrific day for the Herdez Competition team and all my sponsors."

The resident of Boca Raton, Florida, showed his strength early and often, taking just 14 laps to start negotiating slower traffic and ripping off to a monumental lead to put the entire 18-car field in danger of going a lap behind. Fortunately, their salvation came on Lap 50 in a brush with the wall that tightened not only the evening's contest but also the championship race as points leader Sébastien Bourdais lost control while in hot pursuit of a fired-up Rodolfo Lavin. Bourdais hit the Turn Four wall, terminally bending the suspension on his McDonald's Lola.

"When Lavin went low [into the corner] I was already low," explained Bourdais, who failed to finish for the first time since Montreal in August 2003. "He took all of the downforce from my car. I crashed but that's part of the job. It's tough to get experience on an oval when we only race on one per year.

"I'm not worried about the points now," he continued. "Obviously it was good to put the McDonald's car on the front of the standings but there is still a lot of [the] season ahead."

Bourdais' mishap brought out the second caution period of the evening (the first had come on the very first lap when oval neophyte Justin Wilson spun and glanced the wall in Turn Two). Such was Hunter-Reay's astonishing pace that only three other cars remained on the same lap: the two Indeck/Forsythe Championship Racing Lolas of Patrick Carpentier and Paul Tracy, and defending race winner Jourdain who was doing a sterling job for the fledgling RuSPORT Champ Car team. Jourdain, indeed, had snuck past both Bourdais and Lavin on Lap 48 – the lap before Bourdais' accident – and was especially grateful to see the caution lights flash on.

The ensuing restart ended the night for another heavy hitter as Tracy made a move to pass teammate Carpentier on the outside of Turns One and Two. Carpentier wasn't in any mood to allow Tracy easy passage, however, and the defending series champion ran high into the marbles in mid-corner, then into the wall.

"I was a little disappointed," said Tracy, with masterful understatement. "I think Pat could have given me more room, but that's racing."

Carpentier, meanwhile, saw the incident from an altogether different perspective: "On the restart I tried to keep with Ryan and got sideways. I caught it, but that lost me some time and momentum and Paul went around me so we were side-by-side in Turn One. We didn't touch at all and he just went up into the wall.

"I don't think I'm going to talk to him tonight," added the French-Canadian with a wry chuckle. "We get along pretty well. It's very sad that he went up into the wall. Paul races very hard and we all respect him for that but I don't think he expected me to drive it in that deep."

Suddenly, just three cars remained on the lead lap. The middle part of the race continued in the same vein as Hunter-Reay pulled out to a 10-second lead while Carpentier and Jourdain, who had worked his way impressively from ninth on the grid, battled for second and third.

Hunter-Reay was never seriously challenged, but the moment that ensured the battle for second would remain far away from the 2003 Surfers Paradise winner came courtesy of a caution for debris on the race track with 62 laps remaining. A miscommunication with their crews caused Carpentier and Jourdain to miss their chance to pit with Hunter-Reay. Instead they elected to stop with the remainder of the field, which was a violation of Champ Car rules. The ensuing penalty sent both cars to the back of the restart line where they could continue their battle for second place, but effectively ended any outside chance of running down the leader. The fight went all the way to the end of the race, with Carpentier holding off Jourdain to claim the second spot.

"I tried really hard to catch Ryan but it was almost impossible because he had an excellent car," said Carpentier. "I figured that I would have to settle for second when I knew that I wouldn't be able to catch Ryan."

"It is great to be on the podium," added Jourdain. "Third is so good for the RuSPORT team and my sponsor Gigante. The team is just unbelievable. We are making great improvements and becoming strong. The car just got better over the weekend and we had a good car for the race."

Hunter-Reay's teammate Mario Dominguez ran as high as third in the early stages but suffered a broken air-gun during his second scheduled pit stop. The Mexican had to make an additional visit to the pit lane under green flag conditions, restricting him to an eighth-place finish.

Countryman Lavin also drove an excellent race. He was most unfortunate to incur a penalty when he inadvertently pitted out of sequence following Bourdais' crash, and consequently was banished to the back of the pack. Undeterred, Lavin fought his Corona car back to seventh before getting up into the marbles in Turn Three and brushing the wall just two laps from the finish. Even so he was classified ninth.

Coincidentally, yet another Mexican, Roberto Gonzalez, ran similarly well, rising to ninth in his NII Holdings/PKV Racing Lola until also clouting the wall just a couple of laps from the finish.

Team leader Jimmy Vasser upheld PKV honor in his Gulfstream car, netting his best result since joining the ownership ranks at the beginning of the season.

"It was a struggle in the first half of the race," said the 1996 champion, who started eighth and finished fourth, "but the car seemed to come on in the later stages of the race and it was much better."

The RuSPORT team was already delighted with Jourdain's podium finish – its first – and team owner Carl Russo's joy was compounded when rookie A.J. Allmendinger added his first-ever top-five finish with the #10 BG Products/Red Bull Lola. Allmendinger improved eight spots in climbing to fifth, adding a championship point for gaining most positions in the race and putting himself back in the thick of the Rookie-of-the-Year race.

Bruno Junqueira, meanwhile, adopted a circumspect approach, keeping his PacifiCare car's nose clean all night and finishing in sixth place, giving him the series points lead by one digit over Carpentier.

"My goal this weekend was to finish in the top three and leave here with the championship lead," he explained. "We finished sixth but at least we put the PacifiCare team in the lead."

Fellow veteran Oriol Servia scored his best finish of the year thus far in Dale Coyne Racing's yokeTV.com Lola, moving up four spots to seventh ahead of Dominguez, Lavin and Mario Haberfeld, who led a three-car Reynard brigade with Derrick Walker's #5 Cummins machine.

Jeremy Shaw

Left: The stars were out in Milwaukee as Champ Cars lapped the historic mile during a crisp June evening sky.
Michael Kim/LAT

Below: Forsythe teammates Tracy and Carpentier (inside) battle in Turn One.

Bottom left: Jimmy Vasser,s PKV Racing crew performs routine service on the Œ96 series champion's Gulfstream Lola.
Photographs: Dan Streck/LAT

Above: **Carl Russo's RuSPORT team earned its first-ever podium finish, courtesy of Michel Jourdain Jr.** (below).
Photos: Michael Levitt & Michael Kim/LAT

RuSPORT COMES OF AGE

At its core, the RuSPORT organization is a meticulous entity, one that takes great pains to plan out nearly every step it takes both on and off the track. Team owner Carl Russo had devoted a lot of thought to putting each piece of his racing team in place, relying heavily on the expertise provided by team president Jeremy Dale.

But the best-laid schemes o' mice an' men *gang aft agley*, as Robert Burns taught us, and so it was with RuSPORT when Bobby Rahal's abandonment of the series left Michel Jourdain Jr. without a Champ Car seat. The team stepped up to put together a second car for the Mexican veteran to run alongside American *wunderkind* A.J. Allmendinger less than four weeks before the start of the season.

"To say things came at us 100 mph probably isn't accurate," said Russo. "It was more like 100 miles a second."

But the team got up to speed quickly and put its vast potential on display at Milwaukee. Jourdain ended up as just one of three cars on the lead lap, earning the first-year squad its first Champ Car podium visit, while the rookie Allmendinger showed his ability to learn on the fly, scoring the first top-five finish of his fledgling career.

Jourdain relied on the knowledge gained in 2003 when he won at the Milwaukee Mile, and used that information to help the development of both RuSPORT cars. Fortunately for the team, most of the development would come on race day after qualifying offered no hint of the success to come. Jourdain started ninth while Allmendinger gridded a distant 13th.

"David Brown, my engineer, and I sat down and I told him I didn't know what I wanted out of the race car," admitted Allmendinger. "He said 'Michel's hit on something, let's go after it.' I went down a lap going through traffic on the first stint, but as the race went on I found that my car was really good after about 10 laps on the tires. Everybody was coming back to me. I could catch them and get around them. From then on, it was just pacing myself and not making any mistakes."

Bridgestone Presents Champ Car World Series Powered by Ford

ROUND 3

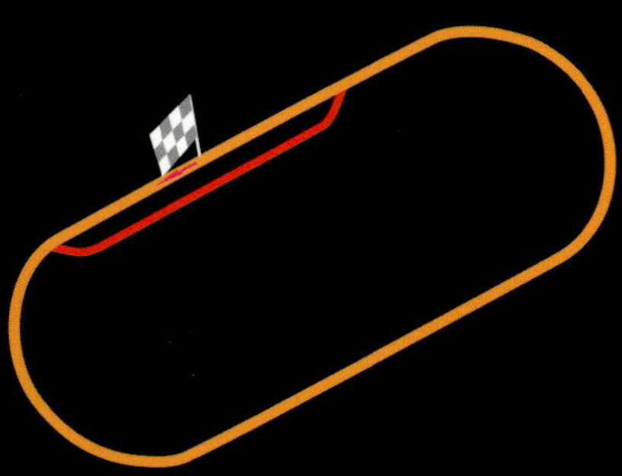

THE TIME WARNER CABLE ROADRUNNER 250

THE MILWAUKEE MILE, STATE FAIR PARK W. ALLIS, WISCONSIN

June 5, 250 laps of 1.032 miles – 258.000 miles

Place	Driver (Nat.)	No.	Sponsor(s) Team Engine/Car	Tires	Q Speed	Q Time	Q Pos	Laps	Time/Status	Ave. (mph)	Pts
1	Ryan Hunter-Reay (USA)	4	Herdez Competition Ford-Cosworth/Lola B03/00	BS	181.150	20.509s	1	250	1h 59m 12.397s	129.859	34
2	Patrick Carpentier (CDN)	7	Indeck Forsythe Championship Racing Ford-Cosworth/Lola B02/00	BS	179.132	20.740s	3	250	1h 59m 18.262s	129.752	27
3	Michel Jourdain Jr. (MEX)	9	Gigante RuSPORT Ford-Cosworth/Lola B04/00	BS	178.085	20.862s	9	250	1h 59m 23.746s	129.653	25
4	Jimmy Vasser (USA)	12	Gulfstream PKV Racing Ford-Cosworth/Lola B02/00	BS	178.153	20.854s	8	249	Running		23
5	*A.J. Allmendinger (USA)	10	BG Products/Red Bull RuSPORT Ford-Cosworth/Lola B03/00	BS	173.998	21.352s	13	249	Running		22
6	Bruno Junqueira (BR)	6	PacifiCare Newman/Haas Racing Ford-Cosworth/Lola B02/00	BS	178.042	20.867s	10	248	Running		19
7	Oriol Servia (E)	11	yokeTV.com Dale Coyne Racing Ford-Cosworth/Lola B2K/00	BS	177.625	20.916s	11	247	Running		17
8	Mario Dominguez (MEX)	55	Herdez Competition Ford-Cosworth/Lola B02/00	BS	178.744	20.785s	4	246	Running		15
9	Rodolfo Lavin (MEX)	3	Corona Forsythe Championship Racing Ford-Cosworth/Lola B03/00	BS	178.538	21.809s	6	245	Accident		13
10	Mario Haberfeld (BR)	5	Cummins Walker Racing Ford-Cosworth/Reynard 02I	BS	172.255	21.568s	15	245	Running		11
11	*Justin Wilson (GB)	34	Mi-Jack Conquest Racing Ford-Cosworth/Reynard 02I	BS	175.378	21.184s	12	244	Running		10
12	*Roberto Gonzalez (MEX)	21	NII Holdings PKV Racing Ford-Cosworth/Lola B02/00	BS	172.937	21.483s	14	243	Oil leak		9
13	Alex Tagliani (CDN)	8	Johnson Controls Rocketsports Racing Ford-Cosworth/Lola B02/00	BS	178.478	20.815s	7	243	Running		8
14	*Nelson Philippe (F)	17	LeasePlan Rocketsports Racing Ford-Cosworth/Lola B02/00	BS	169.219	21.955s	17	240	Running		7
15	*Alex Sperafico (BR)	14	Mi-Jack Conquest Racing Ford-Cosworth/Reynard 02I	BS	165.946	22.388s	18	240	Running		6
16	*Gaston Mazzacane (RA)	19	American Medical Response Dale Coyne Ford-Cosworth/Lola B01/00	BS	169.590	21.907s	16	79	Accident		5
17	Paul Tracy (CDN)	1	Indeck Forsythe Championship Racing Ford-Cosworth/Lola B02/00	BS	178.615	20.800s	5	60	Accident		4
18	Sébastien Bourdais (F)	2	McDonald's Newman/Haas Racing Ford-Cosworth/Lola B01/00	BS	179.765	20.867s	2	50	Accident		3

*Denotes Rookie Driver

Caution flags: Laps 1-4, Wilson spun/stalled; laps 51-59, Bourdais accident; laps 60-63, Tracy accident; laps 83-99, Mazzacane accident; laps 188-201, debris; laps 216-221, debris; laps 249-250, Lavin accident. **Total:** Seven for 56 laps.

Lap leaders: Ryan Hunter-Reay, 1-250 (250 laps). Total: Hunter-Reay, 250 laps.

Fastest race lap: Ryan Hunter-Reay, 21.765s, 170.696 mph on lap 8.

Championship positions: 1 Junqueira, 76; 2 Carpentier, 75; 3 Hunter-Reay, 66; 4 Bourdais, 65; 5 Dominguez, 62; 6 Tracy, 53; 7 Wilson, 50; 8 Tagliani, 46; 9 Jourdain Jr., 45; 10 Vasser, 37; 11 Allmendinger, 35; 12 Lavin, 32; 13 Servia & Haberfeld, 30; 15 Gonzalez, 29; 16 Philippe, 26; 17 Sperafico, 15; 18 Marques, 6; 19 Mazzacane, 5.

MILWAUKEE SNIPPETS

• Eric Bachelart's Mi-Jack Conquest Racing team opted to field one of its trusty Reynard chassis for ex-Formula 1 driver Justin Wilson's first-ever oval race, rather than run the risk of damaging its lone Lola. Smart move. The Englishman (below) qualified a respectable 12th, comfortably outpacing the similar cars of Mario Haberfeld and Alex Sperafico, but his inexperience surfaced on the very first lap of the race when he went spinning in Turn Two. "I just got too close to the car in front of me and lost [control of] the rear and the Mi-Jack car just went around," related Wilson, who was fortunate to emerge without any significant damage and went on to finish 11th. "Then you are playing catch up... or not, after that. Every time I got in traffic I'd lose the downforce and I couldn't do anything. We just weren't quick in traffic, but when I was on my own I was OK. I survived and that is good."

• Newman/Haas Racing co-owner Paul Newman enjoyed a full day of competition even before flying to Milwaukee for the Saturday evening Champ Car race. At the ripe age of 79, Newman guided his Chevrolet Corvette to the pole for an SCCA GT-1 race at his home track, Lime Rock Park in Connecticut, and set fastest lap en route to a second-place finish. His Champ Car drivers didn't fare nearly so well, with Sébastien Bourdais crashing out early and Bruno Junqueira being content to drive to a steady sixth-place finish.

• Ryan Hunter-Reay's runaway victory marked the first time since 1992 that anyone led every lap of a Champ Car oval event. The last driver to accomplish the feat was Bobby Rahal, who led all 200 laps en route to a win at Phoenix International Raceway.

Michael Levitt/LAT

Michael Kim/LAT

• Hunter-Reay, Jimmy Vasser and A.J. Allmendinger (above) ensured that three American drivers finished among the top five positions in a Champ Car race for the first time since Memo Gidley, Bryan Herta and Vasser did so at Cleveland in 2001.

• A marked improvement in the weather by comparison to the inaugural Milwaukee Mile night race in 2003 saw a total of 46,532 fans turn out for the three-day event – an increase of 28 percent over the previous year. "We are very pleased to have a substantial increase in attendance," said Milwaukee Mile Vice President & General Manager Mark Perrone. "For the first time, our race fans really responded to the season ticket packages we've offered them, and we were happy to accommodate hundreds of first-time infield suite guests."

• The first driver change of the season was effected in time for The Time Warner Cable Road Runner 250, with Tarso Marques stepping out of Dale Coyne's #19 American Medical Response Lola in favor of Argentine rookie Gaston Mazzacane. A veteran of the European open-wheel ranks who had a stint in Formula 1 in 2000-01 – since when he had sat on the sidelines -- Mazzacane predictably found the transition rather difficult. Nevertheless, he qualified ahead of both Nelson Philippe and Alex Sperafico and was running 15th when he spun into the wall in Turn Two after 79 laps. "It's really, really crazy because it's completely different from all the other races in my career," said the amiable Mazzacane, grinning broadly.

• Patrick Carpentier's second-place finish – allied to his fourth-place run at Monterrey and Paul Tracy's win at Long Beach – catapulted Canada into the lead of the Nation's Cup standings after three races. Brazil maintained second, trailing 82-74, while Mexico rose to third on 71. Previous pacesetter France slipped to fifth, equal on points with Team USA on 65.

BRIDGESTONE PRESENTS
THE CHAMP CAR WORLD SERIES POWERED BY FORD • ROUND 4

PORTLAND

In the shadow of Mt. Hood, Sébastien Bourdais leads his teammate Bruno Junqueira and Paul Tracy at Portland.
Paul Abbott/LAT

QUALIFYING

Sébastien Bourdais watched Newman/Haas teammate Bruno Junqueira set the pace during first-round qualifying for the Champ Car Grand Prix of Portland, but he and his McDonald's-sponsored machine made up the distance and then some during the final session on Saturday afternoon. Bourdais took advantage of a penalty that led to Junqueira abandoning his final attempt and posted a chart-topping lap of 59.229 seconds (119.678 mph). The pole was his second of the season and the seventh of his young career – a remarkable effort given that Portland represented only his 22nd start.

"The Newman/Haas team has been great this whole weekend for both Bruno and myself," said Bourdais. "We had a good [pre-race] test and have a good car setup."

Junqueira (below) maintained second place on the grid (by virtue of leading Friday qualifying), despite stepping out of his car just five laps into the final session. He had received a penalty from Champ Car stewards after being adjudged to have impeded another competitor's qualifying lap. Realizing that Junqueira would have needed to post two flying laps in order to secure the pole, the team eschewed further qualifying in order to save tires for the race.

"It is frustrating," said the Brazilian, "but the PacifiCare team has worked real hard and the car is good."

Added Junqueira, optimistically, "I guarantee that I will be the first car into the Festival Curves tomorrow and that I will lead the first lap!"

Defending series champion Paul Tracy also hit trouble, literally, after ending his run for the pole against the tire wall at Turn Seven. The mishap brought out the red flags and caused him to forfeit his fastest lap, but he had already done enough to secure a place on the inside of the second row of the grid.

Rookies Justin Wilson and A.J. Allmendinger acclimated quickly to the Portland layout, earning the fourth and the fifth starting spots ahead of Mario Dominguez, 2003 Portland podium finisher Alex Tagliani and Michel Jourdain Jr., who continued the momentum he had gained by his Milwaukee podium with his best qualifying run of the season thus far.

NEWMAN/HAAS RACING clasped an iron grip on the Champ Car Grand Prix of Portland. Sébastien Bourdais and Bruno Junqueira monopolized the front row of the grid for team owners Paul Newman and Carl Haas, separated by a scant 0.037 seconds, and the pair continued to dominate in the 94-lap race. Bourdais used a strong mid-race run -- and a softer set of Bridgestone "alternate" tires -- to build a gap of more than eight seconds over his teammate, then withstood a furious late-race rush when his Brazilian counterpart also switched to the faster rubber, claiming the win by just 1.247 seconds.

"The Newman/Haas team and McDonald's crew did an excellent job today," praised Bourdais. "The McDonald's car was consistent and we were able to pull away. I knew that Bruno would have a shot to catch me at the end when he put on a set of the alternate tires because those tires were so fast and I had the primary tires on because I used up my alternate tires. However, we were able to pull it off."

Forsythe Championship Racing's Paul Tracy comfortably outpaced the remainder of the field but couldn't offer a serious challenge to the Newman/Haas pair, finishing more than 40 seconds adrift in third place.

It took a couple of attempts before Bourdais could begin his romp around the 1.969-mile Portland International Raceway layout, as the predictably raucous Festival Curves chicane brought out a yellow flag on the first time through. Michel Jourdain Jr. (#9 Gigante Lola) was unfortunate enough to be the only victim of the usual bumping and grinding as the 18-car field of 750hp turbocharged machines slowed from 175 mph to approximately 50 mph to negotiate the tight trio of turns. The Mexican lost a lap before being restarted and so was effectively out of contention already.

The restart was equally fraught as Mario Dominguez lost control of his Herdez Lola coming onto the front straightaway and gyrated directly into the path of an innocent Rodolfo Lavin (#3 Corona Lola). Both drivers were forced out of the race as the caution flags waved one more time.

"I had a good car and my best starting position so far at this track [sixth], so I was really looking forward to the race," related a crestfallen Dominguez. "Unfortunately, I made a mistake. I used the push-to-pass and with the extra boost I had too much wheelspin and I spun and hit the wall. I am very disappointed because I think I had a good shot at a strong finish."

Fortunately for the fans, that proved to be the final caution of the day as the remaining 86 laps were left to the drivers and teams. Bourdais again jumped out to the lead over Junqueira and Tracy, widening his advantage with each passing lap and building a comfortable margin as the frontrunners prepared for their first round of pit stops. Junqueira and Bourdais pitted, respectively, three and four laps before Tracy, but slower traffic prevented the defending series champion from making any noticeable gains on the leaders.

Top rookie Justin Wilson led the chase of the top trio, once again doing a sterling job for Eric Bachelart and Mike Lanigan's Mi-Jack Conquest Racing team. Alex Tagliani held down fifth for Rocketsports Racing in the early stages, having gotten around A.J. Allmendinger's RuSPORT car on the very first lap.

The middle stages of the race saw lapped traffic cause some fluctuations at the front of the field. Junqueira closed to within a second of the leader at one point as Bourdais lost some time while attempting to pass a slower car; but the Brazilian was unable to get close enough to contemplate a passing attempt. The battle a little farther back also persisted as rookies Wilson and Allmendinger (who had repassed Tagliani during the first round of pit stops) fought tooth-and-nail for a top-five finish in a war that included a side-by-side drag race along the pit lane following their second pit visits.

Patrick Carpentier, meanwhile, had begun to move into the picture after employing a different pit stop strategy in an attempt to overcome a troubled qualifying session with the second Indeck/Forsythe Championship Racing Lola. The French-Canadian, who started 13th, made the first of his mandatory three green-flag pit stops as early as Lap Nine and proceeded to capitalize on a clear track by turning a series of fast laps. The ploy cost him some time when he encountered a group of slower cars at one stage, but he still was able to work his way steadily forward.

Carpentier, running fourth, was the first of the lead-lap cars to make his third and final pit stop, after 68 laps, and while he briefly went a lap down to the Newman/Haas pacesetters, he was secure in the knowledge that everyone in front of him had to make one more visit to the pit lane.

Junqueira stopped with 18 laps remaining, at which point he was 8.8 seconds behind Bourdais. The Brazilian's crew bolted on his last set of Bridgestone alternate tires, which gave him a fighting chance of running down his teammate. He quickly put the softer rubber to good use, lopping nearly a half-second per lap off of the lead. He shaved the deficit to four seconds with nine laps to go and had it under two seconds with four orbits left after posting a string of fastest laps, but it still wasn't quite enough to catch Bourdais.

"The PacifiCare car was good throughout the whole race," noted Junqueira after notching his fourth straight top-six result. "The alternate tires that Bridgestone provided us were real fast and had a lot of grip. I thought I would catch him in the end, however I ran into more traffic and ran out of time. But we only finished a second behind Sébastien, so it was close."

Tracy's pit stop strategy enabled him to lead a few laps, earning a welcome championship bonus point and a much-needed strong finish to rebound from his accident in the previous race at Milwaukee.

"I feel good," said the Canadian, who stood on the podium for the first time since winning at Long Beach. "It was a good finish but not as good as we would have liked. The Indeck car was good. We started on qualifying [alternate] tires, knowing the Newman/Haas team was starting on stickers. I thought it would be hard to stay even with them at the start. Our strategies were different; ours was to go longer than them, however we got caught behind traffic and they were able to pull away from there on. We had the speed in the car, just got hung up the whole time. I am happy to finish on the podium.

Above: Michel Jourdain is hit from behind in the always crowded first turn at Portland.
Michael Levitt/LAT

Center left: Jimmy Vasser and Oriol Servia look to see what's happening in the pit lane.
Maria Grady/LAT

Left: Gaston Mazzacane rides the curb in his AMR-sponsored #19 Dale Coyne Lola.
Paul Abbott/LAT

Below: Father's Day is celebrated by two generations of Jourdain, Allmendinger, Junqueira, Lavin and Gonzalez.
Michael Levitt/LAT

Now we are in a groove and hopefully we will be winning races soon."

Teammate Carpentier's strategic gamble worked out well as he moved ahead of the battling Wilson and Allmendinger following the final round of pit stops to keep his championship challenge on track.

"The changes [race engineer] Eric [Zeto] and the crew made were great and the car was flying," declared Carpentier, who had been hindered by gearbox problems in qualifying. "There was a lot of traffic, and fighting the backmarkers, that definitely held me up, but I pushed the whole afternoon. I'm just glad to have had such a strong finish from 13th."

The battle between Wilson and Allmendinger went on throughout the final half of the race. They went side-by-side into the Festival Curves on more than one occasion, but the 2003 Toyota Atlantic champion could never quite find a way to get around 2001 F3000 title-holder Wilson.

"The pace of our car was not what we hoped for, but my crew gave me excellent [pit] stops," noted Wilson after adding a fifth-place finish to his pair of sixths in the opening two races of the year. "All things considered I'm pretty pleased."

Ditto Allmendinger: "We had the fourth best car today," reckoned the 22-year-old Californian. "Justin, that guy is hard to pass, but it was completely fair. We were way faster but it's tough to pass here. He was good enough coming onto the straightaway that I couldn't get a good run on him. That guy broke so deep! It was fun to race him."

Tagliani and Jimmy Vasser followed in seventh and eighth respectively, while Mario Haberfeld and Roberto Gonzalez rounded out the top 10.

Jeremy Shaw

PAYING FOR WHAY YOUR SAYING

BRUNO Junqueira and Paul Tracy finished second and third, respectively, in the Champ Car Grand Prix of Portland, but their propensity to fill reporters' notebooks earned them $10,000 fines for making what were deemed inappropriate remarks aimed at Champ Car Chief Steward Chris Kniefel and other officials. Meanwhile, Alex Tagliani didn't say nearly as much after the race but paid an even stiffer penalty as he was docked a pair of valuable championship points for on-track violations. In addition, Tracy incurred a $5,000 fine for making improper gestures toward an official.

Junqueira and Tracy were fined in accordance with Champ Car Rule 2.8.8 which concerns criticism of officials and personal demeanor. Junqueira was upset with officials after Saturday qualifying, claiming the penalty cost him a shot at challenging Newman/Haas teammate Sébastien Bourdais for the pole.

"It's very frustrating, because they always make mistakes against me," he said of the race officials. "They did it to me in Milwaukee, and in Vancouver and Surfers Paradise last year. [Talking to officials is] a waste of time, you know, because you always talk with them and they don't listen to us."

Tracy's disagreement with the officials came on Sunday when he got caught behind the lapped car of Tagliani (below) while attempting to chase down the Newman/Haas duo late in the race. By rule, once he had been lapped, Tagliani should have allowed Tracy to pass, but the French-Canadian refused to acquiesce.

Tracy was upset initially at the absence of a blue move-over flag for Tagliani, and after making a series of lewd hand signals as he sped beneath Starter J.D. Wilbur's flag stand, later claimed to have a solution to the problem: "Change the chief steward and the flagman," he railed. "We were radioing in to the chief steward every lap and never got a response back. You know, we keep talking over and over in the drivers' meetings about guys obeying the blue flags, but if [the officials] don't even show it, then [the responsibility is] not even on the driver. It's really down to the officiating."

The blue flags eventually were displayed to Tagliani, but his tardy response led to a series of black flags too, which again he chose to ignore, in violation of Champ Car Rule 2.8.5. Hence the two-point deduction from his point total.

Dan Streck/LAT

ALTERNATE ENDING

BRIDGESTONE introduced an innovative feature to its successful Champ Car tire program in 2004, developing softer-compound "alternate" tires -- alongside its "primary" rubber – for a selection of races as a means of giving the teams an extra card in their strategy deck on race day. The intention was to promote more overtaking maneuvers.

Revised regulations allowed each team to be issued two sets of alternate tires in addition to six sets of primary tires. Each car was required to utilize at least one set of alternates in the race, with the majority of teams electing to use the second set in final qualifying.

The stickier tires – which had red markings on the sidewalls so that the fans could easily distinguish them from the regular shoes – were making their second appearance on the 2005 trail, having made their bow in Long Beach (when they were initially dubbed "option" tires). But it was in Portland that the softer tires had their first real impact.

Sébastien Bourdais chose to exploit his alternate Bridgestone Potenzas early in the race, building a cushion of more than eight seconds by the race's halfway point. But his lead quickly evaporated when Newman/Haas Racing teammate Bruno Junqueira's crew bolted on his alternates for the race's final stint. The margin between them shrank to just 1.2 seconds in the waning minutes, but Bourdais was able to outlast his hard-charging stablemate for the win.

"The Bridgestone tires were great here," declared Bourdais. "The regular tires were just fine but the alternate tires were much better. Not only were they quicker but they were durable as well. I was faster between three-tenths and five-tenths (of a second) from the middle to the end of the stint, so it was perfect."

"We definitely saw a noticeable difference between the performance of the alternate spec as compared to the primary spec Bridgestone tires," said Joe Barbieri, Project Supervisor, Bridgestone Motorsport. "We will certainly continue to work on improvements to the concept. Both Sébastien and Bruno put on quite a show at the end and made this an exciting race for the Portland fans."

Michael Levitt/LAT

ROUND 4

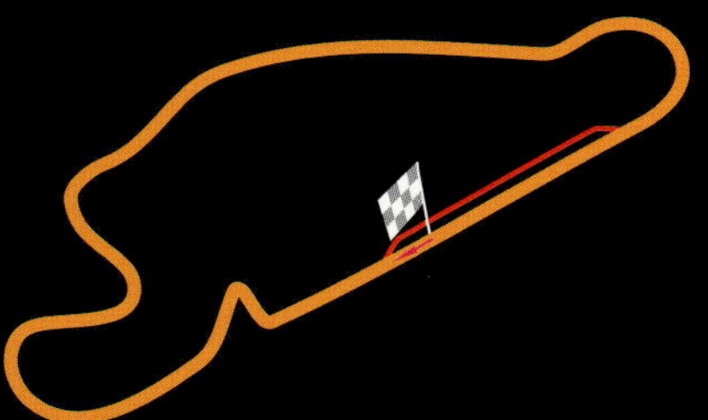

CHAMP CAR GRAND PRIX OF PORTLAND

PORTLAND INTERNATIONAL RACEWAY PORTLAND, OREGON

JUNE 20, 94 laps of 1.969 miles – 186.086 miles

Place	Driver (Nat.)	No.	Sponsor(s) Team Engine/Car	Tires	Q Speed	Q Time	Q Pos	Laps	Time/Status	Ave. (mph)	Pts
1	Sebastien Bourdais (F)	2	McDonald's Newman/Haas Racing Ford-Cosworth/Lola B01/00	BS	119.678	59.229s	1	94	1h 45m 50.461s	104.293	33
2	Bruno Junqueira (BR)	6	PacifiCare Newman/Haas Racing Ford-Cosworth/Lola B02/00	BS	119.603	59.266s	2	94	1h 45m 51.708s	104.902	29
3	Paul Tracy (CDN)	1	Indeck Forsythe Championship Racing Ford-Cosworth/Lola B02/00	BS	119.506	59.314s	3	94	1h 46m 30.527s	104.265	26
4	Patrick Carpentier (CDN)	7	Indeck Forsythe Championship Racing Ford-Cosworth/Lola B02/00	BS	117.783	1m 00.182s	13	94	1h 46m 42.817s	104.065	24
5	*Justin Wilson (GB)	34	Mi-Jack Conquest Racing Ford-Cosworth/Lola B02/00	BS	119.305	59.414s	4	94	1h 46m 48.890s	103.966	21
6	*A.J. Allmendinger (USA)	10	BG Products/Red Bull RuSPORT Ford-Cosworth/Lola B03/00	BS	118.825	59.654s	5	94	1h 46m 49.798s	103.952	19
7	Alex Tagliani (CDN)	8	Johnson Controls Rocketsports Racing Ford-Cosworth/Lola B02/00	BS	118.337	59.900s	7	93	Running		17
8	Jimmy Vasser (USA)	12	Gulfstream PKV Racing Ford-Cosworth/Lola B02/00	BS	118.294	59.922s	9	93	Running		15
9	Mario Haberfeld (BR)	5	Cummins Walker Racing Ford-Cosworth/Reynard 02I	BS	116.820	1m 00.678s	15	93	Running		13
10	*Roberto Gonzalez (MEX)	21	NII Holdings PKV Racing Ford-Cosworth/Lola B02/00	BS	118.166	59.987s	11	93	Running		11
11	Oriol Servia (E)	11	yokeTV.com Dale Coyne Racing Ford-Cosworth/Lola B2K/00	BS	117.736	1m 00.206s	14	92	Running		10
12	Ryan Hunter-Reay (USA)	4	Herdez Competition Ford-Cosworth/Lola B01/00	BS	118.286	59.926s	10	92	Running		9
13	*Gaston Mazzacane (RA)	19	American Medical Response Dale Coyne Ford-Cosworth/Lola B02/00	BS	116.522	1m 00.833s	16	92	Running		8
14	Michel Jourdain Jr. (MEX)	9	Gigante RuSPORT Ford-Cosworth/Lola B04/00	BS	118.337	59.900s	8	92	Running		7
15	*Nelson Philippe (F)	17	LeasePlan Rocketsports Racing Ford-Cosworth/Lola B02/00	BS	115.200	1m 01.531s	18	91	Running		6
16	*Alex Sperafico (BR)	14	Mi-Jack Conquest Racing Ford-Cosworth/Reynard 02I	BS	115.572	1m 01.333s	17	90	Running		5
17	Mario Dominguez (MEX)	55	Herdez Competition Ford-Cosworth/Lola B02/00	BS	118.620	59.757s	6	2	Accident		4
18	Rodolfo Lavin (MEX)	3	Corona Forsythe Championship Racing Ford-Cosworth/Lola B02/00	BS	117.945	1m 00.099s	12	2	Accident		3

*Denotes Rookie Driver

Caution flags: Laps 1-3, Jourdain spun/stalled; laps 4-8, Dominguez/Lavin accident. Total: Two for 8 laps.

Lap leaders: Sebastien Bourdais, 1-29 (29 laps); Paul Tracy, 30-32 (3 laps); Bourdais, 33-56 (24 laps); Tracy, 57-62 (6 laps); Bourdais, 63-94 (32 laps). Total: Bourdais, 85 laps; Tracy, 9 laps.

Fastest race lap: Bruno Junqueira, 1m 00.573s, 117.022 mph on lap 92.

Championship positions: 1 Junqueira, 105; 2 Carpentier, 99; 3 Bourdais, 98; 4 Tracy, 79; 5 Hunter-Reay, 75; 6 Wilson, 71; 7 Dominguez, 66; 8 Tagliani, 63; 9 Allmendinger, 54; 10 Jourdain Jr. & Vasser, 52; 12 Haberfeld, 43; 13 Servia & Gonzalez, 40; 15 Lavin, 35; 16 Philippe, 32; 17 Sperafico, 20; 18 Mazzacane, 13; 19 Marques, 6.

PORTLAND SNIPPETS

Gavin Lawrence/LAT

• PKV Racing had effected a shuffling of its crew prior to arriving in Portland. Veteran chief mechanic Skip Faul had taken charge of Jimmy Vasser's #12 Gulfstream Lola, while Chris Schofield had been moved across to oversee the two-seater program, which continued to give media members and sundry dignitaries a taste of what a 750hp Champ Car is all about. Since the Portland event coincided (as usual) with Father's Day, current drivers' fathers Greg Allmendinger, Jose Junqueira (above), Nick Hunter-Reay and Roberto Gonzalez Sr. were taken for a high-speed ride, and all emerged beaming with admiration and pride.

• The controversy following final qualifying began when three drivers – Bruno Junqueira, Alex Sperafico and Gaston Mazzacane -- were adjudged to have impeded a rival. In accordance with Champ Car Rule 6.17.4, the transgressors forfeited their fastest lap times. Junqueira, in particular, was incensed by the call. "I started my first run on regular Bridgestone tires and got a lot of traffic," he related. "I came up on Sperafico who is always two or three seconds off the pace. It screwed up my lap and that was supposed to be my fast one. I backed off to build a gap and a PKV car [Roberto Gonzalez's] was not even close behind me."

• Patrick Carpentier endured a dismal couple of days of practice and qualifying as his Indeck/Forsythe Championship Racing Lola was continually jumping out of gear. His crew tried everything they could think of to alleviate his complaint, but to no avail...until they fitted an entirely new gearbox and transmission in time for the final warmup practice on race morning. Finally, Carpentier was able to display his true colors. The French-Canadian drove an excellent race, employing a creative pit stop strategy to rise from 13th on the grid to fourth at the finish.

• Determined to build upon its impressive showing at Milwaukee, which netted a third-place finish for Michel Jourdain Jr. and a career-best fifth for rookie A.J. Allmendinger, the RuSPORT team tested for a day at the California Speedway road course in Fontana en route to Portland. Allmendinger completed around 400 miles of running, in very hot conditions, and was a factor all weekend long at Portland, claiming a season-best fifth on the grid and then going to finish sixth.

• By claiming his eighth straight top-10 finish in the previous race at Milwaukee, Mario Dominguez had established a new record for Mexican drivers, eclipsing the previous mark set by Adrian Fernandez and Michel Jourdain Jr. Sadly, the streak came to an early end at Portland when he lost control and crashed at the first restart.

• Bruno Junqueira's second-place finish, along with the extra point for posting fastest lap, enabled him to extend his championship lead. Patrick Carpentier trailed by six points (105-99) after four races, while Bourdais was a further one point adrift. Britain's Justin Wilson also maintained his lead in the Rookie-of-the-Year chase with 71 points to the 54 of primary challenger A.J. Allmendinger.

• Sébastien Bourdais (below) had been busy during the week off since Milwaukee, traveling to his hometown of Le Mans, France, to contest the classic 24-hour sports car race. Bourdais played a starring role, providing one of the few serious challenges to the dominant Audi R8s with one of the Pescarolo Sport team's Judd-powered Courages. He was equally impressive on his return to the open-wheel ranks, first of all equaling the record established by Paul Tracy in 2003 by qualifying on the front row of the grid for each of the first four races of the season, then romping to another accomplished victory.

Mike Levitt/LAT

Right: Sébastien Bourdais celebrates for the second straight year at the airport track.

Below: The Cleveland skyline always ensures a spectacular backdrop for the Champ Cars.

Photographs: Michael Kim/LAT

CLEVELAND

CALAMITY CORNER STRIKES AGAIN

TURN One at Cleveland's Burke Lakefront Airport track – especially on the opening lap of the race – has long been acknowledged as a near certainty to make any season's highlight reel. The start routinely features a pack of cars running at full throttle along a wide runway that can feasibly allow them to spread out seven-wide on the approach to the first turn. However, the flat-out dash ends abruptly, funneling the field into a 130-degree right-hand hairpin that is a crucial launch point for the fast back section along the shores of Lake Erie.

The list of drivers that have had promising days ended in the first turn reads like a Who's Who of Champ Car racing. Jimmy Vasser, Michael Andretti and Patrick Carpentier are just a few of the men that have come to grief in Turn One, and the 2004 edition claimed a couple more.

It was a bit more poignant this time, however, as the customary melee ended the dreams of a series veteran as well as a young driver and team that had a legitimate shot at their first podium, if not their first win. Defending series champion Paul Tracy had annexed the pole for Forsythe Championship Racing, while alongside on the front row at the start was Mi-Jack Conquest Racing rookie Justin Wilson.

The vastly experienced Tracy headed for the far left as the green flag flew, watching in his mirrors what unfolded behind him while setting himself up for a clean entrance to the turn on the normal racing line. Wilson, meanwhile, found himself in no man's land. Approaching the hairpin he ducked out to the right, only for the late-braking Alex Tagliani to come steaming down the inside directly into his path.

Wilson was knocked sideways by the contact with Tagliani, resulting in a spin that pushed him into Tracy and ended the day for both cars. Tagliani survived the collision and went on to finish third while Tracy and Wilson spent the rest of the day watching on television.

"I was clear [going] into the first corner – two to three-car lengths ahead – and I braked at the same point I do for qualifying and turned in... it was my corner," declared Tracy. "Then Tagliani goes by at 100 mph, way too fast into the corner where there was no opportunity, and Wilson had nowhere to go so [he] took me out."

Above: Paul Tracy was not at all happy after being punted from behind in Turn One.
Michael Levitt/LAT

Above left: Incriminating evidence? Three abreast in Turn One, and Alex Tagliani (on the inside) had started from fifth on the grid.

Left: Bourdais threads the needle to get through the first-turn melee unscathed.
Photographs Greg Feistman/LAT

Above: After the drop of the green flag, the field spreads out across the tarmac before funneling into the tight Turn One.
Michael Kim/LAT

Right: **Rookie A.J. Allmendinger quickly gets up to speed at Cleveland, impressing many with his fourth place starting position.**
Michael Levitt/LAT

QUALIFYING

Champ Car's youth movement made its presence felt in final qualifying as three of the top four spots on the starting grid went to relative newcomers to the series. But in the end it was the experience of reigning champion Paul Tracy that carried the day.

Tracy scored his first pole of the season on a warm Friday afternoon, circulating the 2.106-mile Burke Lakefront Airport layout in 57.546 seconds, an average speed of 131.749 mph.

"Everything was just timed perfectly today," he said. "We waited a bit before going out in hopes to get a clear track. I had five good laps, then the red flag came out; it worked out perfectly for us."

The Canadian's pole run put him ahead of a trio of young lions for the 97-lap Saturday evening event. Rookie points leader and 2001 FIA International Formula 3000 champion Justin Wilson earned the best starting spot of his young career and the first front-row spot for Mi-Jack Conquest Racing. Wilson held the pole briefly, vaulting to the top of the charts on his seventh lap, and then, as lap times tumbled, used the last of his 15 laps to secure second on the grid.

Sébastien Bourdais, the 2002 F3000 champion and reigning Champ Car Rookie of the Year, rebounded from a Thursday penalty that cost him a front-row starting spot to set the third fastest time. Bourdais rued his decision to make a setup change but still remained ahead of 2003 Toyota Atlantic Champion A.J. Allmendinger, who claimed the best qualifying result of his young Champ Car career despite a quick spin in the waning moments after his car bottomed out on the bumps in the final chicane.

"I'm happy and still a little disappointed because the car was better," reckoned Allmendinger. "I don't think I could have beat Paul but I could have contended for the front row. The car was really good and I was just trying to challenge it even more. I got greedy and lost it."

At least he kept going, which was more than could be said for Ryan Hunter-Reay, who brought out the red flags with just two minutes remaining in the session. Alex Tagliani ended up fifth ahead of points leader Bruno Junqueira, who, unfortunately, was midway around what would have been comfortably his best lap when the session came to a premature halt.

SÉBASTIEN Bourdais won the U.S. Bank Presents The Champ Car Grand Prix of Cleveland for the second year in a row, taking advantage of a first-corner melee and then cruising to a clear victory aboard Newman/Haas Racing's #2 McDonald's Lola.

Bourdais led 88 of the 97 laps around Cleveland's Burke Lakefront Airport on a Chamber of Commerce weather day on the North Coast. The Frenchman's third win of the year – and his second in succession – spearheaded the season's third 1-2 finish for Newman/Haas Racing, mirroring the result from Portland as Bruno Junqueira guided his #6 PacifiCare entry home in second place.

"This was probably the easiest race of my short Champ Car career," admitted Bourdais. "There was the pileup in Turn One at the start of the race. All I could see was smoke. I aimed for the apex, then realized there was no one around me.

"The McDonald's car was good all weekend and my team did a great job giving me a good car. It is a great sensation to be back here in Cleveland and win for the second time."

A first-corner fracas is a common occurrence on the fast, wide-open airfield road course, where the track narrows from well over 100 feet wide into a tight, right-handed turn. The 2004 edition was no exception. The only real surprise was that for the first time in the race's history, dating back to 1982, both front row starters – polesitter Paul Tracy (#1 Indeck/Forsythe Championship Racing Lola) and Justin Wilson (#34 Mi-Jack Conquest Racing Lola) – fell victim to the mayhem after Wilson was clipped by Alex Tagliani, then caromed into an innocent Tracy.

Predictably, opinions were divided as to how the accident was triggered. Most fingers pointed toward Tagliani, who had started fifth, but the French-Canadian didn't concur: "I had a couple of cars in front of me that were slower, so I wanted to get by them. I went into first gear to make the turn and locked my brakes. I almost made it and then Wilson came out from nowhere and touched me a little bit and then I went into the grass."

Wilson, meanwhile, saw it from a different perspective: "I know how late I braked," he said. "I turned in and all of a sudden I saw a blue flash to my right..."

Whatever the cause, the outcome was indisputable: Bourdais emerged from the first turn with the lead, both Tracy and Wilson ended up heading home and Tagliani fell far back in the pack after going off course. Junqueira, too, lost many positions after taking evasive action.

So it was that Patrick Carpentier, who had started seventh in his Indeck Lola, suddenly found himself in second place for the restart, followed by A.J. Allmendinger (Red Bull/BG Products Lola) and Oriol Servia. The Spaniard had vaulted from 13th to fourth in Dale Coyne's yokeTV.com Lola, and soon demoted Allmendinger after the rookie performed a quick 360-degree spin in Turn Eight on the 13th lap.

Allmendinger's RuSPORT teammate Michel Jourdain Jr. snuck past fellow Mexican Mario Dominguez for fifth right away at the restart, while Tagliani's day appeared to have gone from bad to worse when he lost control coming through the final chicane just prior to taking the green flag. He resumed a distant last.

Fellow countryman Carpentier also was out of luck, his run of four straight top-four finishes ending in a cloud of smoke after 19 laps following a rare Ford-Cosworth engine failure.

"That's very unusual indeed," noted Carpentier. "The Ford engines are so strong. I don't know what happened."

Bourdais gave up the lead briefly to Servia and then Jourdain during pit stops but reclaimed the point after the stops cycled through and continued to run away from the field. His lead reached a mammoth 33 seconds by Lap 39 before the caution flags waved because of debris on the race track.

The full-course yellow then was extended by a few laps after Ryan Hunter-Reay spun in Turn Four on the restart lap while battling Servia for third place.

"I passed Oriol and he tried to get past me and we touched while racing side by side," recounted the American, who stalled the engine and lost a lap before he could be restarted.

"That's how racing goes," he added philosophically, "but we were racing hard. I enjoyed it."

Bourdais was unfazed by the interruptions and once again sprinted away from his pursuers at the restart. Impressively, Junqueira had battled his way back to second place following his early delay, leaving Jourdain and Servia to enjoy a lengthy squabble over third.

The pair again led briefly during the second round of pit stops. Jourdain, however, had earlier brushed the wall in Turn Eight, and when he came into the pits for his second of three mandatory pit stops on Lap 60, his crew found the left-front suspension irreparably damaged. Jourdain's hopes of another podium finish to complement his third place at Milwaukee had been extinguished.

"RuSPORT and the Gigante crew proved to everybody what we already knew," he declared. "It was just a matter of time before this team competed for its first Champ Car victory."

Jourdain's untimely retirement shifted the focus instead onto Tagliani, who had been charging through the pack a prodigious rate and was now up into third place, despite his two earlier mishaps. His progress was assisted by shrewd strategy, the Rocketsports crew having called him into the pits for a quick fuel top-up during the previous caution period.

"I was at the end of the line anyway," reasoned Tagliani. "We had a really quick car and I was using the push-to-pass all the time. And I started running [laps] consistently in the 59s when everybody [else] was doing 60s in front of me, and that's where we made up all of our ground."

Bourdais was one of the first drivers to complete his final pit stop, after 71 laps. He resumed without losing the lead and rattled off the remaining laps to win comfortably.

Junqueira at one stage started to whittle away at his teammate's advantage. He posted the fastest lap of the race on a late charge, until a scare while lapping a slower car sent him into a slide in Turn Eight (where he had survived a major incident during practice), prompting him to settle for the bridesmaid's role.

"I decided that's it, [I] already had a crash there and I'm second, let's keep this position," he said. "Just kind of keep a good pace but keep the second position and keep a lead on the championship. I mean, from last to second, that was a good result.

"I kept a good pace during the race and it is good to keep the lead in the championship," continued Junqueira. "We've been consistent and the approach to every weekend is to win. That win will come eventually."

Tagliani's fine comeback to third thrust him right back into the thick of the points race, allowing him to overhaul Tracy and Wilson for the fourth spot after five races.

Servia also drove impressively, notching a magnificent fourth for the perennially underfunded Dale Coyne Racing team – its best result since Roberto Moreno took the squad's lone podium finish at Michigan in 1996.

"We all have worked hard and I am happy for the guys on the team and our sponsors," said Coyne. "Now we need to keep this level and make the next step to climb the podium ladder."

Jimmy Vasser earned his second top-five placing of the year, chased home by rookie Allmendinger, who rebounded from his early indiscretion to take sixth.

"We had the car too low early in the race and it was hitting the ground too much, but I was still trying to be aggressive," said Allmendinger. "I don't know how I didn't hit the [barriers] because it was just like what happened to me in practice [during the first session on Thursday when he spun into the tire wall]. I'm happy for sixth because I thought I was going [to crash]. We should have at least had third though. We have the speed, so we'll just have to move on from this and go get them in Toronto."

Jeremy Shaw

Above: Bruno Junqueira finished second, but can't yet afford a Gulfstream biz-jet.
Mchael Kim/LAT

Main photgraph: Oriol Servia (heading Ryan Hunter-Reay) turned in a spectacular performance to finish fourth for Dale Coyne.
Michael Levitt/LAT

MR. WILSON, WELCOME TO CLEVELAND

JUSTIN Wilson possessed impeccable credentials when he signed up to drive in the 2004 Champ Car World Series. A champion previously in Formula Palmer Audi and Formula 3000, the 6-foot-3-inch Englishman had competed in Formula 1 in 2003, driving first for Minardi and later Jaguar.

Wilson, 25, soon awakened the Champ Car paddock to his vast talent, finishing sixth on his debut at Long Beach despite having had just one full test day with his Mi-Jack Conquest Racing team prior to the season opener. He followed that with another sixth in Monterrey and a stirring fifth in Portland before heading to a Cleveland track that was unlike anything he had ever seen.

The Briton promptly earned the first front-row start of his career on the fast and challenging airport road course, as well as the first for the second-year team owned by former Indy Lights champion Eric Bachelart and Mi-Jack's Mike Lanigan.

"It is great to know we can compete at the same level as some of the more established teams in the series," declared Bachelart. "We have been getting better as the season progresses, and I am thrilled to see how well Justin has responded driving at most of these tracks for the first time. Our engineers have been doing a fantastic job with the setups and the crew is extremely reliable with our pit stops. With what I have seen so far, I expect great things from Justin and our team tomorrow and throughout the year."

Sadly, their expectations for the Champ Car Grand Prix of Cleveland were dashed within seconds of the drop of the green flag, following contact with both Alex Tagliani and polesitter Paul Tracy. Wilson, however, retained his lead in the Rookie of the Year standings, albeit by a meager one point over a fast-closing A.J. Allmendinger. He also remained upbeat despite his disappointment, recognizing the fact that his performance boded well for the immediate future.

"Obviously, this is not the way we wanted to finish the race," he said. "But we had a fast car all weekend long, and now I know we can compete with any of the teams in the series."

After his first-turn trouble, Tagliani flew back through the field to finish a fine third.
Dan Streck/LAT

ROUND 5

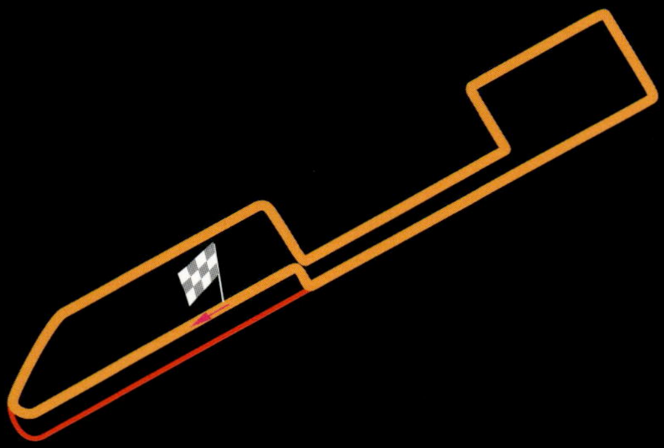

U.S. BANK PRESENTS THE CHAMP CAR GRAND PRIX OF CLEVELAND

BURKE LAKEFRONT AIRPORT, CLEVELAND, OHIO

JULY 3, 97 laps of 2.106 miles – 204.282 miles

Place	Driver (Nat.)	No.	Sponsor(s) Team Engine/Car	Tires	Q Speed	Q Time	Q Pos	Laps	Time/Status	Ave. (mph)	Pts
1	Sebastien Bourdais (F)	2	McDonald's Newman/Haas Racing Ford-Cosworth/Lola B01/00	BS	130.641	58.034s	3	97	1h 48m 16.056s	113.209	32
2	Bruno Junqueira (BR)	6	PacifiCare Newman/Haas Racing Ford-Cosworth/Lola B02/00	BS	130.210	58.226s	6	97	1h 48m 31.186s	112.946	28
3	Alex Tagliani (CDN)	8	Johnson Controls Rocketsports Racing Ford-Cosworth/Lola B02/00	BS	130.367	58.156s	5	97	1h 48m 43.640s	112.731	25
4	Oriol Servia (E)	11	yokeTV.com Dale Coyne Racing Ford-Cosworth/Lola B2K/00	BS	128.197	59.140s	13	97	1h 48m 54.252s	112.548	25
5	Jimmy Vasser (USA	12	Gulfstream PKV Racing Ford-Cosworth/Lola B02/00	BS	129.514	58.539s	10	97	1h 48m 57.957s	112.484	21
6	*A.J. Allmendinger (USA)	10	BG Products/Red Bull RuSPORT Ford-Cosworth/Lola B03/00	BS	130.398	58.142s	4	97	1h 48m 58.414s	112.476	19
7	*Roberto Gonzalez (MEX)	21	NII Holdings PKV Racing Ford-Cosworth/Lola B02/00	BS	127.931	59.263s	14	97	1h 49m 14.719s	112.196	17
8	Mario Dominguez (MEX)	55	Herdez Competition Ford-Cosworth/Lola B03/00	BS	129.002	58.771s	11	96	Running		15
9	Rodolfo Lavin (MEX)	3	Corona Forsythe Championship Racing Ford-Cosworth/Lola B02/00	BS	127.722	59.360s	15	96	Running		13
10	*Nelson Philippe (F)	17	LeasePlan Rocketsports Racing Ford-Cosworth/Lola B02/00	BS	127.240	59.585s	16	95	Running		11
11	Ryan Hunter-Reay (USA)	4	Herdez Competition Ford-Cosworth/Lola B01/00	BS	129.536	58.529s	9	95	Running		10
12	*Gaston Mazzacane (RA)	19	American Medical Response Dale Coyne Ford-Cosworth/Lola B02/00	BS	125.905	1m 00.217s	18	94	Running		9
13	*Alex Sperafico (BR)	14	Mi-Jack Conquest Racing Ford-Cosworth/Reynard 02I	BS	125.969	1m 00.186s	17	93	Running		8
14	Mario Haberfeld (BR)	5	Cummins Walker Racing Ford-Cosworth/Reynard 02I	BS	128.985	58.779s	12	80	Gearbox		7
15	Michel Jourdain Jr. (MEX)	9	Gigante RuSPORT Ford-Cosworth/Lola B04/00	BS	129.729	58.442s	8	61	Suspension		7
16	Patrick Carpentier (CDN)	7	Indeck Forsythe Championship Racing Ford-Cosworth/Lola B02/00	BS	129.926	58.353s	7	20	Engine		5
17	Paul Tracy (CDN)	1	Indeck Forsythe Championship Racing Ford-Cosworth/Lola B02/00	BS	131.749	57.546s	1	2	Accident		6
18	*Justin Wilson (GB)	34	Mi-Jack Conquest Racing Ford-Cosworth/Lola B02/00	BS	130.821	57.954s	2	0	Accident		3

*Denotes Rookie Driver

Caution flags: Laps 1-4, Wilson/Tracy & others accident; laps 40-43, debris; laps 44-47, Hunter-Reay spun and stalled. **Total:** Three for 12 laps.

Lap leaders: Sebastien Bourdais, 1-25 (25 laps); Oriol Servia, 26-27 (2 laps); Michel Jourdain Jr., 28 (1 lap); Bourdais, 29-53 (25 laps); Jourdain, 54-59 (6 laps); Bourdais, 60-97 (38 laps).
Totals: Bourdais, 88 laps; Jourdain, 7 laps; Servia, 2 laps.

Fastest race lap: Bruno Junqueira, 58.960s, 128.589 mph on lap 95.

Championship positions: 1 Junqueira, 133; 2 Bourdais, 130; 3 Carpentier, 104; 4 Tagliani, 86; 5 Tracy & Hunter-Reay, 85; 7 Dominguez, 81; 8 Wilson, 74; 9 Vasser & Allmendinger, 73; 11. Servia, 65; 12 Jourdain Jr., 59; 13 Gonzalez, 57; 14 Haberfeld, 50; 15 Lavin, 48; 16 Philippe, 43; 17 Sperafico, 28; 18 Mazzacane, 22; 19 Marques, 6.

CLEVELAND SNIPPETS

• The youngest driver in the field (by far), Nelson Philippe again languished toward the back of the pack in Rocketsports Racing's LeasePlan Lola, but the 17-year-old Frenchman at least expressed himself a little happier after switching to a longer-wheelbase setup. "The car feels a lot smoother," he said on Thursday. "I feel more confident about the car's handling and was consistently faster each lap – I wish I'd had this stuff sooner in the season." Philippe (below) kept his nose clean in the race and recorded another top-10 finish, mirroring his result from Monterrey.

Michael Levitt/LAT

• Fastest in final qualifying, reigning series champion Paul Tracy became only the ninth driver in the history of Champ Car racing to win 20 poles. The feat vaulted Tracy past 1988 champion Danny Sullivan and 1940-41 title winner Rex Mays into eighth place on the all-time Champ Car pole list, tying 1976 champion Gordon Johncock.

• The contentious new-for-2004 rule empowering Champ Car stewards to penalize a driver in qualifying if he was found to have impeded a rival, whether intentional or not, reared its head again several hours after the first session had been concluded: Both provisional polesitter Sébastien Bourdais and fourth-fastest Patrick Carpentier were indicted and convicted. Their best laps were duly forfeited, dropping them to fourth and ninth, respectively, in the provisional order.

• Before his Thursday penalty had been assessed, Bourdais said he felt he could extract more speed from his car during final qualifying. As it turned out, he couldn't, and therefore missed an opportunity to establish a new record of five consecutive front row starts to begin a Champ Car season. Bourdais had made some setup changes to his McDonald's Lola during the earlier practice session and wasn't quite as happy with the handling, so the best he could manage was third on the grid. "If a bad day is qualifying P3," he said with a smile, "I'll take it."

• Ongoing braking difficulties hampered Gaston Mazzacane's efforts in Dale Coyne Racing's #19 American Medical Response Lola. The Argentine rookie found some improvement in the final warmup on race morning and set his fastest lap of the weekend despite running with a full tank of fuel. Then his crew discovered a warped brake rotor which had to be changed for the race.

• Mexican rookie Roberto Gonzalez continued to make steady progress for PKV Racing. He wasn't at all happy on Thursday, qualifying a lowly 16th in the first session, but he found a lot more speed for the final period on Friday after adopting the same setup used by teammate Jimmy Vasser. Gonzalez went on to finish seventh, despite a quick spin, marking a new career-best performance and capping his third top-10 finish in the last four races.

• Rodolfo Lavin was sixth quickest in the opening practice, seventh in the pre-qualifying warmup and then ninth on Friday morning. But he didn't get his act together for qualifying and wound up a lowly 15th on the grid. Race day was better. "The car felt great and I was putting in good times every lap," he related. "In the end I finished ninth – not what I wanted, but after starting 15th it was better than nothing. The car was good all weekend and I felt really comfortable. I'm learning so much [from the Forsythe Championship Racing team] and am feeling much smoother in my driving."

• Championship leader Bruno Junqueira set the pace in Thursday's opening practice, clocking the fastest time before spinning off and crashing in Turn Eight. Damage to the right side of the #6 PacifiCare Lola was extensive, but his crew, headed by Donny Hoevel, had everything back together again in time for Junqueira to post the third fastest time in qualifying. Incredibly, he crashed again on Friday morning, depositing his car into the tires at the Turn Three/Four complex. This time it was the left side which took the brunt of the impact. Again he bounced back in final qualifying, and the Brazilian (pictured above after his shunt) reckoned he was on a lap that would have been good enough for the front row of the grid when the red flags waved after Ryan Hunter-Reay also crashed.

Dan Streck/LAT

Right: American Jimmy Vasser pushes hard to earn his first podium finish of the year
Dan Streck/LAT

Below: It was anything but a ticker-tape parade in Toronto for Sébastien Bourdais as he captured his third straight win.
Michael Levitt/LAT

BRIDGESTONE PRESENTS
THE CHAMP CAR WORLD SERIES POWERED BY FORD • ROUND 6

TORONTO

Right: JD Wilbur shows the green flag to the field to start the 19th Champ Car race run through the streets of Exhibition Place.

Center right: Bruno Junqueira relaxes prior to strapping into his 750hp Champ Car.
Photographs: Michael Levitt/LAT

Far right: Junqueira and Dominguez make contact forcing both drivers out early.
Photographs: Phil Abbott/LAT

MOLSON
CANADIAN LIGHT
PKVracing.com
BOSCH
NEXTEL

ONTARIO

DODGE

QUALIFYING

Canadian drivers claimed the lion's share of the media coverage during the first day of practice and qualifying for the 19th annual Molson Indy Toronto, with Patrick Carpentier posting the fastest time in morning practice and then countryman Paul Tracy snaring the provisional pole; but, as so often in 2005, Sunday morning's headlines were centered upon Sébastien Bourdais.

Final qualifying took a few minutes to get rolling as the main pole challengers delayed their runs, aware that the track would be at its best with more rubber laid down. It was worth the wait as fans were greeted with a flurry of changes atop the score sheets. Five drivers traded the pole during the session before Bourdais put it beyond reach.

The supremely gifted 25-year-old Frenchman earned his third pole of the season and the eighth of his nascent career as he snapped off a blistering lap of 58.558 seconds (107.893 mph) to lead the 18-car field on a sunny Saturday afternoon in Exhibition Place. Bourdais used his fifth lap of the day to set the best time and then had to sweat out nearly 10 more minutes while the rest of the field took their shots at unseating him.

"I really have to thank the McDonald's team because they did a great job with the setup," said Bourdais, who became the first driver since Juan Pablo Montoya in 2000 to start each of the season's first six races from the top three. He also claimed the coveted Greg Moore Pole Award.

"You just try as hard as you can so I am glad it was good enough," he said.

Tracy was "only" fourth quickest in the final session but already had second on the grid locked up by virtue of his Friday effort. Bourdais' teammate Bruno Junqueira jumped from sixth to third on his very last lap, nipping Mario Dominguez who had the toughest break of the day but still posted his best qualifying effort since Milwaukee. Dominguez was the first driver of the weekend to break the 59-second barrier, with a best lap of 58.899 seconds, but had to take to a runoff area on his very next pass due to a massive gearbox meltdown.

Rookie points leader Justin Wilson also had been quickest for a few moments before having to settle for fifth and his fourth top-five start of the season. It was another strong effort from the Formula 1 refugee following his front row qualifying spot one week earlier in Cleveland.

SÉBASTIEN Bourdais was a dominant force in the Molson Indy Toronto. He accelerated directly into the lead from the pole and was able to keep Newman/Haas Racing's #2 McDonald's Ford-Cosworth/Lola at the top of the charts on a day that featured seven caution flags and five penalties, as well as numerous bruised egos and a pile of broken race-car parts.

The Frenchman led 75 of the day's 84 laps and fought off repeated restart challenges, including one with two laps to go, to take the victory in front of a bumper crowd of 72,561. His fourth win of the season, coupled with first-lap trouble for teammate Bruno Junqueira, enabled him to turn a three-point deficit into a 28-point advantage in the championship standings.

"We had a great car today and things are going really well for us right now," said Bourdais. "But I want to stay focused on the target which is winning the championship. Things can change very fast in racing. Just when you think you're on top the worst things can happen. We've still got a long way to go."

The action came early and often on a day of perfect weather on the shores of Lake Ontario. As Bourdais bolted into the lead ahead of fellow front-row qualifier -- and local hero -- Paul Tracy, Junqueira and Mario Dominguez attempted to go two-wide through the first turn and ended up running out of real estate. Neither was able to continue after their collision, leaving a distraught Junqueira to tumble from his perch atop the series standings.

"At the start I was inside Paul and could have made an attempt to pass but I didn't want to take a chance so early in the race so I backed off and Mario put his nose in there," he recounted. "I was leading the championship and couldn't afford a risk like that. The kid had nothing to lose because he did not have as many points as I did."

"It's too bad," countered Dominguez. "I was on the outside; Bruno didn't give me any room and he turned in on me."

After a lengthy clean-up, Bourdais and Tracy stayed within reach of each other throughout the next 15 laps, chased by Justin Wilson and Patrick Carpentier. The top four cars were still blanketed by less than four seconds when the second full-course caution of the day heralded the demise of season debutant Memo Gidley who had nosed his Rocketsports Lola into the tire wall at Turn Three.

The first set of green-flag pit stops began on Lap 34, after which Wilson resumed in front of Tracy. Sadly, their tussle came to an abrupt end soon after a restart on Lap 42 when the Englishman slipped a little sideways in Turn Three and was tagged into a spin by Tracy. Directly behind, Oriol Servia was bundled off by Alex Tagliani as the pair disputed fifth place. Caution again. Wilson and Servia came off worst, losing laps before their stalled machines could be restarted, while both Tracy and Tagliani were assessed drive-through penalties for "initiating avoidable contact."

The shenanigans played into the hands, particularly, of Jimmy Vasser, who gratefully took over second place in PKV Racing's #12 Gulfstream Lola.

"For me it was just a matter of keeping our nose clean," the 1996 series champion said with a chuckle. "I made it through some of the carnage at the first corner, [and] had a good seat for a lot of the fireworks that were just in front of me."

The order after 50 laps saw Bourdais well clear of Vasser and

Above right: **Haberfeld pushes hard to match his career-best finish. The fourth-place result for Walker Racing was the highest finish for a Reynard in 2004.**
Phil Abbott/LAT

Right: **Paul Tracy and Justin Wilson collide in Turn Three. It was a rough event for Canadian hero Tracy, who was penalized twice for over-aggressive driving.**
David Chesson/LAT

fellow American Ryan Hunter-Reay. RHR was enjoying an excellent run for the Herdez Competition team, despite being assessed a drive-through penalty very early in the proceedings after inadvertently passing rookie A.J. Allmendinger while the yellow flags were waving (and punting his BG Products/Red Bull car into a spin for good measure). Michel Jourdain Jr. ran fourth, also doing a fine job for RuSPORT and taking full advantage of an alternate pit stop strategy necessitated by an early pit stop to change a nosecone that was damaged on the first lap.

Hunter-Reay was the first to make his second and final scheduled pit stop, on Lap 59. Bourdais followed him in a handful of laps later, handing the lead briefly to Vasser, who pitted on Lap 69, and then the remarkable Tracy who had been charging along after his earlier indiscretion.

Bourdais assumed the lead once more when Tracy took on service after 73 laps. The Frenchman was followed by Vasser, Hunter-Reay and Carpentier, who was making up for lost time after stalling during his pit stop. Tracy, meanwhile, anxious for a good result on his hometown track, shot out of the pits and promptly rammed into Jourdain at the exit of Turn One, sending the unfortunate – and rightly irate – Mexican into the barriers.

"It's a shame Paul Tracy doesn't know how to compete fairly," fumed Jourdain. "I gave him enough room to race and he didn't return the favor."

The Champ Car Stewards clearly agreed with Jourdain's assess-

HABERFELD HEATS UP

Mario Haberfeld made a major splash in the Champ Car World Series in 2003, scoring a fourth-place finish in his very first start with Mi-Jack Conquest Racing and showing no fear in a wheel-to-wheel shoving match with Bruno Junqueira at close to 170 mph.

The personable Brazilian went on to put together a respectable campaign before switching over to Walker Racing for 2004. The Indianapolis squad carried the burden of being the only single-car team in the series -- and furthermore was saddled with the unfashionable Reynard chassis -- so elected to spend most of its track time working on race setups rather than tweaking the car in qualifying trim. Consequently, Haberfeld was doomed to start in the back half of the field more often than not, inevitably leaving him with much to do on race day.

Toronto was no different as the Cummins/Walker car gridded 14th, but Haberfeld's deft maneuvering through the first-lap incidents promoted him to ninth right off the bat. He stayed there through the first half of the race, waiting for another opportunity.

"Toronto is famous for accidents, so our main concern was to run until the end avoiding getting caught in the various incidents," Haberfeld said.

As predicted, things really broke loose in the second half of the race as Justin Wilson, Paul Tracy, Alex Tagliani and Oriol Servia all ran into trouble virtually simultaneously. A second penalty for Tracy with six laps to go bumped Haberfeld into the top five behind Patrick Carpentier.

Carpentier then set his sights on the third-place car of Ryan Hunter-Reay, whereupon contact between them resulted in the American limping toward the pits with a punctured tire. Haberfeld thereby moved into fourth, matching his career high from the aforementioned 2003 season opener in St. Petersburg. In addition, Haberfeld earned a bonus championship point for gaining the most positions during the race.

"I'm ecstatic! The result was better than what we had hoped for, but it shows that we can be competitive in the series," he said. "Perhaps this will be the turning point of our season, and we will continue to progress throughout the rest of the year."

Right: Canadian Carpentier noses into the tire barrier, but recovered to finish fourth.
David Chesson/LAT

Below: Alex Sperafico earns a career-best 10th-place finish with Mi-Jack Conquest.
Michel Levitt/LAT

Bottom: Mazzacane brought home a sixth-place finish for Dale Coyne Racing.
Phil Abbott/LAT

MAZZACANE'S MILESTONE

SOMETHING of a young prodigy in his early days of open-wheel racing (no small feat coming from the country that produced the legendary Juan Manuel Fangio), Gaston Mazzacane climbed through the ranks to reach the International F3000 championship at the age of 21, and was serving as a Formula 1 test driver for Minardi at age 24. He went on to secure a full-time F1 seat just one season later, driving for Minardi and then the ill-fated Prost team in the first four grand prix of 2001.

Three years later, the Argentine pilot known as "Mad Dog" in his homeland joined the Champ Car ranks with Dale Coyne Racing, teaming up with Spaniard Oriol Servia (who, ironically, he had beaten out for the Prost seat). The now 29-year-old Mazzacane quixotically made his first-ever Champ Car start on the tricky Milwaukee Mile oval, where, predictably, he crashed; but he soon showed his skills on the road and street courses that followed.

He made up three positions from his grid placing in Portland, and six in Cleveland, but Toronto was his coming-out party. He started 16th after a lackluster qualifying session but gained five positions after patiently picking his way through the first-lap incidents.

He soon found his rhythm on the Exhibition Place circuit, running in the top 10 by the race's halfway point. Canny pit stop strategy enabled him to slide briefly into fourth ahead of reigning champion Paul Tracy for four laps, whereupon he was shuffled back to eighth by Lap 50. Mazzacane battled fiercely to stay on the lead lap for the next 25 orbits – a move that would pay off when a caution came out on Lap 74.

Mazzacane was able to regain touch with the rest of the field, and restarted in ninth. He moved up to eighth when Roberto Gonzalez sputtered, and was promoted to sixth when Alex Tagliani and Patrick Carpentier tangled. The sixth-place finish was Mazzacane's highest-ever result in a top-tier series and came as a welcome birthday present for Dale Coyne, who had turned 50 the previous week.

"I am very happy for this great finish with this great team," commented Mazzacane. "The car, pit stops, strategy were all perfect. I am very thankful to Dale for this wonderful opportunity and for me an emotional result."

ment of the incident, and Tracy's crew soon was informed that he would be required to make yet another unscheduled visit to the pit lane. And this time he would be held for five seconds before being allowed to continue.

Tracy had to wait until the remnants of Jourdain's Gigante Lola had been scraped off the wall (necessitating another full-course caution), before serving his penance. He did so immediately after the restart on Lap 80, and even then he still resumed in seventh place!

Then came yet another caution, after Rodolfo Lavin's Corona Lola stalled on the track, out of fuel.

The myriad interruptions caused the race to be shortened (by 11 laps) due to television constraints, and when the green flags were shown again, there was only enough time for a two-lap dash to the checkers. Bourdais remained untroubled, edging away from Vasser, but there was more drama in their wake as Hunter-Reay and Carpentier made contact on Lakeshore Boulevard with little more than a lap and a half remaining. To the relief of the crowd – but not Hunter-Reay – it was the American who came off worst, limping into the pits to change a punctured rear tire.

"I was hit so hard I could feel the car jump and I am lucky I kept it off the wall," related RHR, who soldiered on to finish a disgruntled eighth.

"I wanted to get that third-place finish," affirmed Carpentier. "I had two seconds of 'push-to-pass' left. Once you push it, if you lift, then you don't have it any more. I pushed it and then I went to the left [to pass], he went to the left; I went to the right, he went to the right – left, right and I couldn't lift so I hit him. Then that was it. Made the pass!"

Carpentier also claimed that he considered himself immune to a penalty because, in his opinion, Hunter-Reay had been unfairly robust in his defense of the position and, if anything, his rival should have been disciplined for "blocking." The stewards apparently concurred. No more penalties were issued and Carpentier kept his third-place finish.

"It's fantastic to do well in Toronto," he said. "I've never been lucky here and this is my best result ever. I'm so happy."

The other two podium finishers were equally delighted, with Bourdais heaping praise on his Newman/Haas crew following yet another superlative performance and Vasser rejoicing at his PKV team's first-ever top-three finish.

"I am really happy with the energy in the team," enthused Vasser after taking the checkered flag 1.396 seconds adrift of the Frenchman. "I have been working with them and it really is starting to come around."

Mario Haberfeld matched his career best by guiding Walker Racing's #5 Cummins Reynard to fourth, while Tracy held on for fifth following what might charitably be described as an "eventful" afternoon.

Gaston Mazzacane scored comfortably his best finish to date, netting sixth for Dale Coyne Racing ahead of Tagliani and Hunter-Reay. Servia never recovered from going a lap down in the early stages, while Alex Sperafico kept out of trouble to claim his first top-10 finish.

Jeremy Shaw

ROUND 6

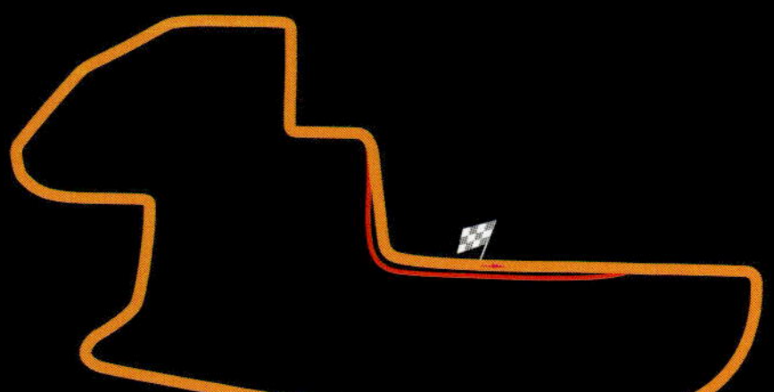

MOLSON INDY TORONTO

EXHIBITION PLACE, TORONTO, ONTARIO, CANADA

JULY 11, 84 laps of 1.755 miles – 147.420 miles

Place	Driver (Nat.)	No.	Sponsor(s) Team Engine/Car	Tires	Q Speed	Q Time	Q Pos	Laps	Time/Status	Ave. (mph)	Pts
1	Sebastien Bourdais (F)	2	McDonald's Newman/Haas Racing Ford-Cosworth/Lola B01/00	BS	107.893	58.558s	1	84	1h 45m 36.930s	83.749	34
2	Jimmy Vasser (USA)	12	Gulfstream PKV Racing Ford-Cosworth/Lola B02/00	BS	106.237	59.471s	11	84	1h 45m 38.326s	83.731	28
3	Patrick Carpentier (CDN)	7	Indeck Forsythe Championship Racing Ford-Cosworth/Lola B02/00	BS	106.723	59.200s	6	84	1h 45m 43.661s	83.660	25
4	Mario Haberfeld (BR)	5	Cummins Walker Racing Ford-Cosworth/Reynard 02I	BS	104.696	1m 00.346s	14	84	1h 45m 44.822s	83.645	24
5	Paul Tracy (CDN)	1	Indeck Forsythe Championship Racing Ford-Cosworth/Lola B02/00	BS	107.038	59.026s	2	84	1h 45m 46.595s	83.622	23
6	*Gaston Mazzacane (RA)	19	American Medical Response Dale Coyne Ford-Cosworth/Lola B02/00	BS	103.354	1m 01.130s	16	84	1h 45m 50.932s	83.564	19
7	Alex Tagliani (CDN)	8	Johnson Controls Rocketsports Racing Ford-Cosworth/Lola B02/00	BS	106.240	59.469s	9	84	1h 46m 05.374s	83.375	17
8	Ryan Hunter-Reay (USA)	4	Herdez Competition Ford-Cosworth/Lola B01/00	BS	106.615	59.260s	7	84	1h 46m 20.105s	83.182	15
9	Oriol Servia (E)	11	yokeTV.com Dale Coyne Racing Ford-Cosworth/Lola B2K/00	BS	106.240	59.469s	10	83	Running		13
10	*Alex Sperafico (BR)	14	Mi-Jack Conquest Racing Ford-Cosworth/Reynard 02I	BS	103.146	1m 01.253s	17	83	Running		11
11	*A.J. Allmendinger (USA)	10	BG Products/Red Bull RuSPORT Ford-Cosworth/Lola B03/00	BS	106.401	59.379s	8	82	Running		10
12	*Justin Wilson (GB)	34	Mi-Jack Conquest Racing Ford-Cosworth/Lola B02/00	BS	107.032	59.029s	5	80	Running		9
13	*Roberto Gonzalez (MEX)	21	Nextel PKV Racing Ford-Cosworth/Lola B02/00	BS	103.894	1m 00.812s	15	80	Accident		8
14	Rodolfo Lavin (MEX)	3	Corona Forsythe Championship Racing Ford-Cosworth/Lola B03/00	BS	105.522	59.874s	13	78	Out of fuel		7
15	Michel Jourdain Jr. (MEX)	9	Gigante RuSPORT Ford-Cosworth/Lola B04/00	BS	106.035	59.584s	12	73	Accident		6
16	Memo Gidley (USA)	17	LeasePlan Rocketsports Racing Ford-Cosworth/Lola B02/00	BS	102.737	1m 01.497s	18	36	Accident		5
17	Mario Dominguez (MEX)	55	Herdez Competition Ford-Cosworth/Lola B03/00	BS	107.268	58.899s	4	0	Accident		4
18	Bruno Junqueira(BR)	6	PacifiCare Newman/Haas Racing Ford-Cosworth/Lola B02/00	BS	107.732	58.842s	3	0	Accident		3

*Denotes Rookie Driver

Caution flags: Laps 1-6, Junqueira/Dominguez/Allmendinger accident; laps 22-24, Gidley spun and stalled; laps 38-41, Gidley accident; laps 42-45, Servia/Wilson accident; laps 47-48, debris on course; laps 74-79, Jourdain accident; laps 81-82, Lavin stalled on course. **Total:** Seven for 27 laps.

Lap leaders: Sebastien Bourdais, 1-63 (63 laps); Jimmy Vasser, 64-68 (5 laps); Paul Tracy, 69-72 (4 laps); Bourdais, 73-84 (12 laps). **Totals:** Bourdais, 75 laps; Vasser, 5 laps; Tracy, 4 laps.

Fastest race lap: Sebastien Bourdais, 1m 00.304s, 104.769 mph on lap 58.

Championship positions: 1 Bourdais, 164; 2 Junqueira, 136; 3 Carpentier, 129; 4 Tracy, 108; 5 Tagliani, 103; 6 Vasser, 101; 7 Hunter-Reay, 100; 8 Dominguez, 85; 9 Allmendinger & Wilson, 83; 11 Servia, 78; 12 Haberfeld, 74; 13 Jourdain Jr. & Gonzalez, 65; 15 Lavin, 55; 16 Philippe, 43; 17 Mazzacane, 41; 18 Sperafico, 39; 19 Marques, 6; 20 Gidley, 5.

TORONTO SNIPPETS

Dan Streck/LAT

• Memo Gidley (above) returned to the Champ Car fray for the first time since the end of the 2001 season, taking up a late call to replace Nelson Philippe in Rocketsports Racing's #17 LeasePlan Lola. "Contractual problems" were cited for the young Frenchman's absence, and after Roberto Moreno regretfully declined the invitation to drive because he was in the hospital undergoing a minor surgical procedure, Gidley was summoned. He didn't arrive until Friday evening, and after a late-night seat fitting he took to the track for the first time on Saturday morning. Under the circumstances, the American acquitted himself very respectably and was instantly quicker than Alex Sperafico and Gaston Mazzacane. Unfortunately, his lack of familiarity with the car caught him out in Sunday's race and he ended up parked against the wall.

• Sébastien Bourdais' pole was the eighth of his career, tying him with teammate Bruno Junqueira, Jimmy Vasser, Jack McGrath and Texan Lloyd Ruby for 30th on the all-time Champ Car list. He went on to notch his seventh race victory, equaling the tally of such all-time greats as Dan Gurney, Eddie Rickenbacker and Gil de Ferran. To put his strike rate (.29) into perspective, Bourdais achieved the mark in just 24 races, compared to two-time series champion de Ferran's 129 starts.

• Gorgeous weather conditions all weekend, allied to the strong performances of Canadian heroes Paul Tracy and Patrick Carpentier, attracted the usual huge crowds to the Molson Indy, with a three-day event total attendance of 164,218.

• "This has always been the biggest race for me," commented Tracy after earning himself a championship point by virtue of his provisional pole on Friday. "Always has been, always will be." Tracy, of course, was born and bred in the Toronto suburbs, and he certainly lived up to his nickname – "The Thrill from West Hill" – in the race, attracting not one but two penalties for violating Rule 6.27, which pertains to "avoidable contact" with other competitors.

• One week after qualifying on the front row at Cleveland, rookie Justin Wilson once again set the cat among the pigeons by clocking the fastest lap during practice on Saturday morning. The Briton also was quickest for a while during final qualifying, and ended up fifth on the grid for Eric Bachelart's rapidly improving Mi-Jack Conquest Racing team. "I'm a bit disappointed that we couldn't qualify higher, as we expected," Wilson said. "Due to some traffic I encountered during my last laps, I was unable to improve my time, [but] I felt the car was capable of a top-three grid position."

• Wilson's main rival for rookie-of-the-year honors, A.J. Allmendinger, endured one of his least competitive weekends but still drew level on points with the Englishman after Wilson was knocked out of the race in the early stages. Allmendinger wasn't feeling 100 percent due to a slight cold, and his predicament wasn't helped by his car: "We're slow," he said on Friday. "Just can't find any grip." A switch to RuSPORT teammate Michel Jourdain Jr.'s setup helped, and Allmendinger turned some competitive laps in the race -- but not before an early skirmish had cost him a lap.

• Bourdais' win elevated France into the lead of the Nation's Cup standings, by a margin of 163 points to 158 over defending champions Canada. Brazil lay third after six races on 151, followed by the United States on 132 and Mexico on 107.

• "Man, these street races are a blast!" exclaimed Jimmy Vasser (below), echoing the thoughts of the usual huge crowd after notching his first podium finish since taking on a new role and joining Kevin Kalkhoven and Dan Pettit as a part-owner of PKV Racing. "I guess the key of the race was that I didn't run into anybody – a little bit of old man wisdom I suppose!"

Paul Abbott/LAT

Main photograph: Ever the showman, Paul Tracy accepts the crowd's plaudits following a fine drive to victory – and an equally impressive display of donuts.
Leland Hill/LAT

Above right: False Creek has provided a setting for the Champ Cars since 1998.

Right: Carl Russo greets Michel Jourdain Jr. after taking a magnificent second place.
Photographs: Lesley Ann Miller/LAT

Below: Rookie A.J. Allmendinger is properly initiated after his first podium.
Michael Levitt/LAT

RUSPORT CLIMBS THE LADDER

RuSPORT owner Carl Russo had to fight back the tears after his drivers Michel Jourdain Jr. and A.J. Allmendinger finished second and third in Vancouver. The double podium marked a new watershed for the Colorado-based outfit that had graduated to Champ Cars in 2004 after decimating the Toyota Atlantic competition the previous year with its young lion Allmendinger.

"The guys have worked so hard and so intelligently," praised Russo, very much a hands-on team owner and motivational guru. "We've stuck to our core principles and persevered through thick and thin."

The original plan for '04 had been to field a single-car effort for Allmendinger, but when Jourdain became a free agent following his former employer Bobby Rahal's defection to the IRL, Russo decided the opportunity to bring a proven race winner on board was too good to pass up. The 11th-hour timing of the deal – it was announced on March 31, just 18 days before the season-opener at Long Beach! – presented the team with a daunting logistical challenge, but Jourdain's experience proved an invaluable asset as it negotiated the inevitable steep learning curve.

"This weekend demonstrates again why Michel was a championship contender last year," declared Russo. "He executed well on the racetrack, but what people don't see is how much he has meant to this team off the racetrack."

Allmendinger, too, paid tribute to Jourdain's contribution: "Without Michel we would have been a single-car team and I would have been completely lost. Having his knowledge and experience helps everyone in the team to know a little bit more about what we want out of the cars and how to get to that point."

Fittingly, the result was the product of a true team effort, with shrewd strategy, faultless pit stops and prodigious race pace all playing their part in hauling the two drivers up the lap chart from the sixth row of the grid.

"It's fantastic for Carl and everybody on the team," enthused Jourdain. "You know, they work so hard. I felt bad when I came in because they had everything so organized, and in three days they had to hire a lot more people, equipment, I mean everything... We are still missing a lot of people and the guys work every day until 10 p.m. back at the shop. So this is fantastic for them."

VANCOUVER

Forsythe
INDECK
INDECK
Forsythe
INDECK
Ford
INDECK
BRIDGESTONE
BRIDGESTONE

QUALIFYING

Paul Tracy has had a strong affinity for the demanding Concord Pacific Place street circuit on Vancouver's downtown waterfront ever since it was reconfigured in 1998, and the Canadian was in peerless form during provisional qualifying on Friday.

Mindful that finding a gap in the traffic is a chancy business around the twisty 1.781-mile layout, Tracy wisely opted to venture out relatively early in the session and lay down a marker for his rivals to aim at. No one succeeded in usurping him from the top of the charts and he duly bagged the coveted bonus point and guaranteed front-row slot – despite having to forfeit his best time after officials deemed him guilty of blocking.

"We didn't get off to a good start this morning, but we made a few small changes in the afternoon and the car came alive," related Tracy.

Saturday's final qualifying was anti-climactic as a pair of untimely red-flag interruptions prevented the session from developing a real rhythm and meant that many drivers relied on their provisional times for their grid placings.

Not so Rodolfo Lavin, who sprang one of the biggest upsets of the season by topping the session in his Corona-backed Lola and joining Forsythe teammate Tracy on the front row. The unheralded Mexican, whose previous best qualifying effort had been sixth at Milwaukee, was the last to arrive at the top-three press conference, prompting Tracy to quip, "He doesn't know how to get here because it's his first time!"

"We've worked really, really hard since the start of the season," said Lavin, grinning from ear to ear. "We went in the right direction on setup today and now we are starting to show what we can do with a good car and a good team. Hopefully this is only the beginning of good results for me."

Newman/Haas Racing's Sébastien Bourdais set the pace in practice on Saturday morning but was thwarted by the red flags in qualifying and had to settle for third. Mario Dominguez vaulted from eighth on the overnight grid to fourth in the leading Herdez Competition entry, while Memo Gidley qualified a splendid fifth on his second outing for Rocketsports Racing.

PAUL Tracy was the toast of a typically enthusiastic 63,000-strong crowd after winning the Molson Indy Vancouver in barnstorming style. The defending series champion started from pole position and controlled the first three-quarters of the race more or less at will. But he was forced to dig deep into his reserves when it became clear that he would have to make an unscheduled pit visit a handful of laps from the end due to a refueling glitch at his last planned stop.

Driving with the panache that makes him Champ Car's most dynamic performer when he's firing on all cylinders, Tracy reeled off a sequence of blistering laps which built him enough of a cushion to emerge still in the lead. His 28th career victory and first since Long Beach in April went some way toward putting his title defense back on track, as well as defusing criticism of his Toronto antics a fortnight earlier.

"It wasn't the demonstration I wanted it to be," joked Tracy. "Obviously I just wanted to maintain my lead. I wasn't too happy when the team came on the radio and told me that I didn't have enough fuel."

There were no such dramas for Tracy in the early stages. He made a perfect getaway to lead into the first corner, although his hopes that Forsythe Championship Racing teammate and surprise front-row occupant Rodolfo Lavin would act as a "rear gunner" were dashed when Sebastien Bourdais immediately demoted the Mexican to third place. Mario Dominguez, an impressive Memo Gidley and Patrick Carpentier followed in grid order, while Bruno Junqueira, who had started a lowly eighth after crashing in final qualifying, outbraked Justin Wilson at Turn Six.

Tracy, as usual, was in his element on cold tires and initially pulled away quite rapidly at the head of the field. But before long Bourdais found his rhythm and the gap stabilized at around 2.5 seconds. It looked like a classic Forsythe v. Newman/Haas duel was on the cards when a full-course yellow intervened on Lap 22.

The caution was triggered by a collision between Carpentier, who had inherited fifth place when Gidley spun his Rocketsports Lola a couple of laps earlier, and backmarker Alex Sperafico in the Mi-Jack Conquest Racing Reynard. After moving off-line along the pit straight with the apparent intention of letting Carpentier through to lap him, the hapless Sperafico promptly clouted the #7 Indeck Lola and sent it backward into the tire barrier at Turn One. Carpentier was understandably irate – especially since he had been equally blameless after being eliminated in similar fashion at Vancouver in 2003.

"I was just being patient and saving fuel, using third gear in the second-gear corners, when I was taken out by a guy who was already two laps down by then," railed Carpentier.

Seconds earlier and barely 100 feet up the road, Lavin, who had been hanging on gamely in third place under increasing pressure from fellow countryman Dominguez, had finally succumbed when he lost the back end of his Corona machine and spun down to 14th.

The next segment of the race proved critical, as Tracy bolted away at the restart while Bourdais found himself grappling with the handling of his McDonald's Lola and lost ground at a precipitous rate – just as the first round of pit stops loomed. In successive laps Tracy's lead ballooned from 1.6 seconds to 2.3 to 3.7 to a five full seconds. By the time he peeled into the pits after 32 circuits he was more than six seconds to the good.

Bourdais stopped one lap later and his crew sent him away with less than a full tank of methanol in a bid to regain some of the lost time – but the damage was done and the Frenchman found himself embroiled in traffic for the remainder of the afternoon.

Into the breach stepped the RuSPORT team, which rolled the dice by short-filling A.J. Allmendinger and Michel Jourdain Jr. in order to gain track position. The ploy worked a treat, as the pair leapfrogged Bourdais, Dominguez and Junqueira to assume second and third places respectively. Moreover, both drivers found their cars were handling to perfection and soon put some distance between themselves and Bourdais.

By Lap 42 the points leader had fallen into the clutches of Rocketsports Racing's Alex Tagliani, who had already displaced Junqueira during the pit stop shuffle – although the Newman/Haas duo regained the upper hand after Tagliani made an early final stop on Lap 53.

Tracy still enjoyed a comfortable cushion over Allmendinger, who had nevertheless taken full advantage of the clear racetrack afforded by RuSPORT's pit strategy to trade fastest laps with his mentor in the high 1m 01s range. Jourdain, too, wasn't hanging about, only losing a tenth of a second here and there to the two leaders. The Mexican's frugal fuel consumption paid dividends when he was able to eke out three more laps than Allmendinger on his second tank. The extra laps on hot tires and a low fuel load were enough to release him in front of his teammate in a clear second place. Bourdais, paying the price for his earlier short-fill, lost out to Junqueira for the same reason.

Tracy's stop, meanwhile, had passed without incident – or so it seemed. The fuel hose was attached for a mere seven seconds, but at 25 laps the final stint was set to be slightly shorter than the previous two. Then the realization dawned on the Forsythe engineers that something was amiss; a refueling malfunction had left Tracy seven gallons short of the amount he needed to complete the 85-lap distance.

"We don't know exactly what happened," admitted vice-president of operations Neil Micklewright. "There was a problem with the fueling system and not enough fuel went in."

The bad news was swiftly relayed to Tracy, who at that stage had a 15-second buffer over Jourdain but needed something like 25 seconds in hand if he was to make an additional "splash-and-dash" pit visit and rejoin without losing the lead.

"I had everything under control until the miscue on the second pit stop," recounted the Canadian. "I couldn't believe it! They told me I needed to pull out a 25-second gap. I put my head down and just

Right: An incensed Patrick Carpentier strides back to the pits after tangling with hapless rookie Alex Sperafico in Turn One.
Lesley Ann Miller/LAT

Top right: Jourdain used all his experience on the unforgiving streets of Vancouver

Far right: Rookie teammate Allmendinger rewarded his crew's hard work with third.
Photographs: Michael Levitt/LAT

9
GIGANTE G
Office

INDECK
Corona

Right: Paul Tracy dutifully serves as one of the judges of the traditional "Miss Indy" contest, won this year by Jessica Sulidis.

Below: His task was not an easy one...
Photographs Dan Streck/LAT

Bottom: Memo Gidley got right back in the swing of being a Champ Car driver, qualifying an excellent fifth before jetting off to race his Ford Focus at Portland.
Michael Levitt/LAT

went for it, driving every lap like a qualifying lap."

Undeterred by a brush with the tire barrier on the exit of Turn Six, Tracy moved ever closer to his target margin with a string of new fastest laps. By the time he eventually called at the pits on Lap 77 his lead had swollen to 28.2 seconds. It was more than enough, enabling him to resume with a still-comfortable six-second advantage over Jourdain. But it was still a closer-run thing than Tracy would have liked.

"If there had been another yellow the race would have been over for us," he conceded. "Plus at the end my tires were done. I went from doing 1m 01s laps to mid-1m 03s, so really over the last six or seven laps I was just hanging on."

Jourdain and Allmendinger posted the best result so far for the burgeoning RuSPORT outfit by coming home second and third, Jourdain overcoming fading brakes and Allmendinger admitting to fatigue in the waning stages as he battled to keep a closing Junqueira at bay.

"My engineers David Brown and Chris Lerch gave me an awesome car," beamed Allmendinger in the afterglow of his first podium finish. "Actually they gave me a little too much grip on the last stint because I felt like it was going to rip my arms off the last 20 laps. You know, actually if I was two laps down I might have pulled in because I was so tired, but I wasn't going to give up a podium spot."

Junqueira was reasonably content to salvage fourth place after his qualifying setback. Bourdais' pace was curiously inconsistent but he felt the prevailing fuel regulations were his biggest enemy.

"I'm frustrated about the rules because the race is all about fuel economy now," he complained. "No one could pass – they just had to save fuel. We had to short-fill to keep our position. Then the others pitted later on a different strategy and were able to get ahead of us. We had a car to finish second but we weren't able to take advantage of it."

A slow first pit stop put Dominguez behind the eight-ball and he had to settle for sixth, while Herdez Competition teammate Ryan Hunter-Reay narrowly failed to relieve Tagliani of seventh. Mario Haberfeld was the last of the unlapped runners in Derrick Walker's Reynard.

Alex Sabine

SUPERSUB TURNS SUPERHERO!

IF points were awarded for effort and dedication alone, Memo Gidley would be a multiple Champ Car title-holder by now. Instead the popular 33-year-old has spent his top-level career living a hand-to-mouth existence, scraping together temporary drives with a veritable Who's Who of teams but never enjoying the benefit of a season-long campaign with the same outfit.

Like Roberto Moreno before him, Gidley has been dubbed "Supersub" for his dependability in substitute roles. Even by his standards, however, the call-up from Paul Gentilozzi to drive the second Rocketsports entry in Toronto had come at short notice (on Friday of the race meeting). Furthermore, Gidley had no prior experience of a current-generation Champ Car with its 12,000 rpm rev-limit and higher turbo boost.

A second outing with the #17 Lola in Vancouver therefore provided the first representative gauge of the Californian's pace. He came through with flying colors. After posting the ninth fastest time on Friday, Gidley was one of the stars of Saturday's fragmented final qualifying session, claiming a sensational fifth on the grid – four places ahead of teammate Alex Tagliani.

He had no time to savor the moment, though, since he was determined to keep a prior commitment to race a Ford Focus, sponsored by the U.S. Air Force Reserve (which also supported his Champ Car effort), in the SPEED World Challenge touring car event at Portland International Raceway.

Immediately after clambering out of his Rocketsports machine at 2.45 p.m., Gidley hot-footed it to the airport by police escort, jumped on a Learjet to Portland and then was transported by helicopter to the circuit, arriving with less than a minute to spare before the 4.15 p.m. start! He went on to win the Hard Charger award after climbing from the back of the 34-car field to 11th place.

If nothing else the exercise was a testament to Gidley's unquenchable passion for the sport. Alas, he was brought down to earth with a bang when he stepped back into his Champ Car on Sunday, spinning out of fifth place on Lap 19.

"I just locked the rear tires in Turn Four and that was it," he confessed after coming home a disappointed 11th. "We tried to regain positions with a different strategy, but it's not as easy to do that these days with the rule requiring green-flag pit stops."

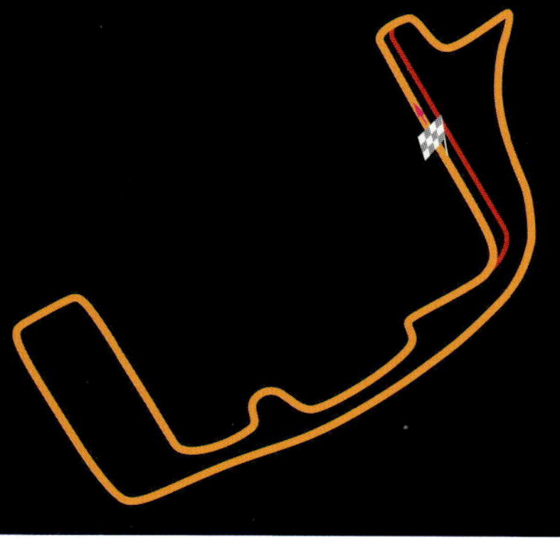

ROUND 7

MOLSON
INDY VANCOUVER

CONCORD PACIFIC PLACE, ONTARIO, BRITISH COLUMBIA, CANADA

JULY 25, 85 laps of 1.781 miles – 151.385 miles

Place	Driver (Nat.)	No.	Sponsor(s) Team Engine/Car	Tires	Q Speed	Q Time	Q Pos	Laps	Time/Status	Ave. (mph)	Pts
1	Paul Tracy (CDN)	1	Indeck Forsythe Championship Racing Ford-Cosworth/Lola B02/00	BS	105.333	1m 00.870s	1	85	1h 34m 42.849s	95.900	34
2	Michel Jourdain Jr. (MEX)	9	Gigante RuSPORT Ford-Cosworth/Lola B04/00	BS	103.786	1m 01.777s	12	85	1h 34m 48.406s	95.806	29
3	*A.J. Allmendinger (USA)	10	BG Products/Red Bull RuSPORT Ford-Cosworth/Lola B03/00	BS	104.105	1m 01.588s	11	85	1h 34m 48.988s	95.797	25
4	Bruno Junqueira (BR)	6	PacifiCare Newman/Haas Racing Ford-Cosworth/Lola B02/00	BS	104.323	1m 01.459s	8	85	1h 34m 49.393s	95.790	23
5	Sébastien Bourdais(F)	2	McDonald's Newman/Haas Racing Ford-Cosworth/Lola B01/00	BS	105.153	1m 00.974s	3	85	1h 34m 57.080s	95.661	22
6	Mario Dominguez (MEX)	55	Herdez Competition Ford-Cosworth/Lola B03/00	BS	104.820	1m 01.168s	4	85	1h 34m 58.683s	95.634	20
7	Alex Tagliani (CDN)	8	Johnson Controls Rocketsports Racing Ford-Cosworth/Lola B02/00	BS	104.188	1m 01.539s	9	85	1h 35m 15.017s	95.360	17
8	Ryan Hunter-Reay (USA)	4	Herdez Competition Ford-Cosworth/Lola B01/00	BS	104.142	1m 01.566s	10	85	1h 35m 15.468s	95.353	15
9	Mario Haberfeld (BR)	5	Cummins Walker Racing Ford-Cosworth/Reynard 02I	BS	103.562	1m 01.911s	14	85	1h 35m 26.520s	95.169	13
10	Jimmy Vasser (USA)	12	Gulfstream PKV Racing Ford-Cosworth/Lola B02/00	BS	103.520	1m 01.936s	15	84	1h 45m 38.326s	83.731	11
11	Memo Gidley (USA)	17	LeasePlan Rocketsports Racing Ford-Cosworth/Lola B02/00	BS	104.483	1m 01.365s	5	84	Running		10
12	Oriol Servia (E)	11	yokeTV.com Dale Coyne Racing Ford-Cosworth/Lola B2K/00	BS	103.573	1m 01.904s	13	84	Running		9
13	*Roberto Gonzalez (MEX)	21	Nextel PKV Racing Ford-Cosworth/Lola B02/00	BS	103.142	1m 02.163s	16	83	Running		8
14	*Justin Wilson (GB)	34	Mi-Jack Conquest Racing Ford-Cosworth/Lola B02/00	BS	104.366	1m 01.434s	7	80	Running		7
15	Rodolfo Lavin (MEX)	3	Corona Forsythe Championship Racing Ford-Cosworth/Lola B03/00	BS	105.143	1m 00.980s	2	66	Gearbox		7
16	Patrick Carpentier (CDN)	7	Indeck Forsythe Championship Racing Ford-Cosworth/Lola B02/00	BS	104.427	1m 01.398s	6	21	Accident		5
17	*Alex Sperafico (BR)	14	Mi-Jack Conquest Racing Ford-Cosworth/Reynard 02I	BS	101.214	1m 03.347s	17	19	Accident		4
NS	*Gaston Mazzacane (RA)	19	American Medical Response Dale Coyne Ford-Cosworth/Lola B02/00	BS	100.563	1m 03.757s	18	-	Accident		0

*Denotes Rookie Driver

Caution flags: Lap 1, yellow start/Mazzacane accident; laps 22-25, Carpentier/Sperafico accident. **Total:** Two for 5 laps.

Lap leaders: Paul Tracy, 1-32 (32 laps); Sébastien Bourdais, 33 (1 lap); Mario Dominguez, 34 (1 lap); Michel Jourdain Jr., 35-36 (2 laps); Tracy, 37-85 (49 laps). **Totals:** Tracy, 81 laps; Jourdain Jr., 2 laps; Bourdais, 1 lap; Dominguez, 1 lap.

Fastest race lap: Paul Tracy, 1m 01.755s, 103.823 mph on lap 71.

Championship positions: 1 Bourdais, 186; 2 Junqueira, 159; 3 Tracy, 142; 4 Carpentier, 134; 5 Tagliani, 120; 6 Hunter-Reay, 115; 7 Vasser, 112; 8 Allmendinger, 108; 9 Dominguez, 105; 10 Jourdain Jr., 94; 11 Wilson, 90; 12 Servia & Haberfeld, 87; 14 Gonzalez, 73; 15 Lavin, 62; 16 Philippe & Sperafico, 43; 18 Mazzacane, 41; 19 Gidley, 15; 20 Marques, 6.

VANCOUVER SNIPPETS

Michael Levitt/LAT

• Blessed by blue skies and near-record temperatures throughout the weekend, the Molson Indy Vancouver drew its usual bumper attendance. The three-day turnout of 158,420 was only fractionally down on the 2003 total despite Champ Car's well-publicized troubles over the off-season, further testifying to the sport's popularity north of the 49th parallel.

• Notwithstanding the continued success of the event, the paddock rumor mill suggested that 2004 might turn out to be Champ Car's swan-song in British Columbia. The race's future had been in doubt since Vancouver won its bid to host the 2010 Winter Olympic Games. The street circuit runs through the downtown False Creek area which will be redeveloped to house the Athletes' Village, and with much of the metropolitan area under construction, finding an alternative site was likely to present a problem from 2007 onward. Promoter Molson Sports and Entertainment was understood to be seeking funding from the city to continue staging the event for the intervening two years, but sadly their efforts came to naught.

• Bruno Junqueira crashed heavily during final qualifying when his right-front suspension collapsed at the tricky chicane complex before the pits, sending the #6 PacifiCare Lola nose-first into the tire barrier. Suspecting that the failure had been caused by the heavy punishment meted out over the curbs at several points around the Concord Pacific Place street course where the cars are highly-loaded, Newman/Haas Racing opted to replace its own lightweight wishbones with the beefier standard Lola components on Saturday evening. The mechanics labored into the small hours carrying out the modifications as well as scheduled engine changes.

• Gaston Mazzacane's race was over before it began after he lost control of his American Medical Response Lola while warming his tires on the first parade lap and clouted the wall. The incident brought a depressing sense of *déjà vu* to team owner Dale Coyne, who one year earlier had suffered the ignominy of seeing both his cars (driven by Geoff Boss and Gualter Salles) eliminated in precisely the same fashion!

• With only a 90-minute window in which to get to Portland International Raceway for his scheduled start in the SPEED World Challenge touring car race (see sidebar opposite), Memo Gidley was understandably brief in his comments after qualifying a fine fifth. "Thanks guys," he told his Rocketsports mechanics. "I gotta run."

• PKV Racing owner/driver Jimmy Vasser was unhappy with the handling of his Gulfstream Lola all weekend, qualifying a disconsolate 15th and finishing a lapped 10th. The 1996 series champion may have set a record for the brevity – and honesty – of his official post-qualifying quote. "Terrible, terrible, terrible," Vasser said, forcing a smile.

• Hockey legend Wayne Gretzky (in car with Paul Newman) served as the honorary starter for the 15th running of the Vancouver event.

Lesley Ann Miller/LAT

BRIDGESTONE PRESENTS THE CHAMP CAR WORLD SERIES POWERED BY FORD • ROUND 8

ROAD AMERICA

BREAKTHROUGH TIME

THE lucky break that put Alex Tagliani in a position to score his maiden Champ Car victory was as overdue as it was deserved. For years the French-Canadian had been the series' equivalent of the best golfer who hadn't won a major. At least four races that he seemed destined to win – Rio and Road America in 2000, Vancouver in '01 and Montreal in '03 – had slipped from his grasp within tantalizing reach of the checkered flag, in three of those cases due to factors outside his control.

Imagine, then, the butterflies in his stomach over the final, 4.048-mile lap of Road America as he prepared to banish those demons to the history books.

"That last lap was the longest of my life," he confirmed. "The longest track, too! A lot of things went through my mind. I've been waiting such a long time."

Tagliani's weekend began on an inauspicious note when he crashed heavily in the fast Hurry Downs section during Friday morning practice and was forced to sit out the afternoon's qualifying session. He didn't fare much better on Saturday, when a balky gearbox restricted him to 13th on the grid.

"The only problem-free day was Sunday, and it was the day that counted," grinned Tagliani, whose breakthrough win was also the first for the Rocketsports team owned by OWRS principal Paul Gentilozzi. The Lansing, Michigan-based outfit – already a fixture in the Trans-Am ranks, where Gentilozzi had forged a highly successful career as a driver – was one of a flurry of teams to join the Champ Car fray in 2003. Despite the inevitable teething troubles it had made a generally favorable impression, although Tagliani conceded it was yet to blossom into a *bona fide* front-runner.

"I think we have a great team, we just lack a little bit of consistency," he said. "We cannot be fast at every race track. We're still searching for the best setup. But, you know, it's only been a year and a half since this team was created. There's still a lot of things to learn. I think to be here right now, it's already a big achievement for us. If we keep going in that direction, I think there's a lot more to come from this team."

Main photograph: Alex Tagliani speeds beneath J.D. Wilbur's checkered flags to score a long-overdue maiden victory.
Dan Streck/LAT

Inset: There is always a strong Canadian influence at Road America, making Tags' moment of triumph all the more sweet.
Mike Levitt/LAT

LAVIN MAKES HIS MARK

TWO weeks after qualifying on the front row in Vancouver, unfancied Mexican Rodolfo Lavin once again confounded his detractors with an assured and combative performance at Road America that netted a career-high second-place finish.

It was an open secret that Lavin's place at Forsythe Championship Racing for 2004 owed more to the good offices of his long-time sponsor Corona, a leading Mexican brewery, than to the team's estimation of his talent. Few pundits imagined that he would ever climb a Champ Car podium on the evidence of an unconvincing rookie year with Walker Racing in 2003. Five lackluster seasons in Indy Lights and two middling Atlantic campaigns didn't exactly suggest a reservoir of untapped potential, either.

However, presented with a golden opportunity to prove that he belonged at this level, Lavin had gradually begun to find his feet during his sophomore year and really hit his stride with that morale-boosting qualifying run at Vancouver. He wasn't quite able to reproduce that form during qualifying in Wisconsin, but played a starring role in the race, holding his own in wheel-to-wheel combat with Formula 1 refugee Justin Wilson and battling for the lead with eventual winner Alex Tagliani in the closing stages.

"It feels great," exclaimed the likeable 27-year-old. "I've been working for this for many, many years. The team has been giving me a great car, great tools to work with. I think we've been performing pretty well. Last race in Vancouver we qualified second, so we knew [a good race result] was coming. I think we got some luck with the yellow flag coming after our first pit stop. Then it was just a case of keeping out of trouble all day and making consistent lap times."

Asked about his scramble to fend off Tagliani following his final pit stop, Lavin said, "Coming out of the pits, obviously my tires were cold, low pressure. I think he was already two laps out there, so he was warm. Well, definitely, I couldn't avoid [being passed], you know. He went much quicker than me through Turn Three and got past me at the end of the straight."

QUALIFYING

Ryan Hunter-Reay upset the 2004 formbook by claiming provisional pole at Road America on Friday, rebounding from a troubled morning practice session to vault to the top of the timing charts in his Herdez Competition Lola.

Normal service was resumed on Saturday, when points leader Sébastien Bourdais cemented his reputation as Champ Car's ace qualifier by securing his fourth pole in eight races – despite an off-course excursion near the end when he strayed a wheel onto the grass turning into the final corner.

Secure in the knowledge that he would start from the front row by virtue of topping the overnight grid, Hunter-Reay elected to save tires for race day and didn't improve on his Friday benchmark.

"The car was pretty good by the end of yesterday, and today we went with a more conservative approach and ran old tires in qualifying," he explained. "On our last run we put on a new set, and we just underestimated the understeer we had in the car. The good news is that we'll have fresh rubber all day tomorrow."

Former teammate Jimmy Vasser did a sterling job to qualify third for PKV Racing. The 1996 series champion looked strong throughout practice and was just 0.328 second slower than Bourdais around the four-mile lap.

"Well, it's certainly the best opportunity to win a race we've had all season," reckoned Vasser. "We found some things over the last couple of weeks with our damper program and we've had a pretty good car since we unloaded here. Obviously it feels good, especially after Vancouver where I qualified a fantastic 15th!"

Two-time Road America winner Bruno Junqueira was less than satisfied to qualify fourth in the second Newman/Haas entry after being stymied by a combination of traffic and untimely red flags. Patrick Carpentier was next up in the leading Forsythe machine, one place ahead of teammate Paul Tracy. The defending series champion had a scrappy session, running wide onto the gravel at Turn One early on and then spinning off at the final corner in a virtual carbon copy of Bourdais' incident. Unlike the Frenchman, however, Tracy was on a flying lap at the time and careered backward into the tire wall at speed, causing heavy rear-end damage to his Indeck Lola.

THE majestic Road America circuit in leafy Wisconsin is a universal favorite of the Champ Car drivers, but it can be a capricious master. While its four-mile layout offers the sort of high-speed adrenaline rush now largely consigned to distant memory elsewhere, it also has an uncanny knack of throwing a joker into the pack. Back in the 1980s its heavy fuel consumption demands produced several late-race upsets; a rash of mechanical failures decimated the field in 1999 and 2000; and in 2001 and '03 the weather gods played havoc with the proceedings.

One man who knew all about the highs and lows of racing at Road America was Alex Tagliani, having come agonizingly close to victory during his rookie Champ Car season in Y2K only to be cruelly denied by a driveshaft failure. Incredibly, four years and countless heartbreaks later, Tagliani was still seeking that elusive maiden win. So when Lady Luck finally smiled on the French-Canadian in his 85th career start, few begrudged him his taste of glory.

This time, indeed, the cards fell squarely in Tagliani's favor in a tactically-framed, topsy-turvy and often confusing race that turned on the timing of yellow flags and Champ Car's new-for-2004 rule that stipulated a minimum number of green-flag pit stops (in this case three by Lap 44). "Tag" found himself in the happy position of having just made his first stop when a full-course caution erased his

Top left: Sure, Rodolfo Lavin had some luck on his side, but he drove very impressively, too.

Inset left: It was the Mexican driver's first big result.

Photographs: Michael Levitt/LAT

Below: A missing shock cover didn't slow down Servia, here leading Wilson, Vasser and Jourdain in their battle for sixth place.

Bottom: Polesitter Bourdais absolutely on the limit as he battles to overcome the vagaries of the full-course caution periods.

Photographs: Michael Kim/LAT

time deficit to the leaders. Even better news was that the frontrunners were down to their last few dregs of fuel and had to pit under the yellow – effectively a wasted visit since it didn't count toward their green-flag tally. The net result was that Tagliani emerged behind only Paul Tracy, with an extra stop in the bank, and duly assumed the lead once the pit-stop exchanges were back in synch.

"I feel good," beamed Tagliani, whose win was also the first for Rocketsports Racing. "Maybe today, honestly, we got a little bit lucky with the way the yellow turned out. But many races we've been unlucky, even this year. In Monterrey we passed basically every car on the racetrack in the first stint, and we ended up losing position in the same kind of deal.

"You know, I think it takes a really fast car, good strategy and a little bit of luck to win a race in this series. And today all the ingredients were there."

The opening lap set the tone for the afternoon, with frantic action giving way to a full-course yellow (the first of five) to retrieve cars from the kitty litter. Sebastien Bourdais led away from the pole, but fellow front-row starter Ryan Hunter-Reay was engulfed by the chasing pack and had slipped behind a fast-starting Bruno Junqueira, Tracy and Jimmy Vasser by the time they arrived at the Carousel.

No doubt frustrated by his tardy getaway, Hunter-Reay set about repassing Vasser's Gulfstream Lola at Canada Corner, but an optimistic lunge down the inside sent both cars spinning. The luckless Patrick Carpentier was drawn into the melee, and although both Hunter-Reay and Vasser managed to stay on the lead lap, the French-Canadian lost two laps while his pit crew effected repairs.

Following a brief green-flag interlude, during which Bourdais and Junqueira were able to establish a small cushion over Tracy, the race was interrupted again on Lap 12 after Roberto Gonzalez buried the second PKV Racing entry in the same Canada Corner gravel trap that had claimed teammate Vasser.

At the restart on Lap 14, Tracy contrived to leapfrog both the leading Newman/Haas cars in a bizarre chain of events that began with the pace car catching Bourdais by surprise in the last corner and forcing him to jam on the brakes, prompting the close-following Junqueira to take to the grass in avoidance. Tracy took full advantage of the confusion, pouncing on Junqueira even before they crested the hill at start/finish and then bravely out-dueling Bourdais around the outside at Turn One. The two made light contact and Bourdais was left to grapple with bent left-front suspension thereafter.

While Tracy could hardly believe his luck, tempers were flaring in the Newman/Haas camp two laps later after Bourdais and Junqueira tangled at the first corner in a virtual mirror image of the previous skirmish. Bourdais continued with his car now in a rather bedraggled state, but Junqueira spun and stalled, ultimately falling two laps in arrears.

"That's not fair... Sebastien made a mistake; he had to let me past," wailed an irate Junqueira over the radio – although from the sidelines the responsibility appeared more evenly balanced.

The ensuing full-course caution proved to be the turning point of the race, handing a priceless advantage to those who had pitted in the two-lap interval before the yellow came out. That group comprised Justin Wilson, Tagliani, Rodolfo Lavin (who snuck in just in the nick of time), Mario Haberfeld, Gaston Mazzacane and Alex Sperafico. Initially Wilson looked to be sitting pretty, but at the restart he ran wide under hard braking for Turn Five and lost out to Tagliani. The Briton, in fact, was finding his Mi-Jack Conquest Racing Lola a real handful as a result of a loose suspension tie-rod,

Above: **The Champ Car Safety Team is widely regarded as the best in the business.**
Michael Levitt/LAT

Top right: **Former Le Mans winner Guy Smith finished 10th in his Champ Car debut.**
Michael Kim/LAT

Above right: **Mario Haberfeld seemed set for a top-four finish until a late miscue.**
Michael Levitt/LAT

Below: **Hunter-Reay uses every inch of the road - and a little bit more - in his ill-fated bid to displace Vasser on the opening lap.**
Brad Bernstein/LAT

and eventually slipped to a disappointed seventh.

Tracy regained the lead when Tagliani, Wilson and company made their second green-flag stops, but once more found himself one stop behind in the pit cycle. Newman/Haas, meanwhile, had taken a different tack, calling Bourdais in for his second green-flag pit visit (and third overall) on Lap 28 – a lap earlier than Tagliani and some eight before Tracy – to avoid getting "snookered" by an untimely caution again. The wisdom of that policy was demonstrated when the yellows flew for the fourth time on Lap 31, neutralizing Tracy's lead and costing him any real hope of being able to build a big margin on a clear road (as he had done so effectively at Vancouver).

If the race's outcome owed rather too much to such twists of fate from a purist's standpoint, the three distinct pit strategies being played out certainly provided plenty of scope for conjecture. Fortunately for the spectators, there was a great deal of good old-fashioned motor racing going on, too, especially in the tricky downhill braking zone for Turn Five.

Nor was the suspense at the front yet over, since Lavin completed two more laps than Tagliani on his penultimate stint, hoping the tactic might be enough to overcome a 2.5-second deficit. It was a bold gamble, since the threat of another yellow loomed like a guillotine; but with his first-ever shot at a Champ Car win on the line, Lavin and his team figured it was worth it.

Sure enough, he emerged from the pit lane around 1.5 seconds ahead of Tagliani. But on cold tires – and with his quota of push-to-pass boost long since exhausted – Lavin was a sitting duck for Tagliani on the long flat-out run to Turn Five. Even so, he didn't give up without a fight, braking as deep as he dared and only just scrabbling around the corner. The Mexican held on to finish a fine second, easily the most impressive accomplishment of his career to date.

Bourdais was relieved to come away with third following his various travails, padding his championship lead over Junqueira to 47 points in the process.

"Well, I don't know what to think about this race, really, because there have been so many things that I don't even know what happened myself," said the Frenchman, summing up the thoughts of many equally nonplussed observers. "All I know is that we were leading the race. Then this yellow came out at the wrong moment. I got passed by a couple of people; I passed a bunch of people. And here I am on the podium, and I have no idea what happened in between."

Hunter-Reay posted a strong recovery drive to climb all the way to fourth place after his opening-lap *faux pas*, helped enormously by the succession of early caution periods. Herdez Competition teammate Mario Dominguez rounded out the top five, while Servia came home sixth for Dale Coyne Racing. The Spaniard made some opportunistic passing moves and at one stage was lying as high as second – ahead of Bourdais – but lost precious ground on his pit stops.

And what of Tracy? The defending champion's hopes of salvaging a useful finish were dashed by an air-gun failure on his final pit stop. For good measure, he later incurred a drive-through penalty for "avoidable contact" with regular sparring partner Junqueira at Turn Five, and went away with only a meager helping of points for 12th place.

Alex Sabine

ROUND 8

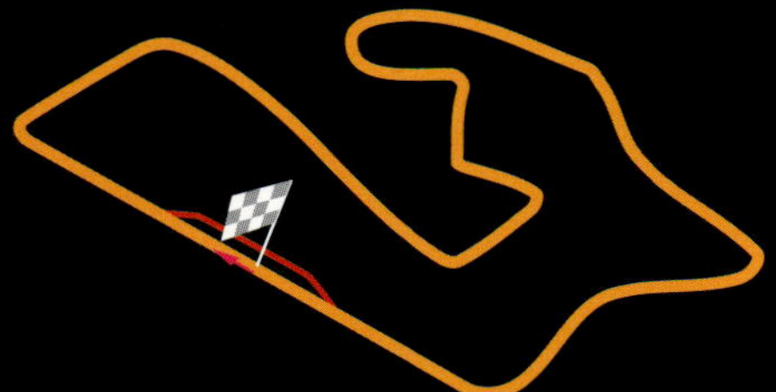

GRAND PRIX OF ROAD AMERICA

PRESENTED BY THE CHICAGO TRIBUNE

ROAD AMERICA, ELKHART LAKE, WISCONSIN

AUGUST 8, 48 laps of 4.048 miles – 194.304 miles

Place	Driver (Nat.)	No.	Sponsor(s) Team Engine/Car	Tires	Q Speed	Q Time	Q Pos	Laps	Time/Status	Ave. (mph)	Pts
1	Alex Tagliani (CDN)	8	Johnson Controls Rocketsports Racing Ford-Cosworth/Lola B02/00	BS	138.562	1m 45.172s	13	48	1h 45m 07.288s	110.903	33
2	Rodolfo Lavin (MEX)	3	Corona Forsythe Championship Racing Ford-Cosworth/Lola B02/00	BS	139.235	1m 44.663s	10	48	1h 45m 09.143s	110.870	28
3	Sébastien Bourdais (F)	2	McDonald's Newman/Haas Racing Ford-Cosworth/Lola B01/00	BS	141.420	1m 43.046s	1	48	1h 45m 10.055s	110.854	27
4	Ryan Hunter-Reay (USA)	4	Herdez Competition Ford-Cosworth/Lola B03/00	BS	140.246	1m 43.909s	2	48	1h 45m 11.102s	110.836	24
5	Mario Dominguez (MEX)	55	Herdez Competition Ford-Cosworth/Lola B03/00	BS	138.136	1m 45.496s	15	48	1h 45m 11.686s	110.825	21
6	Oriol Servia (E)	11	yokeTV.com Dale Coyne Racing Ford-Cosworth/Lola B2K/00	BS	139.982	1m 44.105s	8	48	1h 45m 13.678s	110.790	19
7	*Justin Wilson (GB)	34	Mi-Jack Conquest Racing Ford-Cosworth/Lola B02/00	BS	139.502	1m 44.463s	9	48	1h 45m 15.788s	110.753	17
8	Jimmy Vasser (USA)	12	Gulfstream PKV Racing Ford-Cosworth/Lola B02/00	BS	140.972	1m 43.374s	3	48	1h 45m 15.834s	110.752	15
9	Michel Jourdain Jr. (MEX)	9	Gigante RuSPORT Ford-Cosworth/Lola B04/00	BS	139.176	1m 44.708s	11	48	1h 45m 16.344s	110.744	13
10	*Guy Smith (GB)	17	Rocketsports Racing Ford-Cosworth/Lola B02/00	BS	137.447	1m 46.025s	16	48	1h 45m 17.285s	110.727	11
11	Mario Haberfeld (BR)	5	Cummins Walker Racing Ford-Cosworth/Reynard 02I	BS	138.691	1m 45.074s	12	48	1h 45m 24.013s	110.609	10
12	Paul Tracy (CDN)	1	Indeck Forsythe Championship Racing Ford-Cosworth/Lola B02/00	BS	140.213	1m 43.933s	6	48	1h 45m 33.904s	110.437	10
13	*A.J. Allmendinger (USA)	10	BG Products/Red Bull RuSPORT Ford-Cosworth/Lola B04/00	BS	140.045	1m 44.058s	7	47	Running		8
14	Patrick Carpentier (CDN)	7	Indeck Forsythe Championship Racing Ford-Cosworth/Lola B02/00	BS	140.457	1m 43.753s	5	46	Running		7
15	Bruno Junqueira (BR)	6	PacifiCare Newman/Haas Racing Ford-Cosworth/Lola B02/00	BS	140.656	1m 43.606s	4	46	Running		7
16	*Roberto Gonzalez (MEX)	21	Nextel PKV Racing Ford-Cosworth/Lola B02/00	BS	138.313	1m 45.361s	14	46	Running		5
17	*Alex Sperafico (BR)	14	Mi-Jack Conquest Racing Ford-Cosworth/Reynard 02I	BS	137.064	1m 46.321s	17	46	Running		4
18	*Gaston Mazzacane (RA)	19	American Medical Response Dale Coyne Ford-Cosworth/Lola B02/00	BS	136.350	1m 46.878s	18	29	Accident		3

*Denotes Rookie Driver

Caution flags: Laps 1-4, Hunter-Reay/Vasser accident; laps 12-13, Gonzalez off course; laps 16-18, Junqueira off course; laps 31-33, Mazzacane off course; laps 45-46, Allmendinger/Sperafico spun and stalled. **Total:** Five for 14 laps.

Lap leaders: Sébastien Bourdais, 1-13 (13 laps); Paul Tracy, 14-22 (9 laps); Alex Tagliani, 23-29 (7 laps); Tracy, 30-36 (7 laps); Tagliani, 37-39 (3 laps); Rodolfo Lavin, 40-42 (3 laps); Tagliani, 43-48 (6 laps). **Totals:** Tagliani, 16 laps; Tracy, 16 laps; Bourdais, 13 laps; Lavin, 3 laps.

Fastest race lap: Bruno Junqueira, 1m 45.504s, 138.126 mph on lap 39.

Championship positions: 1 Bourdais, 213; 2 Junqueira, 166; 3 Tagliani, 153; 4 Tracy, 152; 5 Carpentier, 141; 6 Hunter-Reay, 139; 7 Vasser, 127; 8 Dominguez, 126; 9 Allmendinger, 116; 10 Jourdain Jr. & Wilson, 107; 12 Servia, 106; 13 Haberfeld, 97; 14 Lavin, 90; 15 Gonzalez, 78; 16 Sperafico, 47; 17 Mazzacane, 44; 18 Philippe, 43; 19 Gidley, 15; 20 Smith, 11; 21 Marques, 6.

ROAD AMERICA SNIPPETS

• Remarkably, Alex Tagliani became the seventh different driver to score his first Champ Car victory at Road America in the 23-year history of the event. The other members of the club – running the gamut from one-hit wonders to major figures in the sport's pantheon – are Hector Rebaque, Jacques Villeneuve the elder (brother of Gilles), Jacques Villeneuve (son of Gilles), Dario Franchitti, Christian Fittipaldi and Bruno Junqueira.

• On Sunday morning Champ Car officials announced an increase in the allotment of push-to-pass boost available to the drivers from 60 to 75 seconds to make allowance for Road America's long straights, which might otherwise have seen the full quota being depleted in as few as four usages.

• The plethora of full-course yellows meant that the race had to be shortened from its scheduled 52 laps to 48 circuits to fit Champ Car's 1h 45m time limit. Uncertainty over precisely how many laps would be accommodated within that time window added a further dimension to an already complex strategic equation for the teams.

• Mario Haberfeld deserved better than an 11th-place finish after driving the wheels off Walker Racing's unfashionable Reynard all weekend. The Brazilian was one of six drivers to benefit from pitting just before the Lap 16 full-course yellow, and spent most of the race locked in a pitched battle with Justin Wilson and Rodolfo Lavin near the top of the leader board. He was disputing fourth place with Ryan Hunter-Reay soon after the final restart when a braking miscue at Turn Five sent him tumbling down the order.

• There had been another round of musical chairs at Rocketsports Racing since Vancouver, with Britain's Guy Smith stepping into the #17 car in place of Memo Gidley. Smith, who won the 2003 Le Mans 24-hour race with Bentley, hadn't driven a top-line single-seater since competing in Indy Lights in 1999 and admitted he was finding the transition difficult, particularly in terms of extracting the Champ Car's full potential under braking. After qualifying 16th he kept his nose clean on race day to place a respectable 10th.

• Quote of the weekend came from Sébastien Bourdais, who voiced his displeasure at Champ Car's continued attempts to micro-manage the pit stop rules as follows: "It's all about gambling. We're not going to race in Las Vegas until September, but with these rules it's Las Vegas every day."

• Former Wisconsin State Fair Park/Milwaukee Mile CEO Joe Chrnelich had been appointed executive vice-president of development, government affairs and planning for the Champ Car World Series in the run-up to the Road America event. His key responsibilities would be managing the relationships between the series and race promoters, exploring prospective new venues and completing the 2005 schedule.

• Below: More than half the Champ Car driver contingent, together with some 400 professional and casual cyclists, took part in a charity bike ride around Road America on Saturday evening. The "Tour de Road America" raised $18,299 for the Lance Armstrong Foundation, which aims to enhance the quality of life for those living with cancer. The event could not have been better timed, with the inspirational Armstrong having claimed his sixth successive Tour de France victory a fortnight earlier. Most of the participants were content to set a relatively sedate pace, but – surprise, surprise – competitive instincts surfaced in some of the professional sportsmen, and avid cyclist Bruno Junqueira was declared the official winner. The RuSPORT team, meanwhile, carried the banner for the LAF by decking out A.J. Allmendinger's car in its all-yellow livery and "Live Strong" logos throughout the weekend.

• Ryan Hunter-Reay's Sunday got off on the wrong foot when he was caught speeding en route to the circuit (he was running late for the front-row drivers' meeting at the time...) and was slapped with a $205 fine. A collision with Jimmy Vasser on the first lap of the race represented a more serious setback, but, in hindsight, it may have been a blessing in disguise. As a result of his unscheduled visit to the pits on Lap 3, RHR had enough fuel on board not to have to stop under the pivotal full-course caution on Lap 16 – unlike all of the leaders. Once the various strategies had unfolded, he found himself back in contention and charged through impressively to fourth place.

Michael Levitt/LAT

2

Dan Streck/LAT

THE CHAMP CAR WORLD SERIES POWERED BY FORD • ROUND 9

DENVER

JOUR DE GLOIRE!

SÉBASTIEN Bourdais' come-from-behind victory was one of those virtuoso displays that leaves a lingering frisson of exhilaration in the air and has reporters reaching for superlatives. Perhaps inevitably, it prompted comparisons with Alex Zanardi's epic comeback drives from seemingly impossible situations.

Bourdais is an altogether less flamboyant character, both in and out of the car, than the effervescent Italian who bestrode the Champ Car stage during the late 1990s. But the manner in which he put his first-lap spin behind him and proceeded to make mincemeat of the field led many observers to swear they were watching the Target-sponsored Reynard campaigned with such *élan* by Zanardi, rather than Bourdais' familiar McDonald's Lola.

The Frenchman had been pigeon-holed as a smooth, cerebral, even clinical race-winning machine with an engineering brain and a preference for honing his car's setup rather than driving the wheels off it. While that perception wasn't a million miles from the mark, in Denver Bourdais showed that he possessed a wider repertoire of skills than he had been given credit for. The conventional wisdom that he was a peerless front-runner, but when the chips didn't fall his way would tend to wallow in anonymity, had to be thrown out of the window. In fact, as he pointed out, the evidence didn't necessarily support that theory.

"I think I have not been in that position so many times," he said, "but last year it happened two or three times, I guess – Monterrey, when I worked my way from 16th to fifth in, like, 15 laps; and also Portland when we had a puncture at the beginning of the race and worked our way back to third but unfortunately couldn't fight for the win because of a rear wing failure.

"I think I proved today that it's possible to come back [from adversity]. It's obviously very difficult but when I have to do it, I think I showed that I can do it."

Of that there could be little doubt. What made Bourdais' performance even more impressive was the fact that he made up most of his ground without the assistance of either full-course yellows or the kind of zany pit rules that had played havoc with the lap chart at Road America. Quite simply, it was the drive of the season.

Above left: Teammates Junqueira (#6) and Bourdais go wheel-to-wheel into the first corner, and Junqueira emerges ahead.
Anthony Kent/LAT

Above: Later on, same place, different rival as Bourdais sneaks inside Dominguez.
Leland Hill/LAT

Opposite: He carries #2, but on this day Bourdais was #1 on the streets of Denver.
Phil Abbott/LAT

QUALIFYING

Sebastien Bourdais utterly dominated the two days of practice and qualifying in Colorado. After posting a series of new track records on Saturday afternoon, the Frenchman dipped beneath the magic one-minute mark with 10 minutes left on the clock. As a measure of his supremacy, the best anyone else could muster around the low-grip 1.657-mile downtown circuit was 1m 00.525s.

"The McDonald's car has been great since it was unloaded from the truck," enthused Bourdais after sealing his fifth pole in nine races and padding his championship lead to 49 points. "The baseline setup of the car has been very good; we only really changed the wing angle. So it has been a much easier week-end in Denver this year."

Newman/Haas teammate Bruno Junqueira vaulted from fifth on the provisional grid to second in the final line-up courtesy of a late foray on new tires. But having won each of the two previous Denver events he was a little chastened to find himself so comprehensively outpaced by Bourdais.

"I have been struggling this weekend," he admitted. "Bridgestone brought a softer tire here and it is faster, but the setup from last year is not working for us. So we have been making a lot of changes and the car is still not perfect."

Continuing the team formation at the sharp end of the grid, Forsythe stablemates Paul Tracy and Patrick Carpentier annexed the second row. In contrast to Bourdais' yawning 0.6-second advantage, positions two through four were blanketed by a mere 0.07s. Mario Dominguez lined up fifth on the strength of his Friday time, after his Herdez Competition Lola suffered a massive turbo failure in the 15-minute warmup prior to final qualifying. The Mexican, who raised a few eyebrows with a combative drive at Denver in 2003 in which he either overtook or ran into most of the field, had been near the top of the timing charts all weekend and was mortified not to be able to contend for the pole.

"IF that wasn't a race, I don't know what is!" trilled Sébastien Bourdais over the car-to-pits radio moments after turning in the drive of his life to win the Centrix Financial Grand Prix of Denver. And with ample justification; the Frenchman's latest victory – his fifth of the season and the eighth of his young career – was a Herculean triumph over adversity. After a first-lap spin relegated him to the lower ranks of the midfield, Bourdais climbed all the way back up the leader board by the simple expedient of catching and passing anyone who stood in his way.

"It is my most beautiful win for sure," declared a jubilant Bourdais, positively glowing with satisfaction. "When you are on the pole and have a difficult start and then work your way back from 13th to first, I think it's pretty amazing."

Against most expectations, the claustrophobic little track around Denver's Pepsi Center played host to one of the most enthralling street races in recent memory. The drama began at the drop of the green flag, when Bourdais tangled with Newman/Haas teammate Bruno Junqueira in a mirror image of their *pas de deux* at Road America a week earlier.

Junqueira made the better getaway from the outside of the front row and made a beeline for the apex of the first right-hander. Bourdais, however, braked a little deeper and laid claim to the inside line. Two into one didn't go and Bourdais had to pinch his McDonald's Lola across the rumble strips in a vain effort to avoid a collision. The pair made only light contact, but it was enough to tip Bourdais into a spin while Junqueira stole away in the lead.

On the heels of their Road America skirmish, the incident didn't exactly serve to thaw the increasingly frosty atmosphere within the Newman/Haas stable.

"It's a team issue," said Bourdais quietly but firmly when asked for his version of events. "There's going to be a meeting and we'll sort it out later."

Junqueira was slightly more forthcoming, venturing that, "I did a very good start, came on the outside of Sébastien, gave him room... I don't know, I guess he braked too late on the dirty side and we hit."

Bourdais' riposte? "You are very lucky, Bruno, that I am a gentleman because I could be pretty hard on you."

The on-track altercation triggered a chain-reaction accident behind and an immediate full-course yellow. At the restart, Junqueira quickly established a small cushion over Paul Tracy, Patrick Carpentier, Mario Dominguez and Oriol Servia. Meanwhile Bourdais set about salvaging his afternoon from an inauspicious 13th place. He picked off the midfield runners in no time, climbing to eighth by Lap 9. Ryan Hunter-Reay proved a tougher nut to crack, detaining him until Lap 19, but once past he immediately left the young American for dead.

Bourdais' next target was Carpentier, who was struggling with badly worn rear tires – a familiar affliction for the French-Canadian on abrasive street courses – and had fallen into the clutches of Dominguez, Servia and A.J. Allmendinger in the space of one lap. Carpentier finally gave up the unequal struggle and pitted on Lap 25, promoting Bourdais to sixth. Allmendinger was the next to

succumb seven laps later when Bourdais pulled off an audacious move at the slippery Turn Five – not a recognized passing spot.

Meanwhile the battle was joined at the front of the field, Tracy having closed onto Junqueira's gearbox when the Brazilian lost time lapping an ailing Roberto Gonzalez. Dominguez, too, was a beneficiary of the traffic, and the top three concertinaed together just before ducking into the pits for the first of two scheduled stops on Lap 40.

Eager to capitalize on what it knew might be its best opportunity to seize the initiative from Newman/Haas, Forsythe Championship Racing employed a blend of shrewd tactics – taking on slightly less than a full tank of methanol – and brisk pit work to release Tracy ahead of Junqueira and into the lead.

"While I was running behind Bruno I had been saving fuel and I think we had a bit more left in the tank, so our stop was shorter," explained Tracy. "We probably could have gone a lap longer but we didn't want to risk it."

Attacking his first few laps on cold tires with his usual total commitment, Tracy quickly stamped his authority on the race's second stint. Junqueira was powerless to respond, having fallen dramatically off the pace with a long brake pedal and deteriorating handling.

"My car was really bad on the second set of tires," he related. "I couldn't brake and I couldn't attack the corners [as] my car was not comfortable to drive. I just tried to keep it on the track."

Even that modest objective required Junqueira's full attention, as he graphically demonstrated when he had a major sideways moment under braking for Turn Nine at half-distance, allowing a grateful Dominguez through into second place. Meanwhile Bourdais, who had leapfrogged Servia at the pit-stop exchange, was rattling off a succession of fastest laps on a clear track. By Lap 55 he had reeled in his teammate and promptly outbraked him at Turn Nine.

Junqueira's attempt to counter-attack along the start/finish straight got short shrift from Bourdais, who offered a dismissive Gallic gesture before disappearing into the distance.

Lapping more than half a second faster than his nearest rivals, Bourdais whittled the deficit to Dominguez to a handful of car lengths by the time he made an early final pit stop on Lap 68 – some nine laps before the end of the mandatory window, since his flat-out charge had taken its toll on his fuel mileage. Victory still looked like a tall order, as he resumed in fourth place almost 30 seconds adrift of leader Tracy. But such was his superior pace that no one was betting against it – especially since the top three would soon have to head for the pits themselves.

They did so on Lap 75, following a spin by Hunter-Reay in Turn Nine that triggered a full-course caution. In a welcome departure from recent practice, Champ Car officials had shown remarkable restraint in their use of the twin yellow flags all afternoon, but the #4 Herdez Competition Lola was stranded right in the line of fire, leaving them with no option but to deploy the pace car.

At the restart on Lap 79, Bourdais, who had reclaimed third place as a result of Junqueira's pit stop, wasted no time in dispatching Dominguez, surviving a wheel-banging match at the first corner that momentarily threatened to undo all his good work. Instead Dominguez was tapped into a half-spin, but expertly recovered and lost only one more place (to Junqueira).

The impact knocked Bourdais' steering out of alignment but did not adversely affect his car's handling. "I thought it was pretty much over because the front suspension was bent and the steering wheel was not straight any more," he admitted. "But it kind of reduced the car's understeer, so it was helping me out a bit!"

"It was a racing incident," was Dominguez's even-handed verdict. "We both went for the same spot at the same time. I didn't leave him much room and he banzaied the corner. I have no problem with that – I'd have done the same thing!"

Tracy, meanwhile, had been struggling to bring his front tires up to temperature and soon found Bourdais snapping at his heels. When the Canadian ran wide going onto the long back straightaway, Bourdais didn't need a second invitation, diving up the inside under braking for Turn Nine.

"I could see that Paul was struggling so I knew I wouldn't have a hard time to pass him," said Bourdais. "I have to thank him – he gave me plenty of room to try my move and it's been very, very fair with Paul."

Deranged steering and all, Bourdais soon showed a clean pair of heels to Tracy, pulling away to win by 7.4 seconds and setting the fastest lap of the race on the penultimate tour! "Now that's style!" team co-owner Paul Newman admiringly observed.

Tracy admitted he simply didn't have an answer for Bourdais: "It just didn't go our way today. I thought we had the race until the yellow came out. But there wasn't much I could do when Sébastien came up behind me; he had a faster car, as he has done all week-end. Right now everything he touches turns into a Golden Arch, so that's just the way it is..."

Behind Junqueira and Dominguez, Allmendinger came home fifth in the RuSPORT team's home event, having demoted Servia at the final round of pit stops. The Spaniard's Dale Coyne Racing Lola had been emitting ominous wisps of smoke intermittently throughout the race's second half, but fortunately the problem proved to be an air jack dragging on the road surface rather than a terminal engine malaise and he posted his second consecutive top-six finish.

Alex Sabine

Above: **Junqueira led Tracy in the early laps but he couldn't make it three wins in a row in the Mile High City, later slipping to third.**
Dan Streck/LAT

Left: **Patrick Carpentier qualified well but struggled in the race due to heavy tire wear.**
Phil Sedgwick/LAT

THIRD TIME'S A CHARM

AFTER drawing lukewarm reviews during the first two years of its existence, the Grand Prix of Denver came of age under the auspices of title sponsor Centrix Financial in 2004. Champ Car had taken over promotion of the race from the Grand Prix Association of Long Beach and gave Centrix more or less free rein. Refinements to both the track and the facility were complemented by better and more plentiful sideshows and a ramped-up promotional machine, transforming the driver and spectator experience and creating a genuine sense of a "happening" for the first time.

The course itself had been realigned since the previous year, with the start/finish line moved from the pit straightaway along Auraria Parkway to the longer "infield" straight linking the old Turns Five and Six. The corners were renumbered accordingly. Barriers had been moved back in a couple of places to improve drivers' sight lines, while the notorious Mile Wide Corner (formerly Turn Five, now Turn Nine) had been subtly reprofiled.

The facility, too, had been spruced up and given a general "facelift," with concrete walls painted, colorful banners festooning the paddock area, several new spectator bridges and a significant increase in the number and quality of general admission areas. The organizers laid on a wealth of entertainment both on-site and in the city streets, including a concert headlined by Sugar Ray, extreme sports demonstrations, an ice arena inside the Pepsi Center and a makeshift go-kart track. Elsewhere, downtown Denver's Larimer Square was turned into a 24/7 advertisement for the race.

"This event has just got better every year," commented Paul Tracy on Sunday afternoon. "They have basically set the standard for promotion in our series. This race rivals any that we go to, whether it's Australia – everybody talks about how great the Australian race is as an event – [or] the Molson Indys in Canada."

High praise indeed, and Tracy's remarks were echoed by fellow podium finishers Sébastien Bourdais and Bruno Junqueira. In terms of the most important litmus test of all – attendance – the event was also a success. Although no official figures were released, one spokesman described estimates of 105,000 for the three-day meeting as "conservative," while another claimed that Saturday's turnout surpassed the 2003 race day crowd.

ROUND 9

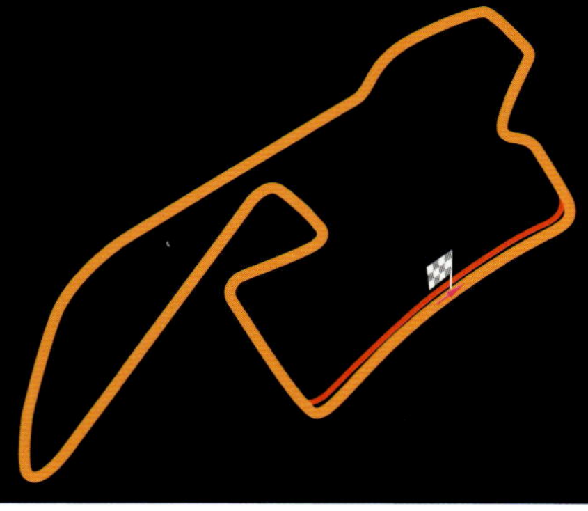

CENTRIX FINANCIAL

GRAND PRIX OF DENVER

PEPSI CENTER, DENVER, COLORADO

AUGUST 15, 90 laps of 1.657 miles – 149.130 miles

Place	Driver (Nat.)	No.	Sponsor(s) Team Engine/Car	Tires	Q Speed	Q Time	Q Pos	Laps	Time/Status	Ave. (mph)	Pts
1	Sébastien Bourdais (F)	2	McDonald's Newman/Haas Racing Ford-Cosworth/Lola B01/00	BS	99.516	59.942s	1	90	1h 40m 25.232s	89.103	35
2	Paul Tracy (CDN)	1	Indeck Forsythe Championship Racing Ford-Cosworth/Lola B02/00	BS	98.455	1m 00.588s	3	90	1h 40m 32.678s	88.993	28
3	Bruno Junqueira (BR)	6	PacifiCare Newman/Haas Racing Ford-Cosworth/Lola B02/00	BS	98.558	1m 00.525s	2	90	1h 40m 33.403s	88.983	26
4	Mario Dominguez (MEX)	55	Herdez Competition Ford-Cosworth/Lola B03/00	BS	98.239	1m 00.721s	5	90	1h 40m 33.793s	88.977	23
5	*A.J. Allmendinger (USA)	10	Western Union RuSPORT Ford-Cosworth/Lola B04/00	BS	97.939	1m 00.907s	7	90	1h 40m 40.873s	88.873	21
6	Oriol Servia (E)	11	yokeTV.com Dale Coyne Racing Ford-Cosworth/Lola B2K/00	BS	98.091	1m 00.813s	6	90	1h 40m 44.488s	88.819	19
7	*Justin Wilson (GB)	34	Mi-Jack Conquest Racing Ford-Cosworth/Lola B02/00	BS	97.367	1m 01.285s	10	90	1h 40m 46.018s	88.797	17
8	Mario Haberfeld (BR)	5	Cummins Walker Racing Ford-Cosworth/Reynard 02I	BS	97.474	1m 01.198s	9	90	1h 40m 49.373s	88.748	15
9	Patrick Carpentier (CDN)	7	Indeck Forsythe Championship Racing Ford-Cosworth/Lola B02/00	BS	98.444	1m 00.595s	4	90	1h 40m 50.603s	88.730	13
10	Alex Tagliani (CDN)	8	Johnson Controls Rocketsports Racing Ford-Cosworth/Lola B02/00	BS	97.366	1m 01.266s	11	89	Running		11
11	Rodolfo Lavin (MEX)	3	Corona Forsythe Championship Racing Ford-Cosworth/Lola B02/00	BS	96.534	1m 01.794s	15	88	Running		10
12	*Roberto Gonzalez (MEX)	21	Nextel PKV Racing Ford-Cosworth/Lola B02/00	BS	95.433	1m 02.507s	18	88	Running		10
13	*Nelson Philippe (FR)	14	Mi-Jack Conquest Racing Ford-Cosworth/Reynard 02I	BS	96.960	1m 01.522s	14	87	Running		8
14	Michel Jourdain Jr. (MEX)	9	Gigante RuSPORT Ford-Cosworth/Lola B04/00	BS	97.240	1m 01.345s	13	86	Running		7
15	*Gaston Mazzacane (RA)	19	American Medical Response Dale Coyne Ford-Cosworth/Lola B02/00	BS	95.578	1m 02.412s	17	86	Running		6
16	Ryan Hunter-Reay (USA)	4	Herdez Competition Ford-Cosworth/Lola B03/00	BS	97.675	1m 01.072s	8	72	Accident		5
17	Jimmy Vasser (USA)	12	Gulfstream PKV Racing Ford-Cosworth/Lola B02/00	BS	97.258	1m 01.334s	12	63	Engine		4
18	*Guy Smith (GB)	17	Rocketsports Racing Ford-Cosworth/Lola B02/00	BS	96.038	1m 02.113s	16	56	Electrical		3

*Denotes Rookie Driver

Caution flags: Laps 1-4, Bourdais/Tagliani/Philippe accident; laps 74-78, Hunter-Reay spun and stalled. **Total:** Two for 9 laps.

Lap leaders: Bruno Junqueira, 1-39 (39 laps); Paul Tracy, 40-79 (40 laps); Sébastien Bourdais, 80-90 (11 laps). Total: Tracy, 40 laps; Junqueira, 39 laps; Bourdais, 11 laps.

Fastest race lap: Sébastien Bourdais, 1m 01.256s, 97.381 mph on lap 89 (new record).

Championship positions: 1 Bourdais, 248; 2 Junqueira, 192; 3 Tracy, 180; 4 Tagliani, 164; 5 Carpentier, 154; 6 Dominguez, 149; 7 Hunter-Reay, 144; 8 Allmendinger, 137; 9 Vasser, 131; 10 Servia, 125; 11 Wilson, 124; 12 Jourdain Jr., 114; 13 Haberfeld, 112; 14 Lavin, 100; 15 Gonzalez, 88; 16 Philippe, 51; 17 Mazzacane, 50; 18 Sperafico, 47; 19 Gidley, 15; 20 Smith, 14; 21 Marques, 6.

DENVER SNIPPETS

Dan Streck/LAT

• It was a big weekend for the first-year RuSPORT team, which is based in nearby Loveland, Colorado, and once again had backing from Denver-based sponsor Western Union for A.J. Allmendinger's car (pictured above). So Allmendinger was somewhat red-faced after nosing his car into the tire barrier without completing so much as a flying lap in Friday qualifying. The gifted rookie redeemed himself on race day with a mature drive to fifth place.

• Oriol Servia's sixth-place qualifying effort represented the best grid position for Dale Coyne Racing since Gualter Salles lined up fourth at Long Beach in 1998. The Spaniard (left) finished in the same position but might have done better still if not for fuel starvation problems, which cost him time at both pit stops.

• In the wake of the confusing race at Road America, Champ Car announced modifications to its mandatory pit-stop rules ahead of the Centrix Financial Grand Prix of Denver. Instead of the previous requirement to make a minimum number of green-flag pit stops by a certain point in the race, the new rule simply called for a single stop for fuel and four tires during a designated window – under either green or yellow-flag conditions. Cars failing to comply with that window, which at Denver ran from Laps 51 to 77, would incur a one-lap penalty.

• Nelson Philippe returned to the saddle after a three-race absence, taking the reins of Mi-Jack Conquest Racing's Reynard in place of Alex Sperafico. The French teenager looked much more assured than in his previous Champ Car stint and even outpaced highly-rated teammate Justin Wilson during Friday practice. His fortunes took a nosedive on race day, however, when he got caught up in the first-corner melee. He soldiered on to finish 13th amid acute discomfort. "I had problems getting comfortable inside the car, and the entire left side of my body went completely numb," he related.

• Jimmy Vasser tied Al Unser Jr. for the all-time record of consecutive Champ Car starts (192) when he took the green flag on Sunday. Aside from that statistical feather in his cap, it was not a weekend Vasser would care to remember. After a promising start on Friday, the 1996 series champion found that the handling of his Gulfstream Lola went awry and he was never again a factor. He was mired in a lowly 14th place when a jammed throttle linkage put him out of his misery on Lap 64.

• Among the many entertaining diversions over the Denver weekend was a go-kart race on Saturday night held on a makeshift track adjacent to the pit straight, in which a motley collection of Champ Car drivers and team owners went head-to-head. The Mi-Jack Conquest Racing duo of Justin Wilson and team owner Eric Bachelart (a former Indy Lights champion) emerged triumphant.

• Paul Tracy arrived in Denver still reeling from the penalty meted out to him for initiating "avoidable contact" with Bruno Junqueira in the closing stages of the Road America race. Tracy remained adamant that he was not to blame and was apparently vindicated after asking his engineers to dig out the telemetry traces, which showed that he had braked earlier for Turn Five on the lap in question than on either of his previous out-laps. The data was brought to the attention of Champ Car stewards Beaux Barfield and Derek Higgins, who were essentially forced to conclude that the incident had been caused not by "red mist" on Tracy's part but by the fact that Junqueira had wandered across in front of him on the approach to the corner, taking air away from his front wings and making contact almost inevitable.

Lesley Ann Miller/LAT

MOLSON DRY
MOLSON DRY
SecureHorizons

After nine races and five podium finishes, Junqueira (pictured leading the Canadian trio of Tracy, Tagliani and Carpentier) took an overdue win on the Ile de Notre Dame.
Paul Abbott/LAT

BRIDGESTONE PRESENTS
THE CHAMP CAR WORLD SERIES POWERED BY FORD • ROUND 10

MONTREAL

QUALIFYING

Rookie A.J. Allmendinger came within a few seconds of claiming his first-ever Champ Car pole. The 22-year-old American rising star's #10 Western Union/RuSPORT Lola stood atop the timing charts as the clock ticked down in the final qualifying session on Saturday afternoon, having posted a lap at 1m 20.272s with a couple of minutes remaining.

His time remained unbeaten when Starter J.D. Wilbur waved the checkered flags, but series points leader Sebastian Bourdais had rushed past just a few seconds earlier so his lap would count. The Frenchman rose to the challenge magnificently, becoming the only driver to dip below the 1m 20s barrier and thereby securing his third successive pole and sixth of the season.

"It was a much harder session today," said Bourdais, who also had earned a championship point for taking the provisional pole on Friday. "I was getting frustrated because I kept running into traffic and then I made a small mistake. I had to put everything together in the end for the McDonald's team.

"[A come-from-behind win in] Denver definitely got the team even more motivated," Bourdais continued. "We really want to win this championship and we showed that we will do everything it takes to do it."

Allmendinger had to be content with the first front-row start of his 10-race Champ Car career: "Every lap my car just kept getting better and better," he said. "It was great to have the pole for a while there, but Bourdais is just unstoppable right now."

The battle for third on the grid also raged on well after the checkered flag fell. Mario Dominguez and Bruno Junqueira had traded the spot back and forth, after each of them holding the pole at one stage. Junqueira, however, ran out of fuel on his final lap and had to watch as Dominguez vaulted past on his own final lap.

Paul Tracy led the Canadian contingent in fifth, despite ending his session 10 minutes early after a brush with the wall damaged his Lola's suspension.

THROUGH the first nine races of the 2004 Bridgestone Presents The Champ Car World Series Powered by Ford, Bruno Junqueira had kept himself in title contention despite the fact he had not won a race and had led a meager total of 45 laps.

In the Molson Indy Montreal, watched by more than 50,000 fans, the Brazilian set the record straight and thrust himself right into the heart of the championship chase by virtue of the sixth victory of his career. Junqueira led the final 25 trips around the 2.709-mile Circuit Gilles Villeneuve, besting local favorite Patrick Carpentier by 6.382 seconds. His win, coupled with an early exit by points leader and Newman/Haas Racing teammate Sebastien Bourdais, slashed the Frenchman's championship advantage from 58 points to 34.

"I'm never going to give up, [and I'll] work very hard, try to catch Sébastien for the championship," declared Junqueira. "I think I can reverse it. Like four races ago, I was leading [the points]. I had three bad races. I hope [now] I can get another three good races."

As usual, Bourdais looked like the man to beat in the early stages. The Frenchman sprinted away from pole at the drop of the flag, leaving everyone else firmly in his wake. The first corner proved eventful for several would-be rivals as Alex Tagliani made contact with Paul Tracy, who then slid through the grass and caromed into hugely impressive rookie A.J. Allmendinger. Tracy got away relatively lightly, tweaking his suspension but losing just a couple of positions. The American, who had qualified a career-best second, wasn't so fortunate. He was forced to make an unscheduled pit stop to replace a punctured tire, rejoining well in arrears.

Mario Dominguez profited from the fracas to move into second place, chased by Junqueira, Tracy and the crowd's two hometown favorites, Tagliani and Carpentier, who had traded positions on the first lap.

The afternoon's only full-course caution came after just a handful of laps when Ryan Hunter-Reay lost control of his Herdez Lola and caught the wall in Turn Nine. The car wasn't badly damaged but the American was done for the day.

The caution erased Bourdais' two-second lead, although he soon established a similar cushion after the restart. But this time Dominguez wasn't about to let him get away, and the gap between the top duo remained fairly constant as they traded fastest laps

Above right: Damaged suspension brought an early end to Sébastien Bourdais' day.
Dan Streck/LAT

Top right: Both on option tires, Mario Dominguez and Bruno Junqueira go wheel to wheel through the first corner as Paul Tracy takes to the grass.

Right: Carpentier enjoyed an excellent day, finishing a solid second in his native Quebec.
Potographs: Mike Levitt/LAT

prior to making their first pit stops of the day.

Bourdais stayed out one lap longer, until Lap 21, but Dominguez's crew took a bit of a gamble by electing not to give their man a full tank of fuel. The few seconds saved, coupled with a slightly lighter car and a very rapid out-lap, enabled the Mexican to nip ahead of the Frenchman going into Turn One on Lap 22.

Out ahead of them both, however, at least for a while, was Allmendinger, who had topped off with fuel during the earlier caution period, allowing him to run a little longer than the others before requiring replenishment. The RuSPORT team's clever tactic enabled him to lead a Champ Car race for the first time in his young career – and thereby claim a bonus championship point. It also gave him a clear race track. Allmendinger took full advantage, turning the fastest lap of the race thus far (1m 21.043s) and building a 14-second cushion before pitting again after 28 laps.

Dominguez then became the day's third different leader, holding a comfortable three-second advantage over Bourdais before it was time for more fuel and another set of fresh Bridgestone tires. Sadly, Dominguez's hopes of victory then took a nosedive when a malfunctioning air gun on the left-front wheel left him stationary for an excruciating 26 seconds.

Bourdais was handed a huge lead when Dominguez pulled into the pits, but he had no intention of taking anything for granted. The Frenchman continued to push hard, and even made a rare error when he slid through the grass in Turn Three on Lap 39. Undaunted, and as if to further underscore his superiority, Bourdais turned what

EMOTIONAL MARIO MAKES GOOD

HERDEZ Competition's Mario Dominguez was a contender throughout the weekend in Montreal. He was fastest in practice on Friday morning (for the second race weekend in a row) and came close to snaring his first provisional pole before overstepping the limit and sliding off the road. He was quick again on Saturday, earning third on the grid, and early in the race became embroiled in a battle for the lead with Sébastian Bourdais.

The 2002 Rookie of the Year successfully passed the Newman/Haas star immediately following his first pit stop, and took over the lead when an out-of-sequence A.J. Allmendinger pulled into the pits after 27 laps. He was looking good.

"I passed Sébastien after the first pit stop, then pulled away from him," noted Dominguez. "That just shows you how good of a car we had. He's been the fastest driver all year. To actually pass him, the Herdez team and I were just working together very well."

However, his luck ran out when he pulled into the pits for his next service and the air gun for his right-front wheel failed. Chief mechanic Daryl Fox scrambled for the spare but, alas, that malfunctioned too. Dominguez pounded the wheel in frustration as his hard-earned advantage slipped away and an agonizing 26 seconds passed before he could resume. The delay restricted him to a nonetheless impressive third-place finish.

"Honestly, I am disappointed because we should have won today," he declared. "We really had the race covered after I passed Sébastian. However, we kept our focus, the team did not let it destroy their day as my last stop was perfect and because of that we were able to recover with a podium finish. I had one of the best cars of my Champ Car career today. My relationship with my engineer Mike Cannon has developed nicely and he made my job easier."

The Mexican had an added emotional reason for wanting this win so badly. In a bittersweet moment, he dedicated his result "to my friend and manager Antonio Marron and Guillermina Pilgram and their son Cristobal, who passed away last week. I really wanted to win for them today, but we couldn't do it, so I dedicate my podium to them."

Michael Levitt/LAT

BACK ON THE WINNING TRAIL

BRUNO Junqueira (above) held high hopes at the beginning of the season. He had finished second in the points for the past two years and fully expected that 2004 would provide his chance to finally grab the championship spoils.

The omens, however, were not too good when he arrived in Montreal. Despite blazing to pole in the season opener at Long Beach, Junqueira had not yet taken the checkered flag. And his previous experience at the Circuit Gilles Villeneuve had not been too special, either. He suffered a mechanical failure in 2002 and finished 13th after spinning twice in 2003.

The early stages of the Molson Indy looked likely to bring more disappointment as Junqueira's Newman/Haas teammate Sebastien Bourdais started from pole ahead of A.J. Allmendinger and Mario Dominguez. Allmendinger dropped back after opening-lap contact with Paul Tracy but benefited from an early fuel stop and was soon back at the front. Dominguez was not so fortunate, losing his chance of a win due to a malfunctioning air gun during a scheduled pit stop.

On Lap 42, Junqueira's fortunes changed, as a collision between Allmendinger and Bourdais led to an early retirement for Bourdais and a penalty for the young rookie. Suddenly, Bruno found himself in the lead. He went on to cross the finish line with almost seven seconds to spare.

"There was at least three races [thus far in 2004] that I was the strongest guy out there and deserved the win, and didn't [win]," said the Brazilian. "Today I felt that I was strong as Mario and Sebastien. We were pretty much on the same level. One of the three of us could win the race. I think the luck came to my side at last, and I'm quite happy for that."

Junqueira's win was well-deserved, and long overdue. It also ensured he would become the first driver to match Bobby Rahal's feat by scoring at least one victory in each of his first four Champ Car seasons, starting in 1982. Nevertheless, he still had a long way to go to match Rahal's achievement of winning in each of his first *eight* campaigns.

was to stand as the fastest lap of the race (1m 20.840s) on the very next lap, just prior to making his second pit stop.

Service was completed with the usual alacrity by his McDonald's crew, and Bourdais was sent on his way. But trouble was looming – in the form of Allmendinger, who had been charging along, still trying to recover from his early setback. Allmendinger saw Bourdais emerge from the pits in front of him and glimpsed his opportunity to make a pass before the Frenchman was able to get his fresh set of Bridgestone Potenza tires up to optimum working temperature.

The fired-up youngster dived for the inside at the Turn 10 hairpin, went in a fraction too deep, and the pair made contact. Allmendinger continued, now in the lead, but the irate Bourdais could only limp back to the pits, suspension broken.

"I'm here to win a championship; I'm not playing a game," fumed Bourdais."I was leaving the pits on cold tires and it's not a sunny day so it takes longer to get them up to temperature. [Allmendinger] fell back in the race and was out of sequence with the leaders. I knew it would be difficult to stay in front of him but I used the push-to-pass button and did not move over to block him or brake desperately late. I gave him room. He was obviously very angry to act that way."

Not at all, said Allmendinger.

"I feel that what happened was really a racing incident," proffered the American. "I'll take partial blame in that I got in a little deep into the corner, but there was a lot of racetrack left [whereby] he could have avoided contact. I wasn't racing Sébastien for the win; I had to make a pit stop in a couple of laps and I was racing for second or third. It was all really unfortunate."

The race stewards sided with Bourdais, however, and assessed a five-second stop-and-wait penalty on Allmendinger, who dropped out of the lead to serve his penance on Lap 45. He resumed in fifth, but still required one more regular pit visit for fuel and tires, which he made on Lap 48.

But once again there was controversy. The regulations for this event called for all drivers to make a pit stop anywhere between the leader's lap 49 and 58. Allmendinger had pitted after 48 laps, and once the mandatory window had passed, the stewards informed his team that he would be assessed a one-lap penalty, dropping him from fifth to 12th in the provisional results. The team duly appealed. And here's where it got complicated. A bulletin issued to all the teams stated that the mandatory window would open "when the leader crosses the blend-in line [at pit entrance] at the completion of leader lap number 48." Allmendinger's team contended that since he had been [ITALIC]behind[END ITALIC] Junqueira when the leader completed his 48th lap, the requirement had been properly met.

Much later, after a stewards' enquiry, RuSPORT's appeal was upheld and Allmendinger's fifth-place finish reinstated.

The initial altercation between Allmendinger and Bourdais promoted Junqueira to the lead for the first time. The Brazilian suddenly found himself with an 11-second advantage, which he had no difficulty in maintaining until the finish.

All eyes, meanwhile, were focused on a fierce battle that had been raging for second place between the two Forsythe cars, the recovering Dominguez and Justin Wilson. Carpentier had the crowd on its feet when he snaked past Tracy for second place on Lap 50, and the hugely popular French-Canadian duly held his position through the final round of pit stops, taking advantage of the softer Bridgestone "alternate" tires and edging clear of Dominguez to secure his best-ever Champ Car result in Canada.

"I'm really happy," he said, beaming broadly. "My crew was great in the pit stops. My last stop was very short to get me back out on the track as soon as possible, but I had to watch the fuel so I couldn't really chase Bruno too hard and I had to keep Mario behind me."

Dominguez's magnificent fight back following his pit lane problems netted an excellent third ahead of Tracy, who had been hampered throughout by handling problems.

"Tagliani had me off on the first corner and my front suspension was badly damaged," declared Tracy. "[The car] was drivable and we decided to drive it rather than lose laps in the pits changing the front. It was crazy. The steering was wild [turning] one way but not the other and it was a very physical race. I just did the best I could."

Poor Wilson encountered yet more misfortune, stranded by a broken gearbox with just 14 laps to go, elevating Allmendinger to fifth. Michel Jourdain Jr. followed his RuSPORT teammate home in sixth, edging out Tagliani, who battled a fuel pickup problem throughout the race, and Jimmy Vasser.

Jeremy Shaw

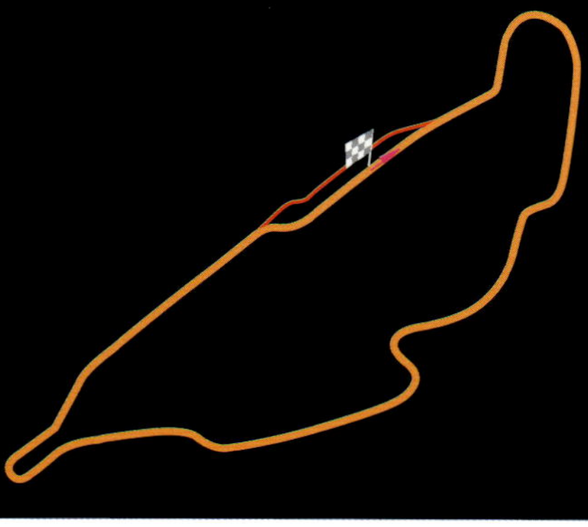

ROUND 10

MOLSON INDY MONTREAL

CIRCUIT GILLES-VILLENEUVE, MONTREAL, QUEBEC, CANADA

AUGUST 29, 69 laps of 2.709 miles – 186. 921miles

Place	Driver (Nat.)	No.	Sponsor(s) Team Engine/Car	Tires	Q Speed	Q Time	Q Pos	Laps	Time/Status	Ave. (mph)	Pts
1	Bruno Junqueira (BR)	6	PacifiCare Newman/Haas Racing Ford-Cosworth/Lola B02/00	BS	121.211	1m 20.458s	4	69	1h 39m 12.432s	113.049	32
2	Patrick Carpentier (CDN)	7	Indeck Forsythe Championship Racing Ford-Cosworth/Lola B02/00	BS	120.644	1m 20.836s	6	69	1h 39m 18.814s	112.928	27
3	Mario Dominguez (MEX)	55	Herdez Competition Ford-Cosworth/Lola B02/00	BS	121.425	1m 20.316s	3	69	1h 39m 23.574s	112.838	26
4	Paul Tracy (CDN)	1	Indeck Forsythe Championship Racing Ford-Cosworth/Lola B02/00	BS	120.694	1m 20.803s	5	69	1h 39m 29.306s	112.729	23
5	*A.J. Allmendinger (USA)	10	Western Union RuSPORT Ford-Cosworth/Lola B04/00	BS	121.492	1m 20.272s	2	69	1h 39m 29.993s	112.716	22
6	Michel Jourdain Jr. (MEX)	9	Gigante RuSPORT Ford-Cosworth/Lola B04/00	BS	119.969	1m 21.291s	12	69	1h 39m 44.688s	112.440	20
7	Alex Tagliani (CDN)	8	Johnson Controls Rocketsports Racing Ford-Cosworth/Lola B02/00	BS	120.565	1m 20.889s	7	69	1h 39m 44.732s	112.439	17
8	Jimmy Vasser (USA)	12	Gulfstream PKV Racing Ford-Cosworth/Lola B02/00	BS	119.981	1m 21.283s	11	69	1h 39m 46.529s	112.405	15
9	Oriol Servia (E)	11	yokeTV.com Dale Coyne Racing Ford-Cosworth/Lola B2K/00	BS	120.145	1m 21.172s	10	69	1h 39m 55.086s	112.245	13
10	*Roberto Gonzalez (MEX)	21	Nextel PKV Racing Ford-Cosworth/Lola B02/00	BS	118.914	1m 22.012s	15	69	1h 40m 21.622s	111.750	11
11	Rodolfo Lavin (MEX)	3	Corona Forsythe Championship Racing Ford-Cosworth/Lola B03/00	BS	119.482	1m 21.622s	14	69	1h 40m 30.515s	111.585	10
12	*Gaston Mazzacane (RA)	19	American Medical Response Dale Coyne Ford-Cosworth/Lola B02/00	BS	116.290	1m 23.863s	18	67	Running		9
13	Mario Haberfeld (BR)	5	Cummins Walker Racing Ford-Cosworth/Reynard 01I	BS	118.199	1m 22.508s	17	65	Running		8
14	*Justin Wilson (GB)	34	Mi-Jack Conquest Racing Ford-Cosworth/Lola B02/00	BS	120.269	1m 21.088s	8	55	Gearbox		7
15	Sébastien Bourdais (F)	2	McDonald's Newman/Haas Racing Ford-Cosworth/Lola B01/00	BS	122.062	1m 19.897s	1	42	Accident		10
16	*Guy Smith (GB)	17	Rocketsports Racing Ford-Cosworth/Lola B02/00	BS	118.797	1m 22.093s	16	27	Engine		5
17	*Nelson Philippe (FR)	14	Mi-Jack Conquest Racing Ford-Cosworth/Lola B01/00	BS	119.667	1m 21.496s	13	21	Accident		4
18	Ryan Hunter-Reay (USA)	4	Herdez Competition Ford-Cosworth/Lola B03/00	BS	120.209	1m 21.129s	9	5	Accident		3

*Denotes Rookie Driver

Caution flags: Laps 6-9, Hunter-Reay accident. **Total:** One for 4 laps.

Lap leaders: Sébastien Bourdais, 1-20 (20 laps); A.J. Allmendinger, 21-27 (7 laps); Mario Dominguez, 28-35 (8 laps); Bourdais, 36-41 (6 laps); Allmendinger, 42-44 (3 laps); Bruno Junqueira, 45-69 (25 laps). **Totals:** Bourdais, 26 laps; Junqueira, 25 laps; Allmendinger, 10 laps; Dominguez, 8 laps.

Fastest race lap: Sébastien Bourdais, 1m 20.840s, 120.638 mph on lap 40.

Championship positions: 1 Bourdais, 258; 2 Junqueira, 224; 3 Tracy, 203; 4 Tagliani & Carpentier, 181; 6 Dominguez, 175; 7 Allmendinger, 159; 8 Hunter-Reay, 147; 9 Vasser, 146; 10 Servia, 138; 11 Jourdain Jr., 134; 12 Wilson, 131; 13 Haberfeld, 120; 14 Lavin, 110; 15 Gonzalez, 99; 16 Mazzacane, 59; 17 Philippe, 55; 18 Sperafico, 47; 19 Smith, 19; 20 Gidley, 15; 21 Marques, 6.

MONTREAL SNIPPETS

• Paul Tracy had an eventful (read expensive) weekend. A trip over the track's unforgiving curbs during the first session on Friday caused severe damage to the chassis of his primary car, forcing him into the backup Indeck Lola for the remainder of the weekend. Then in qualifying he hit the wall solidly enough to punch a rear suspension toe-link clear through the casing of a brand-new gearbox. Saturday was no better, for he slid off the road again in qualifying. The impact contrived to break the engine mountings. "It's not our weekend; everything that can go wrong has gone wrong," lamented PT. Thankfully, he at least brought the car home on Sunday in fourth place – albeit with damaged suspension!

• Champ Car President and CEO Dick Eidswick, Paul Newman, Carl Haas, Sébastien Bourdais, McDonald's USA Director of Alliances John Lewicki and OWRS' Kevin Kalkhoven gathered for a media conference on Friday afternoon (below) to announce that McDonald's would serve as the "Official Fast Food Restaurant of Champ Car" through the 2006 season.

Michael Levitt/LAT

• Mario Haberfeld was obliged to switch over to Derrick Walker's backup Cummins Reynard after his primary car sustained heavy chassis damage from bouncing over the curbs.

• Mi-Jack Conquest Racing had procured a "new" Lola for Nelson Philippe, in place of his aging Reynard. The chassis, B01/00-24, purchased from Rahal-Letterman Racing, had been used solely as a test car in '01, then raced 17 times over the next couple of seasons by Michel Jourdain Jr. Its best finishes were a pair of seconds, at St. Petersburg and Monterrey. Philippe "celebrated" his upgrade by qualifying a career-best 13th. Unfortunately, he crashed the car in the warmup – mercifully without too much damage – then spun off again early in the race in Turn Five after his left-rear wheel fell off, having not been properly tightened at his first pit stop.

• Patrick Carpentier was bitterly disappointed on Friday afternoon when, for the second year running in his hometown race, he was prevented from taking part in the provisional qualifying session after his engine expired during the 15-minute warmup practice. "Never in my [30-year] racing career have I seen exactly the same problem befall the same driver on the same track on the same day in two successive years," said Forsythe Championship Racing Vice President of Operations Neil Micklewright. Carpentier bounced back to qualify sixth on Saturday, then took advantage of others' misfortunes to finish an excellent second.

• The fans again turned out in their droves – 32,912 on Friday, 47,494 on Saturday and a further 53,320 on race day for a weekend total of 133,726.

• Michel Jourdain Jr. was obliged to use a hastily procured white Bell helmet for the weekend, although he did find enough time to add a bit of nationalistic flavor courtesy of some strips of red and green vinyl. Jourdain, you see, had generously presented his usual "skid lid" to Centrix boss (and close family friend) Bob Sutton following the previous weekend's Centrix Grand Prix of Denver, and arrived in Montreal to discover that a new helmet in his regular color scheme had not been delivered on time.

Michael Levitt/LAT

• Montreal represented the 193rd consecutive Champ Car start for Jimmy Vasser (above with framed presentation artwork showing his cars), eclipsing the previous record set by two-time series champion Al Unser Jr. "Obviously it's a huge honor to be mentioned in the same sentence as a great champion such as Al Unser Jr.," said the 1996 Champ Car title-holder.

LAGUNA SECA

Patrick Carpentier celebrates with his crew after a dominant drive in the California sun.
Mike Levitt/LAT

QUALIFYING

Sébastien Bourdais struggled to match the front-running pace during his first visit to the dramatic Mazda Raceway Laguna Seca road course in 2003, so was relatively pleased after posting the second-fastest time during provisional qualifying this time around, just 0.212 seconds adrift of defending pole and race winner Patrick Carpentier.

"I am happy to be second here because we are so close to the pole position," proffered the Frenchman. "The track should be faster tomorrow and we will fight hard to earn the pole position."

He proved true to his word.

Rookie A.J. Allmendinger was the first to dip below Carpentier's Friday time of 1m 09.918s, whereupon Bourdais and then Paul Tracy leapt to the top of the order. In his haste to retaliate, Bourdais overstepped the mark in Turn Two, braking a tad too late and straying all four wheels of his McDonald's Lola into the dirt. The incident damaged his Bridgestone "alternate" tires. Undaunted, Bourdais gathered himself and with time ticking away reeled off two sensational laps, either of which would have been good enough for the pole.

"I had a pretty decent flat spot [on the left front tire] and I figured that was the end of the session for me," related the qualifying master after securing his seventh pole of the season and his fourth in succession. "I prayed it would hold, and put more brake bias to the rear. It was not the ideal situation but we are on pole and that's what matters."

Tracy had been forced to switch to his backup car following an incident during the morning practice which damaged the underside of his primary car's carbonfiber chassis. He did well to rebound by posting the second fastest time in final qualifying. Nevertheless, he was relegated to third on the grid behind Indeck/Forsythe teammate Carpentier by virtue of the latter's provisional pole effort.

Carpentier ran off the track not once but twice on what proved to be his fastest lap in Saturday qualifying, and still posted the fourth quickest time in the session behind the increasingly impressive Allmendinger. RuSPORT teammate Michel Jourdain Jr. also drove well to claim fifth ahead of Alex Tagliani (Rocketsports Racing), Ryan Hunter-Reay (Herdez Competition) and Bruno Junqueira, who, surprisingly, never really got to grips with his PacifiCare car.

IN the late 1990s, Bryan Herta turned Mazda Raceway Laguna Seca into a virtual home from home as he claimed three poles and two wins in Champ Car competition on the famed Northern California road course. Now it appears the mantle has been passed to Patrick Carpentier. The personable Canadian was beaten to the pole by series leader Sébastien Bourdais, then had to follow teammate Paul Tracy for a while (after Tracy had dented Bourdais' challenge by making early contact and causing a puncture), but got his nose in front during the first round of pit stops and hardly looked back. Under a perfect blue sky, Carpentier romped clear of the field at a prodigious rate, stretching his lead to as much as 22 seconds. That advantage was nullified by a late full-course caution, but he fought off a challenge from Bourdais' teammate Bruno Junqueira and once again took control in Jerry Forsythe's Indeck Ford-Cosworth/Lola before sweeping to victory in the Bridgestone Grand Prix of Monterey for the second year in row.

"The Indeck car was good; it got a little loose on the last four or five laps, but no complaints other than that," Carpentier said with a smile after earning the fifth win of his Champ Car career.

The action began shortly after the drop of the green flag as Bourdais led away from the pole and Tracy tucked in close behind to shade second-place qualifier Carpentier on the run to the first corner. The two RuSPORT cars of A.J. Allmendinger and Michel Jourdain Jr. were next, but not for long as Jourdain received a hefty punt from Alex Tagliani as they negotiated the Turn Two hairpin. Both Tagliani and Jourdain were forced to pit for repairs.

There was more contact a little farther around the opening lap, at the infamous Corkscrew turn, between Rodolfo Lavin and Justin Wilson. Lavin continued but the unfortunate Wilson made it only as far as the pits before retiring with extensive damage to his Mi-Jack Lola.

The incident left debris on the track, and as the leaders approached the area next time around, Bourdais opted to take a conservative line into the corner. A close-following – and unsighted – Tracy glimpsed an opportunity to make a move. Moments later there was contact.

"I went around the debris in the area and [Tracy] just ran over it like he didn't care," claimed Bourdais. "Paul rubbed my left rear wheel real hard with his [front] wing and put a big hole in it."

Tracy, who emerged with a slightly second-hand front wing, took over the lead as Bourdais headed for the pit lane to change tires, allowing Carpentier to move up onto his teammate's tail. Allmendinger's bright yellow Lola remained in hot pursuit of the two Indeck cars, while Ryan Hunter-Reay took over in fourth for the Herdez Competition team. Next up were Junqueira, who endured a difficult qualifying and had started a lowly (for him) eighth, and Oriol Servia, who, from 12th on the grid, had picked his way through the early carnage and once again was doing a fine job for Dale Coyne Racing.

Another pair of incidents ensured brief full-course caution periods during the first 15 laps. The first came on the eighth lap when Mario Dominguez spun out of eighth place in Turn Four, and the next just a couple of laps after the restart when Gaston Mazzacane spun and stalled at the top of the Corkscrew. In an unrelated incident, fellow rookie Nelson Philippe gyrated into the tire wall at Turn Two.

Several drivers toward the back of the pack opted to make pit stops during the cautions, but the order up front remained unchanged. Tracy, Carpentier and Allmendinger still led the way.

Carpentier essayed a couple of moves on his teammate following the restart, but on each occasion Tracy slammed the door in his face.

"I was trying to push him to make a mistake," related Carpentier. "He went off little bit going up the hill [through Turn Six]. I tried to go inside at the Corkscrew. [But] I figured that if I made the move, we both probably wouldn't come out of there. So I let him go."

Instead, Carpentier focused his attention on conserving fuel, seeking to complete one more lap than his fellow Canadian before heading for the pit lane for the first time. The strategy worked. Tracy relinquished his lead after 29 laps, which enabled Carpentier to enjoy the advantage of one extra lap at speed before taking on fuel and fresh Bridgestone tires.

With his own service completed, Carpentier emerged from the pits in front of his adversary and quickly began to hammer home his advantage.

Out ahead of them both, however, were Tagliani and Jourdain, who were on different strategies. Both enjoyed a taste of the lead before heading back to the pits for more service.

Tracy continued to chase Carpentier, but only until Lap 38 when he slid off the road in Turn Three, tweaking his already damaged front wing some more and necessitating an unscheduled pit stop for repairs. He resumed a lap down in 11th.

Four laps later there was more drama, this time when Allmendinger – who had lost time when he stalled the engine during his first pit stop – made a somewhat rudimentary attempt to usurp

SERVIA'S GIANT-KILLING ACT

THE man with the widest smile in the paddock on Sunday evening was probably Oriol Servia, who came home a fine third for Dale Coyne Racing. The likeable Spaniard already had four podium finishes to his name in his five-year Champ Car career, but what made this time special was that he did it with a team that defines the term "underdog" – a plucky, hard-trying operation run on a shoestring budget. Not since Roberto Moreno claimed a glorious third at the US 500 in 1996 (when it was co-owned by legendary NFL running back Walter Payton) had Coyne's Illinois-based outfit scaled such dizzying heights.

"It was really a fantastic day!" exclaimed Servia. "We were so close in Cleveland and in so many races, [so] it is great to finally get the result. We still need more speed, but it is great to show what we can do – a team that does not have a huge budget, but a lot of dedication."

Servia was no stranger to life at the lower end of the Champ Car food chain, having driven for Tom Wieringa's newly-formed (and short-lived) Sigma Autosport team in 2001, where he struck up a firm rapport with race engineer David Watson. Now reunited with Watson at DCR, he had posted a number of giant-killing performances in 2004, although minor glitches of one kind or another meant that he hadn't always collected as many points as he should have.

Indeed, Servia's Laguna Seca weekend had been far from trouble-free. A misfire restricted him to 12th on the grid and persisted on race day despite the installation of a fresh Ford-Cosworth power unit (leading the engineers to conclude that the problem must have originated in the fuel system). Fortunately it didn't prove terminal, and Servia employed his usual blend of speed and good racecraft to move smartly through the field, aided by the various indiscretions of the frontrunners.

"We had a good start, there were three guys that went off, but we also passed a lot of people," he said. "The car was so nice to drive, so easy. But since Lap 10 the engine was cutting out at the top of the hill before the Corkscrew; by the end it was like three cuts per straight. So I kept talking to the car, saying 'no, please, keep going,' and thankfully it listened!"

Above right: Oriol Servia brought Dale Coyne his best-ever result on a road course.
Phil Abbott/LAT

Below right: Aside from one slight slip, Patrick Carpentier was flawless at Laguna Seca.
Lesley Ann Miller/LAT

CARPENTIER FINDS HIS RHYTHM

ON the face of it, Patrick Carpentier's second consecutive win at Mazda Raceway Laguna Seca wasn't quite as dominant as the first, when he had started from the pole and was never headed throughout the 87-lap race. If anything, however, it was even more emphatic. In 2003 he had soaked up race-long pressure from Forsythe teammate Paul Tracy and, later, Newman/Haas Racing's Bruno Junqueira. This time around, he had things much easier – at least after he leapfrogged Tracy at the first round of pit stops. While his rivals exited stage left, right and center, Carpentier cruised along in splendid isolation for the rest of the afternoon and won as he pleased.

"The car was really, really good – really planted," declared the French-Canadian. "I could drive very deep into the corners and get back on the power fairly early. It was a smooth ride."

Smooth, that is, aside from one heart-stopping moment when he strayed two wheels onto the sand under braking for Turn 11 with a handful of laps remaining and had to rely upon every last ounce of his talent to keep his Indeck Lola out of the wall.

"When you're running by yourself like that you have a tendency to drift off, and I drifted off a little bit too much," he admitted sheepishly. "I thought I was going to crash – it was really close..."

Once his pulse had returned to normal Carpentier resumed his serene progress to the checkered flag, becoming the fifth different driver to score back-to-back victories at Laguna Seca since Champ Cars began visiting the Monterey Peninsula in 1983. Carpentier had a couple of different theories to explain his success at the hilly 2.238-mile track.

"I really love this place," he said. "It's a rhythm track, like Mid-Ohio [where he won from the pole in 2002]. It has high-speed corners, and I left-foot brake and am able to settle the car down with both feet."

Adopting a more jovial tone, he continued, "Ever since I went over the fence [he vaulted the safety barriers at Turn Four in 2000 after spinning off the track, landing upside-down on the other side], it's been going great for me here. I hope I don't go over the fence again, though."

Above right: **Michel Jourdain Jr. plunges into the Corkscrew during Friday practice.**

Below: **For the second year running, Bruno Junqueira finished second to Carpentier.**

Photographs: Lesley Ann Miller/LAT

Servia from third place at Turn Two.

"It was quite a big hit but I was lucky enough that the car is strongly built," said Servia, who remained in third place while Allmendinger limped back to the pits for repairs to the Western Union car's front wing and suspension.

"It was my fault," admitted Allmendinger, with refreshing honesty. "I'm really sorry for my crew because they did a phenomenal job all weekend and gave me an excellent car. I don't know if I could have beaten Patrick but I certainly could've been right there with him. I'm also really sorry for the contact with Oriol and I'm glad his car wasn't hurt."

The third and final caution period came shortly afterward when Roberto Gonzalez's Nextel/PKV car ground to a halt on the side of the track at the exit of Turn Four, stranded by a fuel pickup problem. All the leaders took the opportunity to make their second and final pit stops, with Carpentier resuming in the lead ahead of Junqueira, Servia and Jourdain, who had gotten out ahead of Hunter-Reay.

The yellow gave Junqueira a glimmer of hope, since it virtually erased Carpentier's commanding lead. Still, there was one lapped car in between the top duo at the restart – the Corona Lola of Carpentier's Forsythe Championship Racing teammate Lavin. Junqueira made short work of passing the Mexican but found his car slithering and sliding as he attempted to push the pace in pursuit of the Canadian, so wisely decided to settle for second place.

"I got a lot of marbles on my tires," explained Junqueira. "The first lap [after the restart] wasn't too good. I know [Pat] was a little bit faster. Third lap, my car slid a little bit. I decided this year I didn't have the speed to race Pat."

Sure enough, Carpentier stretched out his lead to over five seconds by Lap 64. Seven circuits later the gap was up to 7.7 seconds. Then came a rare lapse of concentration as he strayed his car's right-side wheels off the edge of the asphalt under braking for Turn 11 and slid luridly before regaining control.

"I was hoping nobody would see it, but they saw," he recounted later with a chuckle. "For some reason I lost a little bit my focus. I was lucky to be able to save it."

The error certainly caught Carpentier's attention, and there was never any hint of a repetition as he reeled off the remaining laps to score a comfortable victory.

Junqueira's seventh podium finish of the year brought him to within 24 points of Bourdais in the battle for the coveted Vanderbilt Cup, with just three races remaining on the schedule.

"I am happy to finish second," said Junqueira. "The championship is still wide open and I am still fighting hard."

Third place for Servia represented only the second podium appearance for Coyne since he founded the team in 1984. It was no more than either team or driver deserved. Jourdain also drove well to secure fourth despite his early delay and intense pressure from Hunter-Reay in the closing stages. Tagliani, too, was in close proximity at the finish, as was Mario Haberfeld who was gifted seventh place when Bourdais slid wide onto the dirt in Turn Four on the very last lap.

"I wasn't even trying to do anything," said Bourdais. "Maybe I got too close [to Tagliani]. It was a very frustrating race; the result didn't equal the potential."

Jeremy Shaw

ROUND 11

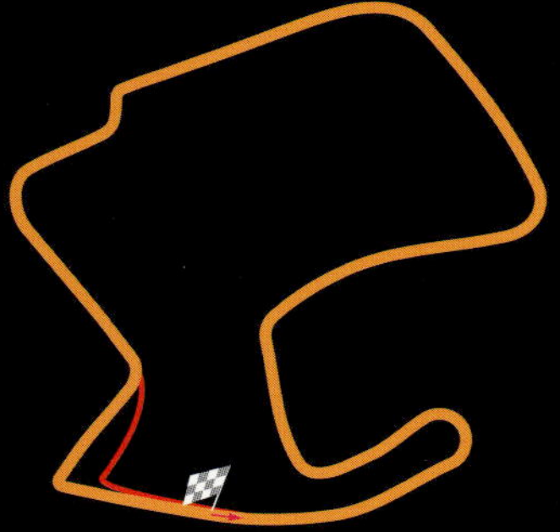

BRIDGESTONE GRAND PRIX OF MONTEREY

MAZDA RACEWAY LAGUNA SECA, MONTEREY, CALIFORNIA

SEPTEMBER 12, 79 laps of 2.238 miles – 176.802 miles

Place	Driver (Nat.)	No.	Sponsor(s) Team Engine/Car	Tires	Q Speed	Q Time	Q Pos	Laps	Time/Status	Ave. (mph)	Pts
1	Patrick Carpentier (CDN)	7	Indeck Forsythe Championship Racing Ford-Cosworth/Lola B02/00	BS	115.750	1m 09.605s	2	79	1h 45m 51.116s	100.217	33
2	Bruno Junqueira (BR)	6	PacifiCare Newman/Haas Racing Ford-Cosworth/Lola B02/00	BS	115.202	1m 09.936s	8	79	1h 45m 56.511s	100.132	27
3	Oriol Servia (E)	11	yokeTV.com Dale Coyne Racing Ford-Cosworth/Lola B2K/00	BS	114.038	1m 10.650s	12	79	1h 46m 11.575s	99.895	26
4	Michel Jourdain Jr. (MEX)	9	Gigante RuSPORT Ford-Cosworth/Lola B04/00	BS	115.569	1m 09.714s	5	79	1h 46m 20.228s	99.759	24
5	Ryan Hunter-Reay (USA)	4	Herdez Competition Ford-Cosworth/Lola B03/00	BS	115.389	1m 09.823s	7	79	1h 46m 20.831s	99.750	21
6	Alex Tagliani (CDN)	8	Johnson Controls Rocketsports Racing Ford-Cosworth/Lola B02/00	BS	115.443	1m 09.790s	6	79	1h 46m 21.547s	99.739	20
7	Mario Haberfeld(BR)	5	Cummins Walker Racing Ford-Cosworth/Reynard 01I	BS	113.843	1m 10.771s	13	79	1h 46m 23.427s	99.709	17
8	Sébastien Bourdais (F)	2	McDonald's Newman/Haas Racing Ford-Cosworth/Lola B01/00	BS	116.163	1m 09.358s	1	79	1h 46m 25.583s	99.676	17
9	*Guy Smith (GB)	17	Rocketsports Racing Ford-Cosworth/Lola B02/00	BS	113.558	1m 10.949s	14	79	1h 46m 37.050s	99.497	13
10	Paul Tracy (CDN)	1	Indeck Forsythe Championship Racing Ford-Cosworth/Lola B02/00	BS	115.900	1m 09.515s	3	79	1h 46m 40.338s	99.446	12
11	Mario Dominguez (MEX)	55	Herdez Competition Ford-Cosworth/Lola B02/00	BS	114.953	1m 10.088s	10	78	Running		11
12	Rodolfo Lavin (MEX)	3	Corona Forsythe Championship Racing Ford-Cosworth/Lola B03/00	BS	114.109	1m 10.606s	11	77	Running		9
13	*Gaston Mazzacane (RA)	19	American Medical Response Dale Coyne Ford-Cosworth/Lola B02/00	BS	112.306	1m 11.740s	17	75	Running		8
14	*Roberto Gonzalez (MEX)	21	Nextel PKV Racing Ford-Cosworth/Lola B02/00	BS	112.079	1m 11.885s	18	52	Out of fuel		7
15	*A.J. Allmendinger (USA)	10	Western Union RuSPORT Ford-Cosworth/Lola B04/00	BS	115.814	1m 09.567s	4	43	Accident damage		6
16	*Nelson Philippe (FR)	14	Mi-Jack Conquest Racing Ford-Cosworth/Lola B01/00	BS	112.825	1m 11.410s	16	11	Accident		5
17	Jimmy Vasser (USA)	12	Gulfstream PKV Racing Ford-Cosworth/Lola B02/00	BS	115.151	1m 09.967s	9	10	Gearbox		4
18	*Justin Wilson (GB)	34	Mi-Jack Conquest Racing Ford-Cosworth/Lola B02/00	BS	113.479	1m 10.998s	15	1	Accident		3

*Denotes Rookie Driver

Caution flags: Laps 8-10, Dominguez spun/stalled; laps 12-16, Mazzacane spun/stalled & Philippe accident; laps 55-57, Gonzalez stalled on course. **Total:** Three for 11 laps.

Lap leaders: Sébastien Bourdais, 1 (1 lap); Paul Tracy, 2-28 (27 laps); Patrick Carpentier, 29 (1 lap); Alex Tagliani, 30-36 (7 laps); Michel Jourdain Jr., 37-40 (4 laps); Carpentier, 41-79 (39 laps). **Totals:** Carpentier, 40 laps; Tracy, 27 laps; Tagliani, 7 laps; Jourdain Jr., 4 laps; Bourdais, 1 lap.

Fastest race lap: Mario Dominguez, 1m 11.727s, 111.326 mph on lap 78.

Championship positions: 1 Bourdais, 275; 2 Junqueira, 251; 3 Tracy, 215; 4 Carpentier, 214; 5 Tagliani, 201; 6 Dominguez, 186; 7 Hunter-Reay, 168; 8 Allmendinger, 165; 9 Servia, 164; 10 Jourdain Jr., 158; 11 Vasser, 150; 12 Haberfeld, 137; 13 Wilson, 134; 14 Lavin, 119; 15 Gonzalez, 106; 16 Mazzacane, 67; 17 Philippe, 60; 18 Sperafico, 47; 19 Smith, 32; 20 Gidley, 15; 21 Marques, 6.

LAGUNA SECA SNIPPETS

• Sébastien Bourdais took his career pole tally to 12, tying him with the legendary Parnelli Jones for 19th on the all-time Champ Car list. The Frenchman also became the first driver since Juan Pablo Montoya in 2000 to win four consecutive poles, and stretched his sequence of top-three starts to an even dozen, eclipsing the record of 11 established by two-time champion Alex Zanardi in 1996-97.

• Patrick Carpentier had a minor setback in the very first practice session when he discovered that fifth and sixth gears had been accidentally transposed within the 'box. After a delay while the error was rectified, the defending race winner lost no time in making his presence felt, vaulting to the top of the timing charts on just his 11th flying lap.

• Bruno Junqueira notched his second runner-up finish in succession at the scenic and challenging road course, but only after surviving an incident on Saturday morning when he crashed in Turn Nine. The incident came after he had made a change to the car setup, unwittingly causing his PacifiCare Lola to bottom out as he negotiated the ultra-quick, downhill left-hander. The Brazilian was fortunate in that damage was pretty much confined to the right front suspension and was easily fixed in time for final qualifying.

• Englishman Guy Smith enjoyed his most competitive outing since joining Paul Gentilozzi's Rocketsports team at Road America. The 2003 Le Mans 24 Hours winner was employing a left-foot braking technique for the first time since his karting days, and his confidence also was boosted by the arrival of new race engineer Harvey Spencer. Surprisingly, given his wealth of experience, fellow Brit Harvey Spencer had never previously worked on a Champ Car, so admitted to relying heavily on input from Brian Ma (engineer for Rocketsports teammate Alex Tagliani), but he did benefit from having worked with Smith previously in Indy Lights, back in 1999. Smith qualified 16th on Friday, improved to 14th on the final grid, then celebrated his 30th birthday on race day by finishing a best-to-date ninth.

• Despite teams being allowed 75 seconds' worth of Cosworth's "push-to-pass" feature (as opposed to the usual 60 seconds) and the reappearance of Bridgestone's equally creative "alternate" tire package, overtaking, as usual, was at a premium at Laguna Seca. Still, the race provided plenty of interesting moments: "We saw teams employ various strategies with Bridgestone's alternate tire, which features a softer, faster compound," noted Bridgestone Motorsport Executive Director Al Speyer. "Those strategies helped improve the racing but we want to work on further developing this technology so that even more passing is possible in the future." Incidentally, Speyer's 35 years with Bridgestone/Firestone was honored with a special presentation following practice on race morning.

Lesley Ann Miller/LAT

• The Cosworth USA engineers had carried out a thorough analysis following an unusual sequence of recent engine gremlins experienced by Jimmy Vasser in Denver, then Patrick Carpentier (during qualifying) and Guy Smith at Montreal, and concluded that they had been unrelated. "We think it was just down to the alignment of the stars more than anything else," said Cosworth Racing Team Manager Ken Deagle. Certainly, there were no recurrences at Laguna Seca.

• Forsythe Championship Racing's already extensive 2004 accident repair bill took another hit on Saturday morning when Paul Tracy understeered into the tire wall at Turn Six. The impact poked a hole in a brand-new chassis (Lola B04/00-04). Indeck teammate Patrick Carpentier also was running a different chassis this weekend (B02/00-26 – which Tracy had used to take the pole in Cleveland and finish second at Denver) after post-race inspection following his second-place result in Montreal revealed that the infamous curbs had caused damage to his regular monocoque (B02/00-18).

BRIDGESTONE PRESENTS

THE CHAMP CAR WORLD SERIES POWERED BY FORD ROUND 12

LAS VEGAS

Main photo: **Under the lights in Las Vegas, the green flies and the race is on! Carpentier leads the way from the pole.**

Left: **A little under 90 minutes later, one car length separates the Newman/Haas pair Bourdais and Junqueira at the finish**

Photographs: Michael Levitt/LAT

QUALIFYING

Less than two weeks after boosting his championship aspirations with a magnificent victory at the Mazda Raceway Laguna Seca road course, acknowledged oval track expert Patrick Carpentier kept the flame flickering by claiming the pole – and a valuable extra bonus point, tying him for third in the standings with teammate Paul Tracy – at Las Vegas Motor Speedway.

Just one practice session preceded late-afternoon qualifying on Friday, and surprisingly it wasn't Carpentier who set the pace for Forsythe Championship Racing. Instead it was his fast-improving teammate Rodolfo Lavin who posted the fastest time at 26.254 seconds, thereby earning the honor of running last in the traditional one-car-at-a-time qualifying session.

When the pressure was on, however, Lavin slipped to sixth on the grid, leaving Carpentier, who had recorded the fourth fastest lap in practice, on top of the pile with a time of 26.190 seconds, an average speed of 206.186 mph.

"The team is getting great momentum these last few weeks," said the Canadian after snaring the fifth pole of his career. "The guys did a great job with the Indeck car today. We made some changes and tweaked a few things with the car after the first practice session. That made a little difference and grabbed us some more speed. The car is stable out there and feels good."

Fellow Las Vegas resident Jimmy Vasser and series leader Sebastien Bourdais took their turn at knocking Carpentier off the top spot, but neither could quite get the job done.

"We ran well (fourth) in the only other oval race in Milwaukee this year, and we're looking to improve upon that run here and get the Gulfstream car to the front when it counts – near the end of the race," said Vasser after securing second on the grid – his best starting position since taking the pole at Long Beach in 2002.

Bourdais extended his streak of top-three qualifying runs to 13, dating back to Surfers Paradise in 2003, edging out teammate Bruno Junqueira by just one-hundredth of a second.

Much was expected of Ryan Hunter-Reay, who dominated the year's only other visit to an oval, in Milwaukee, but the best the American could manage was eighth on the grid.

THERE was no gambling involved in chasing the Bridgestone 400 Presented by Corona victory at Las Vegas Motor Speedway. Just speed. As per usual in 2004, Newman/Haas Racing had that in spades, and the Saturday night race – held in front of 70,000 fans – boiled down to a wheel-to-wheel duel at better than 200 mph between teammates Sebastien Bourdais and Bruno Junqueira.

The pair spent most of the final 15 laps in side-by-side formation, first one then the other taking a turn in the lead. Finally, hugging the inside groove around the smooth, 1.5-mile oval, Bourdais was able to poke his McDonald's car's nose out in front to lead each of the final three laps and score the narrowest victory of the season – by a scant 0.066 second.

"The McDonald's team worked night and day to get this win," praised Bourdais. "They changed an engine before the warmup and again right before the race, and worked their butts off.

"We were a bit down on power to Bruno," he claimed, "but I stuck it on the inside and nobody could pass me."

The result was a severe blow to Junqueira's aspirations of winning the Bridgestone Presents The Champ Car World Series Powered by Ford title, since it allowed his rival to eke out a 27-point advantage with just two races remaining.

"I'm very frustrated with the outcome," said the Brazilian following his sixth runner-up finish of the season. "The high line was a little longer [in distance] and slower and it was a matter of who was ahead."

Patrick Carpentier took sole possession of third in the standings by virtue of a podium finish coupled with the first-lap retirement of fellow Las Vegas resident and Indeck/Forsythe Championship Racing teammate Paul Tracy. The reigning series champion succumbed to a freaky broken spline in his Lola's drivetrain just as the field was coming up for the green flag, formally ending his hopes of a successful title defense.

As Tracy rolled forlornly into the pits at a little after 10.15 pm, Carpentier took advantage of his pole position to head the remaining 17 cars into Turn One. Junqueira jumped immediately from fourth to second, chased by Bourdais, then front row starter Jimmy Vasser (Gulfstream/PKV Racing) and Rodolfo Lavin's Corona Lola as the field jockeyed for position on the opening lap.

The biggest mover in the early stages was Oriol Servia. The Spaniard had started dead last after a persistent electrical gremlin prevented him from making a qualifying run, but Dale Coyne Racing's familiar yellow and black yokeTV.com Lola was up as high as eighth inside the first two laps. Servia then settled into position in the middle of the main pack, battling with the likes of Michel Jourdain Jr. (contesting his 150th Champ Car event), Alex Tagliani and A.J. Allmendinger.

Junqueira made a successful bid for the lead on the seventh lap, taking over from Carpentier and leading the Canadian toward the first round of pit stops, which, according to specific regulations for this event, were required to be made at least every 37 laps. Bourdais still followed in third place when the pit stops began, followed by Ryan Hunter-Reay who had steadily worked his way forward, passing Vasser on the ninth lap and Lavin on the 27th go-round. On his way into the pits, however, the American carried a little too much speed around the apron between Turns Three and Four, having neglected to warm up his carbon brakes (which are used solely on the ovals) beforehand.

"I failed to pump the brake pressure soon enough and when I got to the pit lane speed marker I locked the rears and spun," he explained. "I'm sorry for the team because they gave me a good race car."

Everyone managed to avoid the errant Herdez car, but the yellow lights flashed on as it came to a rest and Hunter-Reay lost several laps before his stalled motor could be restarted. The caution caused confusion in some quarters and led to Tagliani missing his opportunity to pit on the 37th lap. He duly continued around, effectively making a lap on the field before entering the pit lane on Lap 39.

There followed an embarrassing period of chaos as officials tried to determine the correct order for the restart – prompting more than a few fans to head for the exits. (By now it was, after all, close to 11 pm.) Eventually, most of the field was waved past the pace car so that Tagliani could take up his "rightful" position at the head of the pack. Then the restart was delayed two more laps as Tagliani twice attempted to gain a jump on the field. Finally, after 50 laps, the green flag flew and the French-Canadian led away, shadowed by Junqueira, Carpentier and an impressive Lavin, who, as at Milwaukee, was once again displaying his oval prowess.

"The team gave me a great car, great pit stops," said the Mexican. "Everything was great! My sponsor Corona was also the presenting sponsor of the race, and I'm very happy that my #3 Corona/Forsythe car was running so strong in front of the many Corona guests."

Lavin elevated himself to second place on the 56th lap but was

Top right: This pit stop for Tagliani was flawless, but the overall strategy was not.

Bottom right: Nelson Philippe's third outing in a Lola brought his best finish to date: ninth.

Photographs Lesley Ann Miller/LAT

TO PIT, OR NOT TO PIT

FROM a competitive standpoint, Champ Car's debut at Las Vegas Motor Speedway was a major success, delivering 90 minutes of breathless wheel-to-wheel action punctuated by only a single incident -- Ryan Hunter-Reay's spin in the pit entry road on lap 37.

Unfortunately, the ramifications from that apparently minor miscue threw the race into disarray as Champ Car officials struggled to make sense of two conflicting and potentially incompatible provisions in the rulebook.

The first was the stipulation in effect for this race that cars must pit at least every 37 laps. The leaders were in the process of complying with this when Hunter-Reay, lying fourth, lost control of his Herdez Competition Lola.

As is the standard practice whenever there is any kind of incident on an oval track, the yellow lights flashed on to signal a full-course caution. The rules call for the pits then to be closed until the pace car has been deployed. In this case, however, the front-runners had already committed to the pit entry road, and the other drivers on the lead lap duly followed their example.

All but ninth-placed Alex Tagliani, that is, who continued around the race track, effectively making a lap on the competition before finally pitting on Lap 39 – two laps beyond the outer limit of the prescribed window – and emerging in the lead.

The caution dragged on for 12 laps while Champ Car attempted to sort out the confusion and a vigorous discussion took place between officials and Rocketsports team owner Paul Gentilozzi, who claimed that his driver had merely been observing the pit closure rules. The upshot was that Tagliani continued to be scored as the leader through the ensuing restart but was later assessed a stop-and-go penalty, dropping him out of contention for the rest of the evening.

Gentilozzi remained adamant that he had obeyed the letter of the law and later appealed the penalty – to no avail. Instead Tagliani was stripped of the point he had initially earned for leading a lap. To add insult to injury, he was relegated from 14th to 16th in the final classification as penance for failing to heed a black flag for a separate infraction later in the race.

JUMPING OFF THE DEEP END

THE term "steep learning curve" hardly does justice to the scale of the challenge facing Nelson Philippe in 2004. To step into a 750hp Champ Car in only his second year out of karts and pit himself against a field of seasoned veterans at the tender age of 17 was a monumental undertaking.

If he was the most inexperienced, as well as the youngest, driver in Champ Car history, Philippe's short career to date did at least indicate some genuine potential. Having won his spurs in the karting arenas of both Europe and the Americas, he made a successful graduation to cars in 2003, finishing ninth in the competitive Barber Dodge Pro Series.

A marketable personality and profile allied to financial backing from his long-term personal sponsor LeasePlan facilitated Philippe's meteoric ascent from the kindergarten slopes to Champ Cars. After testing impressively for both the moribund Fittipaldi-Dingman Racing team and its sister operation, Mi-Jack Conquest Racing, during the winter, Philippe was snapped up by Paul Gentilozzi's Rocketsports team for the 2004 season, where he would partner proven front-runner Alex Tagliani.

He came down to earth with the proverbial bang over the first five races, qualifying no better than 16th, usually around 1.5 seconds slower than Tagliani (although he did net a pair of 10th-place finishes). Then, immediately prior to the Molson Indy Toronto in July, he abruptly parted company with Rocketsports due to a "contractual dispute."

After three races on the sidelines Philippe resurfaced in Denver, taking Alex Sperafico's place at Conquest Racing – a team he had come close to joining in the first place. The "chemistry" with his new employer, Eric Bachelart, was immeasurably better and it showed in his driving, especially after the team exchanged its outdated Reynard chassis for a Lola at Montreal.

Although he was still prone to expensive rookie mistakes, Philippe proved a much closer match for teammate Justin Wilson than he had for Tagliani. At Las Vegas he even outqualified the gifted Brit, and then parlayed a heads-up drive in the race into a best-to-date ninth-place finish.

"I'm very happy!" he exclaimed. "The car was good, and I feel I could have run with any other cars in the field. My goal was to finish the season strongly, improving with each race, and I really think we can do even better than today in the last two races."

JOHNSON CONTROLS
BOSCH

MI-JACK
LeasePlan

Above: **Jimmy Vasser ponders the prospect of racing in his home town for the first time.**

Above right: **Junqueira explains to his race-winning teammate Bourdais how running on the high line proved to be his downfall.**
Photographs: Lesley Ann Miller/LAT

Below: **Close racing was the order of the night. Lavin holds the preferred inside line while Hunter-Reay tries an outside pass.**
Michael Levitt/LAT

no match for Bourdais who, after losing time during his pit stop, quickly made amends by sweeping through to take the lead for the first time on Lap 58. The Frenchman continued to hold the point until the next round of scheduled pit stops, after 74 laps.

Tagliani, meanwhile, had dropped out of contention after being assessed a stop-and-go penalty for failing to complete his first pit stop within the mandatory window.

The earlier confusion had proven especially unfortunate for Servia, who had been obliged to make an additional visit to pit lane during the caution period. When the pack was reshuffled, Servia abruptly -- and unjustly -- found himself a lap down. He gained small recompense by taking a few laps in the lead (because he was out of sequence with the leading pack), thereby earning a championship bonus point, but try as he did, he was never able to get back into contention.

Servia's next pit stop, after 78 laps, enabled Bourdais to regain the point, where he remained largely unchallenged until the night's only other caution period. Bourdais, indeed, had pulled out a three-second advantage over teammate Junqueira and the rest when the yellow lights flickered on after 124 laps, heralding the end of a strong run by Guy Smith due to engine failure. The Englishman had been running comfortably inside the top 10.

The fourth and final round of pit stops took place during the enforced slow-down. But Mario Dominguez's Herdez team erred under the pressure by calling him in a couple of laps before the final 37-lap window had opened. Consequently, he was forced to make an additional visit to the pits, along with everyone else, on Lap 129. Bourdais' crew, meanwhile, made no such mistakes, ensuring that their man was able to retain his place at the head of the pack. He was followed at the restart by Junqueira, Lavin, Carpentier and Justin Wilson, who had driven impressively all evening and taken advantage of excellent work in the pits by Rich Howard's crew to move up among the top five for the first time.

Bourdais and Junqueira made it a two-horse race from then on, pulling away from the field immediately after the Lap 134 restart. Bourdais planted himself on the low side of the D-shaped super-speedway, leaving Junqueira on the high groove which finally paid off as he poked his nose in front on Lap 149 of the 166-lap affair. The Brazilian's advantage was short-lived, however, as the lapped cars of Tagliani and Gaston Mazzacane gave Bourdais the opportunity to slice through and wrest back the lead from his teammate.

"It was a pretty aggressive move but I had no choice," said Bourdais.

The final 10 laps saw the lead traded back and forth on numerous occasions, with the two teammates never much more than a few inches apart. Finally, though, Bourdais was able to nudge ahead by the slimmest of margins.

"After two frustrating race weekends, it is very rewarding," said Bourdais, who stretched his championship lead at a crucial juncture. "It is another great finish for Newman/Haas Racing; hopefully we can also finish one and two in the championship."

Carpentier overcame a gearbox problem to score his third consecutive podium finish while Lavin claimed an oval-track career-best fourth. Vasser finished almost alongside the Mexican, nosing out Allmendinger, Dominguez and Wilson, whose Mi-Jack Lola picked up an unwanted understeer in the closing stages, costing him several positions.

Jeremy Shaw

ROUND 12

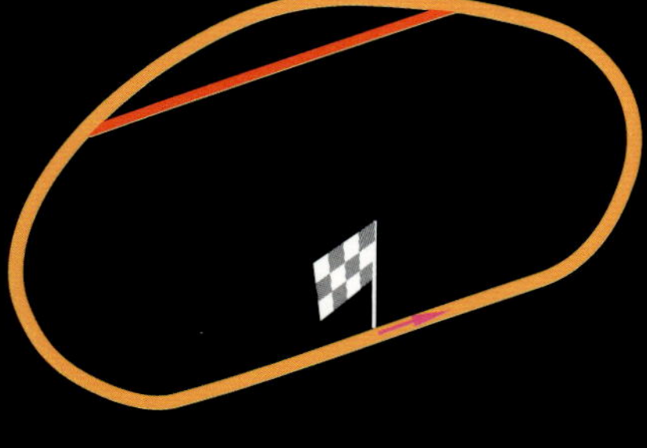

BRIDGESTONE 400
PRESENTED BY CORONA

LAS VEGAS MOTOR SPEEDWAY, LAS VEGAS, NEVADA

SEPTEMBER 25, 166 laps of 1.500 miles – 249.000 miles

Place	Driver (Nat.)	No.	Sponsor(s) Team Engine/Car	Tires	Q Speed	Q Time	Q Pos	Laps	Time/Status	Ave. (mph)	Pts
1	Sébastien Bourdais (F)	2	McDonald's Newman/Haas Racing Ford-Cosworth/Lola B01/00	BS	205.323	26.300s	3	166	1h 29m 01.061s	167.832	32
2	Bruno Junqueira (BR)	6	PacifiCare Newman/Haas Racing Ford-Cosworth/Lola B02/00	BS	205.245	26.310s	4	166	1h 29m 01.127s	167.830	29
3	Patrick Carpentier (CDN)	7	Indeck Forsythe Championship Racing Ford-Cosworth/Lola B02/00	BS	206.186	26.190s	1	166	1h 29m 05.152s	167.703	27
4	Rodolfo Lavin (MEX)	3	Corona Forsythe Championship Racing Ford-Cosworth/Lola B02/00	BS	205.019	26.339s	6	166	1h 29m 07.288s	167.636	23
5	Jimmy Vasser (USA)	12	Gulfstream PKV Racing Ford-Cosworth/Lola B02/00	BS	205.495	26.278s	2	166	1h 29m 07.363s	167.634	21
6	*A.J. Allmendinger (USA)	10	Western Union RuSPORT Ford-Cosworth/Lola B03/00	BS	204.840	26.362s	7	166	1h 29m 07.999s	167.614	19
7	Mario Dominguez (MEX)	55	Herdez Competition Ford-Cosworth/Lola B03/00	BS	203.866	26.488s	9	166	1h 29m 08.002s	167.614	17
8	*Justin Wilson (GB)	34	Mi-Jack Conquest Racing Ford-Cosworth/Lola B02/00	BS	199.409	27.080s	15	166	1h 29m 08.371s	167.602	16
9	*Nelson Philippe (FR)	14	Mi-Jack Conquest Racing Ford-Cosworth/Lola B01/00	BS	201.387	26.814s	13	166	1h 29m 13.040s	167.456	13
10	*Roberto Gonzalez (MEX)	21	NII Holdings PKV Racing Ford-Cosworth/Lola B02/00	BS	203.168	26.569s	10	165	Running		11
11	Michel Jourdain Jr. (MEX)	9	Gigante RuSPORT Ford-Cosworth/Lola B04/00	BS	205.136	26.324s	5	165	Running		10
12	Oriol Servia (E)	11	yokeTV.com Dale Coyne Racing Ford-Cosworth/Lola B2K/00	BS	no speed	no time	18	164	Running		10
13	Ryan Hunter-Reay (USA)	4	Herdez Competition Ford-Cosworth/Lola B03/00	BS	204.530	26.402s	8	164	Running		8
14	Mario Haberfeld (BR)	5	Cummins Walker Racing Ford-Cosworth/Reynard 01I	BS	198.296	27.232s	17	162	Running		7
15	*Gaston Mazzacane (RA)	19	American Medical Response Dale Coyne Ford-Cosworth/Lola B02/00	BS	199.394	27.082s	16	160	Running		6
16	Alex Tagliani (CDN)	8	Johnson Controls Rocketsports Racing Ford-Cosworth/Lola B02/00	BS	202.149	26.713s	21	163+	Running		5
17	*Guy Smith (GB)	17	Rocketsports Racing Ford-Cosworth/Lola B02/00	BS	201.080	26.855s	14	123	Engine		4
18	Paul Tracy (CDN)	1	Indeck Forsythe Championship Racing Ford-Cosworth/Lola B02/00	BS	202.672	26.644s	11	0	Transmission		3

*Denotes Rookie Driver

+Tagliani penalized for violation of Champ Car rules 10.3.6 and 6.23.1

Caution flags: Laps 37-48, Hunter-Reay spun/stalled; laps 49-50, yellow restart; laps 125-133, Smith stalled on course. **Total:** Three for 23 laps.

Lap leaders: Patrick Carpentier, 1-6 (6 laps); Bruno Junqueira, 7-36 (30 laps); Alex Tagliani, 37-57 (21 laps); Sébastien Bourdais, 58-74 (17 laps); Oriol Servia, 75-78 (4 laps); Bourdais, 79-148 (70 laps); Junqueira, 149 (1 lap); Bourdais, 150-157 (8 laps); Junqueira, 158-159 (2 laps); Bourdais, 160 (1 lap); Junqueira, 161 (1 lap); Bourdais, 162 (1 lap); Junqueira, 163 (1 lap); Bourdais, 164-166 (3 laps). **Totals:** Bourdais, 100 laps; Junqueira, 35 laps; Tagliani, 21 laps; Carpentier, 6 laps; Servia, 4 laps.

Fastest race lap: Bruno Junqueira, 26.166s, 206.375 mph on lap 72 (establishes record).

Championship positions: 1 Bourdais, 307; 2 Junqueira, 280; 3 Carpentier, 241; 4 Tracy, 218; 5 Tagliani, 206; 6 Dominguez, 203; 7 Allmendinger, 184; 8 Hunter-Reay, 176; 9 Servia, 174; 10 Vasser, 171; 11 Jourdain Jr., 168; 12 Wilson, 150; 13 Haberfeld, 144; 14 Lavin, 142; 15 Gonzalez, 117; 16 Mazzacane & Philippe, 73; 18 Sperafico, 47; 19 Smith, 36; 20 Gidley, 15; 21 Marques, 6.

LAS VEGAS SNIPPETS

Michael Levitt/LAT

• Patrick Carpentier (above) had won each of the previous two races in which he had started on pole (Mid-Ohio in 2002 and Laguna Seca in 2003), but had to settle for a podium position in Las Vegas. Given that two cogs had been inadvertently transposed within the gearbox (not for the first time this year, it has to be said), third place represented an excellent result. "Just before the start of the race I was checking my gears and I realized fifth and sixth gears were reversed," he related. "I knew that it was going to be difficult on the restarts. We made a few changes on the Indeck car during the race, but overall the car was good. Now we are third in the championship, so I am happy with our results. It was fun, close racing tonight, I really enjoyed myself."

• Forsythe Championship Racing teammate Paul Tracy, by contrast, had a miserable weekend. The defending series champion had high expectations, competing in his hometown for the very first time, but experienced all manner of difficulties and never did get his Indeck car up to speed. Steve Moore's crew changed engines both before and after qualifying, to no avail, and even trying different differential and aerodynamic setups made no appreciable difference. "It's just slow," lamented race engineer Todd Malloy. "It's very frustrating." Unfortunately, matters went from bad to worse on race day. The car was afflicted by a severe understeer in the warmup, then expired virtually at the drop of the green flag when a spline within the drivetrain let go.

• RuSPORT teammates Michel Jourdain Jr. and A.J. Allmendinger qualified fifth and seventh respectively, and were fortunate to retain those grid positions when post-qualifying technical inspection revealed that their cars' carbonfiber brake rotors did not meet the minimum required thickness. A Champ Car official later explained that the team was not penalized because the discrepancy revealed a "gray" area in the rulebook. The brakes on both cars were changed, however, in time for the race.

• When Champ Car hosted a special pre-event test session in mid-August, Mi-Jack Conquest Racing opted to run Reynard chassis for Justin Wilson and Nelson Philippe, rather than their regular Lolas. After the duo propped up the scoring charts, however, the team engineers analyzed all the data and ran simulations in order to compare the relative merits of the different cars. They then decided to concentrate on the Lolas for the race weekend. "It was the right choice but we are still trying to find the right setup for the car," explained Wilson after qualifying a lowly 15th. "We will now review our data and go to work on making the car more competitive for the race." Sure enough, both drivers fared much better on Saturday evening, running strongly in the draft before finishing in eighth (Wilson) and ninth (Philippe).

• The decision to hold a round of the 2004 Champ Car World Series at Las Vegas Motor Speedway was made only in early July, leaving the track and the teams a little more than two months to complete preparations. CCWS officials elected to mandate a high-downforce aerodynamic package for the cars to keep speeds within reasonable bounds and promote close racing. Some drivers expressed their reservations about the decision, complaining that the cars were too easy to drive, but the intensity of the competition and a lack of incidents lent credence to the call.

• Champ Car's decision to join the NASCAR Craftsman Truck series on the billing at Las Vegas proved a sound piece of business acumen, showcasing its brand of turbocharged, rear-engined single-seaters to a new audience while also gaining a toehold in the self-proclaimed entertainment capital of the universe.

• At a press conference after qualifying on Friday evening, Mexican company Roshfrans was named the "Official Lubricant of Champ Car" by Champ Car President Dick Eidswick (pictured below with Mario Dominguez and, right, Roshfrans Commercial Director Sergio Platonoff). Roshfrans, founded in 1955, later reached an additional agreement to sponsor the traditional Rookie of the Year Award.

Michael Levitt/LAT

Vortex
Premium petrol formulated to look after your car.
CALTEX
Coca-Cola
Real Refreshment
70
LEXMARK
LEXMARK
Havoline
Havoline
HERDEZ
HERDEZ
McDonald's

Right: A bird's eye view of the Bartercard Chicane on the Esplanade.
Phil Abbott/LAT

Below: There is no more charismatic venue than the beachside utopia.
Lesley Ann Miller/LAT

BRIDGESTONE PRESENTS THE CHAMP CAR WORLD SERIES POWERED BY FORD • ROUND 13

SURFERS PARADISE

Above from top: The race is run; the Miss Indy contestants add glamour to the already magnetic attraction of the Gold Coast; myriad displays and demonstrations on land, sea and in the air keep the fans enthralled.
Photos: Phil Abbott and Lesley Ann Miller/LAT

Left: As polesitter Tracy leads into the first corner, Bourdais, in second, begins to straight-line the Lexmark Chicane following a slight nudge from behind by rookie A.J. Allmendinger.
Al Munger/LAT

Right: Junqueira's show of strength ensured the title-chase would go down to the wire.
Phil Abbott/LAT

QUALIFYING

Attention was focused on Champ Car World Series title protagonists Sébastien Bourdais and Bruno Junqueira as the two Newman/Haas teammates fought for top honors in the final qualifying session. But in front of a Saturday-record 85,741 fans basking in glorious weather, reigning champion Paul Tracy stole the show by posting a lap of 1m 33.556s (107.551 mph) to earn his first Surfers Paradise pole on his 12th visit to the famed Australian street circuit.

The Canadian's effort represented his third pole of the season and capped a furious battle that had seen each member of the trio hold the top spot during a span of two minutes. Ultimately, however, the drama ended in anti-climax when Roberto Gonzalez ground to a halt, bringing out the red flags three minutes earlier than anticipated.

"I was lucky to put down a fast lap and even luckier to be on top when the red came out at the end of the session," noted Tracy, whose earlier run had been thwarted when Forsythe teammate Rodolfo Lavin collected the wall.

Junqueira, who was only 16th fastest in provisional qualifying on Friday, hindered by a faulty gear position sensor and then an untimely red flag, bounced back impressively to post a time less than two-tenths of a second slower than Tracy.

"I think we put on a good show," said the Brazilian, who would be obliged to line up behind Friday pacesetter Bourdais on the starting grid. "I was fastest then someone beat my time. I moved back up then someone beat it again. I was very happy with the PacifiCare car today but I left a little bit on the table. I was on a very good, mega lap and [clipped] the tires and it cost me some time. It's a shame that the red flag ended the session with three minutes to go. I needed to finish in front of Sébastien but I'm going to try to win the race."

Bourdais' quick time on Friday not only guaranteed him a front row starting position, it also added an extra point to his championship lead.

A.J. Allmendinger stunned the regulars by posting the fourth fastest time (despite a crash during practice on Saturday morning) on his -- and the RuSPORT team's -- first visit to the demanding 2.795-mile Gold Coast street circuit, while 2002 race winner Mario Dominguez edged out Herdez teammate and '03 race winner Ryan Hunter-Reay for sixth.

Top: **Paul Tracy is congratulated by race engineer Todd Malloy after snaring the pole.**

Above right: **Roberto Gonzalez leads the charge off pit lane during a practice session.**

Photographs: Lesley Ann Miller/LAT

VICTORY for Bruno Junqueira in a typically wild Lexmark Indy 300 ensured that the outcome of the 2004 Bridgestone Presents The Champ Car World Series Powered by Ford title-chase would not be decided until the season finale in Mexico City.

The Brazilian's second win of the season, in front of an enthusiastic crowd of 107,321 lining the streets of Surfers Paradise, Australia, was earned through a time-honored combination of outright speed and slick pit work, with a slice of good fortune thrown in for good measure. He qualified only third, behind outgoing champion Paul Tracy and 2004 points leader Sebastien Bourdais, but slipped ahead of his Newman/Haas Racing teammate during the second round of pit stops and profited further when Tracy made an error at two-thirds distance. His task was made a little easier as the race finished under a full-course caution following a dramatic accident from which Patrick Carpentier was fortunate to escape with relatively minor injuries.

"It feels really good to win the race for the PacifiCare team," said Junqueira after taking his seventh career victory. "I'm very happy because the last two years here I led but did not get the win. This year, everything went perfect. I was pushing very hard and my car was just perfect. The Bridgestone tires were great! Every lap I was going 110 percent and they stayed perfect. The track is very fun to drive and this is such a great result for the team."

Bourdais had to be content with second, while surprise 2002 Surfers Paradise race winner Mario Dominguez enjoyed another good day on Queensland's Gold Coast, celebrating his 50th Champ Car start by snaring third for the Herdez Competition team. The first attempt at a start was waved off by J.D. Wilbur after Bourdais was left firmly in the polesitter's wake before the green flag had flown. The field was (arguably) in slightly better order at the second time of asking, although Tracy once again jumped clear to lead the charge toward the first turn.

Allmendinger edged ahead of Junqueira for third, but the rookie promptly left his braking a bit too late for the Lexmark Chicane and lightly rear-ended Bourdais, who had no option but to "straight-line" the left-right-left complex. Luckily, there were no other repercussions and Bourdais remained in second, followed at the end of the first lap by Junqueira who regained his position ahead of Allmendinger at the exit of the Bartercard Chicane. The Herdez cars of Dominguez and Ryan Hunter-Reay led the chase, while Justin Wilson, Jimmy Vasser, Michel Jourdain Jr. and Alex Tagliani completed the top 10 in precisely the same order as they had begun.

The leading trio remained tied together through the opening stint. Matters nearly came to a head on Lap 11, when Bourdais got a run on Tracy along the beachside Esplanade and lined up the Forsythe Lola under braking for the Bartercard chicane. Tracy, however – knowing that Bourdais could not afford to risk contact – hung on gamely around the outside of the left-hand part of the complex, giving him the upper hand in the ensuing right-hander.

A full-course yellow (for debris) on Lap 15 triggered the first round of pit stops, whereupon the only changes among the top 10 saw Dominguez emerge ahead of Allmendinger for fifth and Carpentier slip ahead of Tagliani for 10th. Junqueira was caught napping at the restart and lost nearly four seconds to Bourdais, but gradually began to reel him in again as the Frenchman found his pace controlled by race leader Tracy.

Soon after the green flag, Wilson lost some ground and then tangled with Tagliani in Turn Six, ending the Canadian's day. The incident cost Tagliani a position in the championship standings but he accepted the disappointment pragmatically.

"We've been fortunate to have consistent finishes all season, so we'll take the good with the bad," he said after describing the contact as a "racing incident."

Australian David Besnard, making his Champ Car debut in a Walker Racing Reynard, contrived to spin not once but twice in the early stages – miraculously without making contact with anything solid – and teammate Mario Haberfeld also had an unscheduled gyration on Lap 30. The Brazilian, too, escaped with an undamaged car, but he had stalled the engine and was left stranded in a dangerous location in Turn Nine ensuring another full-course caution.

Again the leaders took the opportunity to make pit stops, only this time a few teams elected not to follow suit. Allmendinger and Carpentier were prime among them, and duly led the way when the green flags waved again after 34 laps.

Tracy followed in third and still appeared to be odds-on favorite for the win. He would require only a splash-and-dash pit stop to reach the finish, while the pair in front would need full service one more time. Wilson also eschewed a pit stop during the caution, moving up to fourth ahead of Junqueira who, crucially, had emerged from the pits ahead of teammate Bourdais.

"The PacifiCare crew did an amazing job today because all of my stops were really good," praised Junqueira. "I was just pushing hard to gain time on Sébastien before heading into the pits, the crew did what they do best and I got out ahead of Sébastien."

Allmendinger paced the field until heading for the pit lane after 37 laps, leaving Carpentier out front for one more lap before he, too, required service. The Canadian's pit stop should have resulted in Tracy regaining the point; but instead he was ruing a mistake on that very same lap in Turn Three, where he had left his braking a fraction too late and skated on down the escape road. There was no physical damage but his hopes of victory had been blown.

"I am very disappointed," said Tracy, who was fortunate to lose

only three positions while performing a slick spin-turn and eventually wound up fourth. "The team did an outstanding job all weekend and we should have capped it off with a win, so I'm a little frustrated right now."

Suddenly, therefore, Junqueira found himself in the lead, albeit with Bourdais hard on his heels in second place. Dominguez held down an excellent third but was unable to match the two Newman/Haas teammates.

For a few laps after the previous caution, Junqueira, like most others, had been in fuel-conservation mode. But after being informed by race engineer Rocky Rocquelin that he would have to make another visit to pit lane in any case, he put his head down and charged.

"There is no better feeling in the world than when you can do that," he declared. "I was putting in qualifying laps every lap and blazing over the chicanes. I just pushed very hard and ran every lap hard to try and pull away from Sébastien."

Not that it proved an easy task. On Lap 43, Junqueira turned the fastest lap of the day thus far at 1m 34.840s. Bourdais responded next time around with a 1m 34.601s. Junqueira then upped the ante to 1m 34.334s, whereupon Bourdais posted a new standard at 1m 34.120s. It was tit for tat. Junqueira, though, proved to be slightly the more consistent of the pair, and after establishing what was to remain as the best lap of the race, 1m 34.017s, on his 49th tour, he extended his cushion to over four seconds.

Junqueira seemed to be in control, but whatever hopes Bourdais might have had of mounting a late challenge were thwarted when Carpentier crashed heavily approaching Turn Three on his 53rd lap.

He had been hindered by a broken front wing for much of the race but, following consultation with his crew via radio, elected not to make a pit stop for repairs. The decision came back to haunt him when the wing came apart – at one of the fastest parts of the track – lodging underneath his front wheels and rendering his input virtually useless. Without steering or brakes, Carpentier's Lola struck the wall a heavy glancing blow on the curving straightaway following the second chicane, then careened straight on at unabated speed into the tire wall at Turn Three.

The Champ Car Safety Team was on the scene quickly to attend to the Canadian, who had been knocked unconscious by the impact. The race duly ended under the caution, with Junqueira trailed home to the checkers by Bourdais, Dominguez and Tracy, all of whom had ducked into the pits for a splash of fuel as soon as the yellow flags had been waved. Hunter-Reay rounded out the top five ahead of Allmendinger and the surprising Besnard, for whom the late caution was a godsend, negating the need for an additional pit stop.

Jeremy Shaw

Above: First-corner action as the Herdez teammates, Dominguez and Hunter-Reay, jostle for fifth position ahead of Wilson.

Left: Alex Tagliani confers with his race engineer, Brian Ma, while Rocketsports boss Paul Gentilozzi also is deep in thought.

Below: British rookie Guy Smith clips one of the omni-present tire stacks in the Lexmark Chicane.

Photographs: Lesley Ann Miller/LAT

Above: Team owner Derrick Walker and rookie charge David Besnard discuss some of their Reynard's finer details in practice.
Lesley Ann Miller/LAT

Below: On home ground, Besnard displayed the correct blend of aggression and patience.
Phil Abbott/LAT

LOCAL BOY COMES GOOD

The last time the rabid Australian fans had been able to cheer on a local favorite in their home event was in 2000 when Jason Bright enjoyed a fine run for John Della Penna's team, running as high as fifth before being involved in someone else's accident in the closing stages. Four years later, another young man with remarkably similar credentials also gave an excellent account of himself on the streets of Surfers Paradise.

David Besnard, like Bright, began his open-wheel career in the hotly fought Australian Formula Ford Championship. In fact, Besnard won the title in 1996, one year after Bright had lifted the same crown, and like his countryman then looked to further his career in the United States. But while Bright came up just four points shy of winning the U.S. Formula Ford 2000 National Championship in '96, two years later Besnard managed to achieve that goal on the strength of eight victories from 14 races. Sadly, the then 21-year-old native of Sydney, Australia, was unable to raise the finance to continue his career overseas.

Instead -- again like Bright – he set his sights closer to home, eventually securing a ride in Australia's premier class of racing, the V8 Supercar Series. Besnard scored his first (and so far only) victory in the high-quality sedan field at Queensland Raceway in 2001, and for '04 joined a brand-new Gold Coast-based team owned by high-flying businessman Craig Gore. At the age of 37, Gore had established his Wright Patton Shakespeare Financial Group as one Australia's most prominent enterprises with interests ranging from property development and financial services through to agriculture and construction.

Spurred on by the Lexmark Indy 300 promoters and with the full support of Australian-born Champ Car World Series co-owner Kevin Kalkhoven, Gore concluded a deal for Besnard to drive one of Derrick Walker's Reynards. The new combination gelled immediately. Besnard undertook only one brief test at Sebring, Florida, a month or so before making his Champ Car race debut, but after surviving a couple of spins early in the race – from which he thankfully emerged unscathed – the 27-year-old took advantage of Walker's typically shrewd strategy and the timely late full-course caution to finish a highly creditable seventh,

"When I spun on the first lap I was a bit surprised," admitted Besnard. "I just got caught out. But our team did a great job of keeping me settled down and allowing me to get back to business. I really felt comfortable in the car; every lap I felt better and better. I am sure I will look back at this tomorrow and think about how much fun it was, but for now I would liked to have finished a little higher!"

DOWN TO THE WIRE

THREE drivers held at least a theoretical chance of winning the Vanderbilt Cup when the Champ Car World Series embarked on its 14th annual pilgrimage to Queensland, Australia. Patrick Carpentier, however, needed some kind of miracle to take home the coveted trophy, since his only realistic hope of overcoming a 66-point deficit to Sébastien Bourdais would entail garnering the maximum 35 points from each of the two remaining road course races – 31 for the win, plus one point apiece for being fastest on each of the two days of qualifying, one more for leading the race and another for setting fastest lap. Even then he had to hope that Bourdais would pick up a total of just three points. For if they finished the year with an equal tally, the Frenchman would win the tie-breaker by virtue of his greater number of race victories.

All Bourdais needed to do to eliminate Carpentier from the reckoning, therefore, was take the green flag both at Surfers Paradise and Mexico City, because even with Walker Racing entering a second car for the final two events to ensure a 19-car field, the final finisher in each race would earn two championship points.

Bourdais' Newman/Haas Racing teammate Bruno Junqueira was the only other driver who could wrest away the honors. The Brazilian also faced a difficult task, trailing by 28 points, but he at least had fighting chance. He had a realistic game plan too: "We need to have a very good two races, finish strong, and hope that Sébastien has a bad result for us to win the championship. So I'll try to do my best. I'll try to do two good races and see what happens."

Junqueira's aspirations took a hit on Friday when his PacifiCare Lola was afflicted by an electrical gremlin, and worse news was to come when Bourdais took the bonus point for provisional pole. But Junqueira fought back, and a well-judged race win – even with Bourdais finishing in second – kept his slim hopes alive for the season finale.

Junqueira, though, was under no illusions: "I'm going to work very hard in Mexico City to try to fight for the championship," he said. "I know it won't come down to my race alone; Sébastien has to have a problem, but if he does I want to be right there so I can fight for it."

Lesley Ann Miller/LAT

ROUND 13

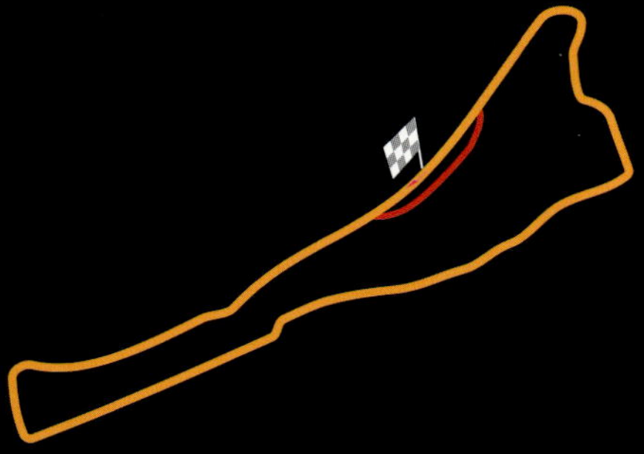

LEXMARK INDY 300

SURFERS PARADISE STREET CIRCUIT, QUEENSLAND, AUSTRALIA

OCTOBER 24, 57 laps of 2.795 miles – 159.315 miles

Place	Driver (Nat.)	No.	Sponsor(s) Team Engine/Car	Tires	Q Speed	Q Time	Q Pos	Laps	Time/Status	Ave. (mph)	Pts
1	Bruno Junqueira (BR)	6	PacifiCare Newman/Haas Racing Ford-Cosworth/Lola B02/00	BS	107.343	1m 33.737s	3	57	1h 46m45.941s	89.53 2	33
2	Sébastien Bourdais (F)	2	McDonald's Newman/Haas Racing Ford-Cosworth/Lola B01/00	BS	106.545	1m 34.439s	2	57	1h 46m 47.140s	89.515	28
3	Mario Dominguez (MEX)	55	Herdez Competition Ford-Cosworth/Lola B03/00	BS	106.956	1m 34.076s	5	57	1h 46m 47.304s	89.513	25
4	Paul Tracy (CDN)	1	Indeck Forsythe Championship Racing Ford-Cosworth/Lola B02/00	BS	107.551	1m 33.556s	1	57	1h 46m 47.857s	89.505	25
5	Ryan Hunter-Reay (USA)	4	Herdez Competition Ford-Cosworth/Lola B01/00	BS	106.381	1m 34.585s	6	57	1h 46m 48.021s	89.503	21
6	*A.J. Allmendinger (USA)	10	Western Union RuSPORT Ford-Cosworth/Lola B04/00	BS	107.194	1m 33.867s	4	57	1h 46m 48.682s	89.493	20
7	*David Besnard (AUS)	15	Wright Patton Shakespeare Walker Racing Ford-Cosworth/Reynard 02I	BS	103.888	1m 36.854s	17	57	1h 47m 02.051s	89.307	18
8	*Justin Wilson (GB)	34	Mi-Jack Conquest Racing Ford-Cosworth/Lola B02/00	BS	106.351	1m 34.611s	7	57	1h 47m 02.716s	89.298	15
9	*Guy Smith (GB)	17	Rocketsports Racing Ford-Cosworth/Lola B02/00	BS	103.793	1m 36.943s	18	57	1h 47m 03.367s	89.289	13
10	*Nelson Philippe (FR)	14	Mi-Jack Conquest Racing Ford-Cosworth/Lola B01/00	BS	105.035	1m 35.797s	14	57	1h 47m 04.146s	89.278	11
11	*Roberto Gonzalez (MEX)	21	NII Holdings PKV Racing Ford-Cosworth/Lola B02/00	BS	104.849	1m 35.987s	15	57	1h 47m 05.319s	89.262	10
12	Jimmy Vasser (USA)	12	Gulfstream PKV Racing Ford-Cosworth/Lola B02/00	BS	106.013	1m 34.913s	8	57	1h 47m 07.445s	89.232	9
13	Oriol Servia (E)	11	yokeTV.com Dale Coyne Racing Ford-Cosworth/Lola B2K/00	BS	no speed	no time	19	57	1h 47m 10.314s	89.192	8
14	Mario Haberfeld (BR)	5	Cummins Walker Racing Ford-Cosworth/Reynard 01I	BS	105.500	1m 35.374s	13	56	Running		7
15	Rodolfo Lavin (MEX)	3	Corona Forsythe Championship Racing Ford-Cosworth/Lola B03/00	BS	105.619	1m35.267s	12	54	Running		6
16	Patrick Carpentier (CDN)	7	Indeck Forsythe Championship Racing Ford-Cosworth/Lola B02/00	BS	105.626	1m35.261s	11	52	Accident		6
17	Michel Jourdain Jr. (MEX)	9	Gigante RuSPORT Ford-Cosworth/Lola B04/00	BS	105.788	1m35.115s	9	31	Accident		4
18	*Jarek Janis (CZ)	19	American Medical Response Dale Coyne Ford-Cosworth/Lola B02/00	BS	104.116	1m 36.642s	16	28	Differential		3
19	Alex Tagliani (CDN)	8	Johnson Controls Rocketsports Racing Ford-Cosworth/Lola B02/00	BS	105.629	1m 35.258s	10	19	Accident		2

*Denotes Rookie Driver

Caution flags: Lap 1, yellow start; laps 15-16, debris on course; laps 17-18, Lavin spun/stalled; laps 31-34, Haberfeld spun/stalled & Jourdain accident; laps 53-57, Carpentier accident.
Total: Five for 15 laps.

Lap leaders: Paul Tracy, 1-31 (31 laps); A.J. Allmendinger, 32-37 (6 laps); Patrick Carpentier, 38-39 (2 laps); Bruno Junqueira, 40-57 (18 laps). **Totals:** Tracy, 31 laps; Junqueira, 18 laps; Allmendinger, 6 laps; Carpentier, 2 laps.

Fastest race lap: Bruno Junqueira, 1m 34.017s, 107.023 mph on lap 49.

Championship positions: 1 Bourdais, 335; 2 Junqueira, 313; 3 Carpentier, 247; 4 Tracy, 243; 5 Dominguez, 228; 6 Tagliani, 208; 7 Allmendinger, 204; 8 Hunter-Reay, 197; 9 Servia, 182; 10 Vasser, 180; 11 Jourdain Jr., 172; 12 Wilson, 165; 13 Haberfeld, 151; 14 Lavin, 148; 15 Gonzalez, 127; 16 Philippe, 84; 17 Mazzacane, 73; 18 Smith, 49; 19 Sperafico, 47; 20 Besnard, 18; 21 Gidley, 15; 22 Marques, 6; 23 Janis, 3.

SURFERS SNIPPETS

• Sébastien Bourdais failed to lead a lap for the first time since Milwaukee in the first week of June, but his hard-fought second-place finish still enabled him to take a 22-point lead over teammate Bruno Junqueira into the final race in Mexico City. Earlier in the weekend, Bourdais rued a slight error in qualifying which, he reckoned, cost him an opportunity of winning his eighth pole of the year. "I locked up the right front [wheel] in the last turn of my fastest lap and nearly put the car in the wall," he explained. "You walk a fine line between being a chicken and being too hungry and I was too hungry today."

• Jimmy Vasser sported a special Troy Lee-designed helmet for the Lexmark Indy 300, and (pictured below left) later presented it to PKV Racing co-owner Kevin Kalkhoven...

Lesley Ann Miller/LAT

• Paul Tracy's fourth-place finish was enough to clinch a second successive Nations Cup for Canada, with one race remaining on the schedule. Tracy, Patrick Carpentier and Alex Tagliani all contributed points to the cause.

• The Sunday attendance of 107,321 didn't quite match the outright single-day record for a Surfers Paradise Champ Car race, but bumper crowds throughout all four days ensured a new event standard of 309,583, marking the second consecutive year that the Gold Coast street party had surpassed the 300,000 mark. (To put that into perspective, the population of the Gold Coast is only 400,000.)

• A.J. Allmendinger was disappointed that his RuSPORT team's race strategy didn't pan out as expected, restricting him to a sixth-place finish, but he gained ample compensation by clinching the Roshfrans Rookie of the Year title with one race remaining. "With contenders like Justin Wilson, it's a pretty great thing to achieve," said the 22-year-old American. "It was one of our goals at the start of the season and we got it."

• Patrick Carpentier spent Sunday night in Gold Coast Hospital after his frightening-looking high-speed accident shortly before the finish, but was released the following morning with a headache but an otherwise clean bill of health.

• When Bruno Junqueira took the checkered flag he continued a remarkable streak by becoming the 14th different driver in as many years to win on the streets of Surfers Paradise, further extending the track's record as the longest-running venue without a repeat winner.

Phil Abbott/LAT

•Sporting a newly shaved head, Oriol Servia (pictured right, above, with fellow "baldy" Michel Jourdain Jr.) was among the pacesetters on Friday, third quickest in the opening session and fourth in provisional qualifying. Sadly, the 30-year-old from Barcelona then crashed during practice on Saturday. The mishap damaged the tub of Dale Coyne's trusty yokeTV.com Lola B2K/00, forcing Andy Green's tight-knit crew to work virtually around the clock to prepare a backup car for action on Sunday.

Phil Abbott/LAT

• Servia had a new teammate for the weekend, with Jaroslav "Jarek" Janis (above) taking over the #19 American Medical Response car from previous incumbent Gaston Mazzacane. Janis, 21, from the Czech Republic, had been racing a Mercedes in the high-profile German touring car (DTM) series in 2004, having previously displayed promise in Formula 3000 competition.

BRIDGESTONE PRESENTS
THE CHAMP CAR WORLD SERIES POWERED BY FORD • ROUND 14

MEXICO CITY

Main photograph: Once the dust settled on the first corner, polesitter Bourdais remained clear of title challenge Junqueira.

Inset: What it's all about: Bourdais hoists the Vanderbilt Cup, which dates to 1904.

Photographs: Dan Streck/LAT

Above: **A.J. Allmendinger impressed once more with a third-place run for RuSPORT**
Dan Streck/LAT

Right: **Four champions in a row: Jimmy Vasser, Paul Tracy, Cristiano da Matta and Emerson Fittipaldi pose for the cameras.**
Phil Abbott/LAT

Bottom right: **Always the bridesmaid, it seems - Junqueira heads for second again.**
Dan Streck/LAT

THE battle for the 2004 Bridgestone Presents The Champ Car World Series Powered by Ford crown boiled down to a straightforward final-round duel between Newman/Haas Racing teammates Sebastien Bourdais and Bruno Junqueira. Of course, Bourdais held a distinct advantage by virtue of his tally of six wins and seven poles from the first 13 races, compared to Junqueira's relatively meager two wins and a solitary pole. He also had a healthy points lead, 335-313, so required no more than a ninth-place finish in the Gran Premio Telmex/Tecate Presented by Banamex to clasp his hands around the historic Vanderbilt Cup trophy.

Junqueira, however, had no intention of giving up without a fight. The Brazilian drew first blood by snaring the provisional pole on Friday, thereby reducing the deficit to 21 points, only for Bourdais to raise the tempo considerably on Saturday by snatching both the pole and a new lap record around Mexico City's celebrated Autodromo Hermanos Rodriguez.

Race day saw the Frenchman in similarly imperious form. True, there was one lapse in concentration when he threw away a big advantage with a quick spin, but Lady Luck was smiling his way. Bourdais rejoined unscathed, recovered his composure and went on to score the victory he so desperately craved.

"I think it cannot be better, to celebrate the championship by winning the race, having done the pole position and set the fastest lap of the race," he declared after perhaps his most dominant performance of the year. "It is a well-deserved championship for the whole McDonald's team and a fantastic achievement from the Newman/Haas Racing team."

Junqueira chased for all he was worth but came up 4.604 seconds shy at the checkered flag. Amazingly, it was his seventh second-place finish of the season. A.J. Allmendinger already had clinched the Roshfrans Rookie of the Year Award but once again underscored his immense promise by finishing a close third to cap an equally impressive first season for Carl Russo's RuSPORT team.

Bourdais made his presence felt right away at the drop of the green flag, scorching directly into the lead and using his push-to-pass button to maximum effect in order to ensure that he could maintain his advantage at the end of the long main straightaway before jumping on the brakes for Turn One. His first hurdle successfully overcome, Bourdais then concentrated on trying to build a cushion over his pursuers, led still by Junqueira.

Before he could do so, however, the yellow flags were flying as the result of a couple of separate incidents, one of which saw

QUALIFYING

The intra-team squabble between Sébastien Bourdais and Bruno Junqueira raged on unabated through the traditional pair of qualifying sessions at the historic 2.786-mile road course in suburban (read hectic) Mexico City. Junqueira did what he had to do on Friday, snaring the provisional pole and the all-important (for him) championship bonus point; but it came at a cost. The Brazilian, you see, had used up one of his two sets of soft, "alternate" Bridgestone Potenza tires to achieve the task, whereas his French rival opted to remain on the standard rubber. Even so, the gap between them was a mere 0.257 second.

"I feel happy with today's result," said Junqueira. "It is important to get the pole; it is especially important to get the championship point and be starting on the front row for the race."

Bourdais, too, was content: "The McDonald's car is definitely looking very good," he asserted. "I think most of the frontrunners have been running on the alternate tires that Bridgestone has brought along. They're definitely much faster."

How much faster? Well, Junqueira had claimed the provisional pole with a time of 1m 27.565s. A little less than 24 hours later, having employed his first set of alternate tires, Bourdais wrapped up his eighth pole of the year. He also added a little salt to the wound, eclipsing Junqueira's two-year-old track record with a lap in 1m 25.919s.

"Well, I feel good, but I know there's still a long way to go," said the 25-year-old from Le Mans. "The hardest part of the season is in front of us. I'm just really, really happy for the boys because they really did a good job. It's not about how fast we can go, it's about how tough we are, how we can stay on the racetrack and have no mechanical issues."

Junqueira had to make do with second on the grid, while Justin Wilson produced his best qualifying performance since Cleveland by annexing third on the grid for Mi-Jack Conquest Racing. That was the good news. The bad news was that he was more than a second slower than the rampant Bourdais!

PKV Racing's Jimmy Vasser vaulted from 15th on the overnight grid to fourth, just 0.022 second slower than Wilson, with Oriol Servia also close behind after his best qualifying show of the year for Dale Coyne Racing. Paul Tracy was the best of the three Forsythe entries in sixth, shadowed by former protégé A.J. Allmendinger, who wasn't happy with the setup changes made to his RuSPORT Lola, slipping from third in the provisional order to seventh.

Below left: Servia played a starring role.
Phil Abbott/LAT

Below center left: Vasser heads for fifth.
Dan Streck/LAT

Roberto Gonzalez spinning his Nextel/PKV car in Turn 14 after being hit from behind by Paul Tracy.

"Tracy came up behind me and I gave him plenty of racing room. The next thing I knew I was turned around," said the Mexican, who resumed at the back of the pack and went on to finish a respectable 12th.

In Tracy's defense, it should be noted that he was already on the comeback trail having himself been "assisted" into a spin following contact with fellow Las Vegas resident (and Gonzalez's teammate) Jimmy Vasser on the first lap in Turn Two.

Mario Dominguez and Tarso Marques, back in Dale Coyne's #19 American Medical Response car for the weekend, also were involved. Both made unscheduled pit stops to change a punctured tire and front wing, respectively.

The restart again saw Bourdais charge off into the lead. The gap grew incrementally at first as he concentrated on making sure he didn't expend too much fuel. Then, once he received the all-clear

VALIANTE'S CHAMP CAR BREAKTHOUGH

ONE of the more feel-good sub-plots of the Mexico City weekend was the impressive debut of Michael Valiante with Walker Racing. Despite the handicap of driving the outclassed Reynard chassis, the 24-year-old Canadian mixed it with the midfield Lola runners and showed a clean pair of heels to his vastly more experienced teammate Mario Haberfeld throughout the meeting.

The modest, soft-spoken Valiante (above) cut his teeth in the Westwood Karting Association, the same club that spawned the late and much lamented Greg Moore. Valiante went on to become a top international karter, winning the North American Formula C 125cc shifter category in 1998 and finishing sixth in the World Championships.

A series of scholarships assisted his progress through the Skip Barber ranks before he graduated to Toyota Atlantic in 2001, contesting a partial season with Lynx Racing. The following year he narrowly missed out on the title, while in 2003 he finished third in the face of the RuSPORT/A.J. Allmendinger juggernaut.

Valiante had been on the cusp of breaking into Champ Cars ever since joining forces with stalwart campaigner Derrick Walker in a sponsorship-seeking effort in the spring of 2003. He was all set to make his debut in the Fontana season finale only for the event to be canceled due to wildfires. During 2004 he had taken an enforced sabbatical after the soft sponsorship market left him high and dry.

So when Walker offered him the opportunity of a one-off appearance at Mexico City, Valiante grabbed it with both hands. He played himself in methodically on Friday before rising to the occasion in the pressure cooker atmosphere of final qualifying, slicing nearly two seconds off his previous best and outpacing Haberfeld by over a half-second to secure 12th on the grid.

The race itself was a little less fruitful, a slow final pit stop and the complete lack of attrition restricting him to a 14th-place finish. If that fell a little shy of his expectations, still it left him one place ahead of Haberfeld in the final reckoning.

"I think the weekend as a whole went really well," he reflected. "I learned a lot. I was a little conservative in the race, but the biggest thing was I had to finish and gain as much experience as I possibly could. In the circumstances it was hard to have asked for more."

Above: Justin Wilson just missed out on a podium place, but once again showed well.
Dan Streck/LAT

from race engineer Craig Hampson, Bourdais stamped his authority on the proceedings and began to pull away by as much as a second per lap.

"You know, really, it was a fuel economy race for 10 laps or so in the first stint," he explained. "And then after that we had a strategy to go as fast as we could to try and enlarge the gap. That was working perfectly. The car was handling as well as we could imagine."

Bourdais continued to leave the rest languishing in his wake, turning the fastest lap of the race one circuit before making his first scheduled pit stop after 26 laps. By then he had stretched his lead to a whopping 16 seconds.

Junqueira clearly had no answer.

"Today's race was kind of hard," he said. "My car didn't have the right balance and I had way too much understeer, especially on the alternate tires. I couldn't follow Sébastien. I made a mistake going into [Turn] 14, so I decided that I was taking too much risk to follow him. So I save a little bit of fuel and let him pull away, and just try to see if he had any problem. I said, I'm set for second, and let's see."

Justin Wilson held an excellent third place prior to the first round of pit stops, chased by Vasser and Oriol Servia -- until Allmendinger came charging into the picture. After starting seventh, the American youngster slipped past the Spaniard into fifth on Lap 21, whereupon the combination of quick lap times, a first pit stop two laps later than his nearest rivals and a short-fill on fuel enabled him to vault all the way into third.

The middle stages of the 63-lap race continued in much the same vein. No one came close to challenging Bourdais, who this day was in a class by himself and driving flawlessly. Until Lap 41, that is. The Frenchman had closed up onto the tail of a surprisingly uncompetitive Dominguez, who was in 15th and about to go a lap down, when all of a sudden the McDonald's car was spinning backward in Turn 14. The lapse was reminiscent of the slip made by Patrick Carpentier at Mazda Raceway Laguna Seca in September. And again the runaway leader emerged unscathed.

"I really just scared myself and probably the rest of [the team] when I spun the car going into the stadium," related Bourdais. "The sun was going down and the shade was gaining on the racetrack. I was trying to pass Mario. I thought he was going to let me by, and he didn't. Then I hit the bump, and when it came back on the racetrack I spun immediately."

Bourdais was lucky. He gyrated onto a wide-open asphalt runoff area, was able to keep the engine running, and rejoined the fray with his lead intact, albeit slashed from 18 seconds to a still-comfortable 5.2 seconds.

Junqueira wasn't happy with the handling of his PacifiCare Lola on the softer Bridgestone "alternate" tires and was unable to take advantage of his teammate's indiscretion. The gap between them actually widened again to a little more than nine seconds prior to their final pit stops, which came in unison after 51 laps. Thereafter, having switched to the harder, primary-compound tire, Junqueira began to make a dent on the Frenchman's lead, but not by enough to cause him any serious concern. There was also the matter of a large group of slower cars to pass, making the Brazilian's task all but impossible.

"It was a shame because the last 10 laps I was racing traffic i nstead of racing Sébastien," reckoned Junqueira. In reality, it didn't matter. Bourdais had the situation well in hand.

Allmendinger, having taken on less fuel than the others during his first pit stop, was the first to make his second visit to pit lane, but such was his pace that he had already consolidated his third place. In fact, he was a little over two seconds behind Junqueira at the finish.

"The car was absolutely amazing throughout the first two stints," he declared. "That's what allowed me to get in third and get to the back of Bruno. Then the last stint, the car just had way too much understeer. But, overall, I'm thrilled with the finish. It's a great way to end the year."

Wilson also was charging along in fourth, just over a second behind Allmendinger and pleased to have scored his best result of the season for Mi-Jack Conquest Racing.

"It's a bit disappointing as we were hoping to put the Mi-Jack car up on the podium to finish out the season, but it was still a competitive weekend for us," related the Briton.

Vasser finished a lonely fifth to round out his first year as an owner-driver, while Patrick Carpentier overcame some lingering effects from his Surfers Paradise accident (which led him to complete only a minimal number of laps prior to the race) to finish an impressive sixth.

Jeremy Shaw

SHOW ME THE MONEY!

ANY racing driver worth his salt wants to win every time he competes, but there was an added incentive to do well in the Gran Premio Telmex/Tecate Presented by Banamex, courtesy of Grupo Modelo S.A. de C.V. – better known to Champ Car fans through its leading brand Corona.

Michael Levitt/LAT

The brewery, whose burgeoning involvement in the series included serving as the primary sponsor of Rodolfo Lavin's #3 Forsythe Championship Racing entry and as a joint sponsor of the recent Las Vegas night race, had created a special initiative to reward the driver who amassed the most points over the two Mexican rounds of the championship. The winner of the 'Corona Cup' would receive a trophy and a cash prize of $100,000.

"As the proud brewers of Corona Extra beer and the fourth largest beverage company in the world, we are proud to present the Corona Cup," said Rene Saraccho, executive vice-president of Grupo Modelo. "This trophy embodies the same principles as our world-famous Corona beer brand – dominate the competition and have some fun along the way."

The award was also designed to recognize the immense popularity of Champ Car racing south of the border, of which there was yet more evidence at Mexico City. Once again the event recorded the highest attendance total of the season, while May's event at Monterrey's Fundidora Park had been on a somewhat smaller scale but still drew a robust crowd of more than 180,000 over the three days. And for sheer partisan enthusiasm, no one can beat the Mexican fans (even if their native sons gave them precious little to cheer in the season finale, much to their collective chagrin!).

No prizes for guessing who collected the bounty – yes, it was newly-crowned champion Sébastien Bourdais. The Frenchman (above with trophy) was odds-on favorite heading into the Mexico City weekend, having swept the board in Monterrey by winning the race, topping both qualifying sessions, leading most laps and posting the fastest lap. He almost pulled off the same feat at the second time of asking, letting just one point slip through his fingers when he was beaten to the Friday pole by Newman/Haas teammate Bruno Junqueira.

Truly, it was game, set and match to Monsieur Bourdais in 2004.

BRIDGESTONE PRESENTS CHAMP CAR WORLD SERIES POWERED BY Ford

ROUND 14

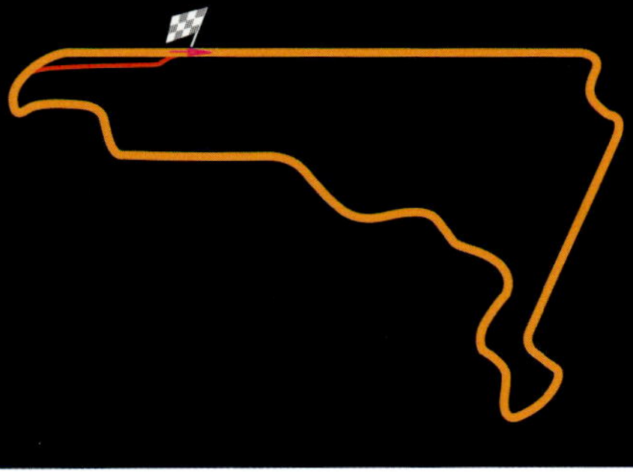

GRAN PREMIO TELMEX-GIGANTE

PRESENTED BY BANAMEX

AUTÓDROMO HERMANOS RODRIGUEZ, MEXICO CITY, D.F. MEXICO

NOVEMBER 7, 63 laps of 2.786 miles – 175.518 miles

Place	Driver (Nat.)	No.	Sponsor(s) Team Engine/Car	Tires	Q Speed	Q Time	Q Pos	Laps	Time/Status	Ave. (mph)	Pts
1	Sébastien Bourdais (F)	2	McDonald's Newman/Haas Racing Ford-Cosworth/Lola B01/00	BS	116.733	1m 25.919s	1	63	1h 39m 02.662s	106.327	34
2	Bruno Junqueira (BR)	6	PacifiCare Newman/Haas Racing Ford-Cosworth/Lola B02/00	BS	115.889	1m 26.545s	2	63	1h 39m 07.266s	106.245	28
3	*A.J. Allmendinger (USA)	10	Western Union RuSPORT Ford-Cosworth/Lola B04/00	BS	115.012	1m 27.205s	7	63	1h 39m 09.442s	106.206	25
4	*Justin Wilson (GB)	34	Mi-Jack Conquest Racing Ford-Cosworth/Lola B02/00	BS	115.262	1m 27.016s	3	63	1h 39m 10.564s	106.186	23
5	Jimmy Vasser (USA)	12	Gulfstream PKV Racing Ford-Cosworth/Lola B02/00	BS	115.232	1m 27.038s	4	63	1h 39m 19.743s	106.022	21
6	Patrick Carpentier (CDN)	7	Indeck Forsythe Championship Racing Ford-Cosworth/Lola B02/00	BS	114.837	1m 27.338s	8	63	1h 40m 00.450s	105.303	19
7	Oriol Servia (E)	11	yokeTV.com Dale Coyne Racing Ford-Cosworth/Lola B2K/00	BS	115.132	1m 27.114s	5	63	1h 40m 23.763s	104.895	17
8	Mario Dominguez (MEX)	55	Herdez Competition Ford-Cosworth/Lola B03/00	BS	114.113	1m 27.892s	15	63	1h 40m 25.389s	104.867	16
9	Michel Jourdain Jr. (MEX)	9	Gigante RuSPORT Ford-Cosworth/Lola B04/00	BS	114.576	1m 27.537s	10	63	1h 40m 34.561s	104.708	13
10	Paul Tracy (CDN)	1	Indeck Forsythe Championship Racing Ford-Cosworth/Lola B02/00	BS	115.055	1m 27.172s	6	62	Running		11
11	Alex Tagliani (CDN)	8	Johnson Controls Rocketsports Racing Ford-Cosworth/Lola B02/00	BS	114.179	1m 27.841s	13	62	Running		10
12	*Roberto Gonzalez (MEX)	21	Nextel PKV Racing Ford-Cosworth/Lola B02/00	BS	114.480	1m 27.610s	11	62	Running		9
13	Rodolfo Lavin (MEX)	3	Corona Forsythe Championship Racing Ford-Cosworth/Lola B03/00	BS	114.121	1m 27.886s	14	62	Running		8
14	*Michael Valiante (CDN)	15	Wildlife Conservation Network Walker Racing Ford-Cosworth/Reynard 02I	BS	114.438	1m 27.642s	12	62	Running		7
15	Mario Haberfeld (BR)	5	Cummins Walker Racing Ford-Cosworth/Reynard 01I	BS	113.714	1m 28.200s	17	62	Running		6
16	*Nelson Philippe (FR)	14	Mi-Jack Conquest Racing Ford-Cosworth/Lola B01/00	BS	112.617	1m 29.059s	19	62	Running		5
17	*Guy Smith (GB)	17	Rocketsports Racing Ford-Cosworth/Lola B02/00	BS	112.941	1m 28.804s	18	62	Running		4
18	Tarso Marques (BR)	19	American Medical Response Dale Coyne Ford-Cosworth/Lola B01/00	BS	114.004	1m 27.976s	16	60	Running		3
19	Ryan Hunter-Reay (USA)	4	Herdez Competition Ford-Cosworth/Lola B01/00	BS	114.713	1m 27.432s	9	58	Running		2

*Denotes Rookie Driver

Caution flags: Laps 3-4, Gonzalez spun/stalled; lap 5, yellow restart. **Total:** Two for 3 laps.

Lap leaders: Sébastien Bourdais, 1-63 (63 laps). **Total:** Bourdais, 63 laps.

Fastest race lap: Sébastien Bourdais, 1m 28.794s, 112.954 mph on lap 25.

Final championship positions: 1 Bourdais, 369; 2 Junqueira, 341; 3 Carpentier, 266; 4 Tracy, 254; 5 Dominguez, 244; 6 Allmendinger, 229; 7 Tagliani, 218; 8 Vasser, 201; 9 Hunter-Reay, 199; 10 Servia, 199; 11 Wilson, 188; 12 Jourdain Jr., 185; 13 Haberfeld, 157; 14 Lavin, 156; 15 Gonzalez, 136; 16 Philippe, 89; 17 Mazzacane, 73; 18 Smith, 53; 19 Sperafico, 47; 20 Besnard, 18; 21 Gidley, 15; 22 Marques, 9; 23 Valiante, 7; 24 Janis, 3.

MEXICO CITY SNIPPETS

• Sébastien Bourdais became the first Champ Car driver since Michael Andretti in 1991 to win as many as eight poles in a single season. Andretti also achieved the feat with Newman/Haas Racing -- from a total of 17 races, compared to just 14 events in 2004. The outright record for poles in a single season stands to A.J. Foyt, who was the fastest qualifier on 10 occasions in the 18-race 1965 campaign.

• Patrick Carpentier missed the first 45 minutes of the opening practice session on Friday, waiting for medical clearance as a result of the concussion he suffered in a huge crash at Surfers Paradise two weeks earlier. He almost missed the start of the Saturday morning session too, but for an entirely different reason: "I was getting changed in the transporter and they didn't realize I was in there and locked the door," he related with a grin. "Luckily I had my cell phone with me and I was able to call the guys and get them to come let me out!"

• The Ford-Cosworth XFE engines had been run relatively conservatively at the Mexico City event in 2003, including a richer-than-optimal air/fuel mixture in order to ensure there would be no overheating problems in the thin air caused by the high altitude (over 7000 feet). For 2004, the Cosworth Racing engineers made a special effort to maximize the motors' efficiency, including the production of a new electronic map. The motors also ran with reduced boost compared to all other road course events (just 39 inches of manifold pressure, which is the same as is run routinely on the ovals), but the other enhancements ensured that lap times were almost identical. The teams also were permitted a full 180 seconds of push-to-pass (three times more than usual), due to the extremely long main straightaway. Impressively, and for the first time in Champ Car history, every car that started the race was still running at the finish.

• RuSPORT Technical Director David Brown relinquished his usual race engineer duties for A.J. Allmendinger to his regular assistant, Chris Lerch, for the weekend. The new combo worked just fine. Allmendinger was third-quickest on Friday and, after slipping to seventh on the grid, bounced back in the race to claim the final podium position. "This weekend has been great overall," he summarized. "We made a mistake in qualifying yesterday with the car setup, and that's what put us back in seventh. But overall, the team has done a great job throughout the whole year -- rookie team trying to learn the series, finding out how difficult it is. I'm thrilled with the finish."

Anthony Kent/LAT

• Surprisingly, and to their intense dismay, none of the four Mexican drivers played a starring role on home ground, although at least they managed to share local honors. Roberto Gonzalez was the highest-placed Mexican qualifier on Friday, in sixth, while Rodolfo Lavin posted an impressive fourth best overall practice time on Saturday morning. Michel Jourdain Jr. ended up best-placed on the grid (a disappointing 10th), and Mario Dominguez emerged as the top finisher in eighth.

• Brazilian Tarso Marques received a late call to drive for Dale Coyne Racing after Jarek Janis' management team elected not to complete their originally scheduled two-race arrangement. Marques, who drove just two races with the team at the beginning of the season, quickly got back in the groove and was a promising fifth quickest in the race morning warmup. He encountered problems in the race but again displayed his proficiency by posting the eighth fastest lap (1m 29.599s), and was appreciably quicker than teammate Oriol Servia (1m 30.158s).

• A total of 345,428 fans filed through the gates during three-day event, marking the highest attendance of the 2004 season. "You can't help being pumped up for this race," said outgoing series champion Paul Tracy after the race, echoing the feelings of every Champ Car driver. "The Mexican fans are incredible. The grandstands were full and the noise was amazing!"

TOYOTA ATLANTIC CHAMPIONSHIP REVIEW

COMEBACK KING

by Merrill Cain

Top left: Principal title contenders Dalziel and Fogarty pose with the highly valued championship trophy at Monterey.
Lesley Ann Miller/LAT

Above: Fogarty and Dalziel (#28) lead the field along Shoreline Drive to start the season in Long Beach, California.
Michael Kim/LAT

Right: Danica Patrick completed every lap run by the series – a remarkable feat.
Phil Abbott/LAT

Below: Top Rookie Andrew Ranger finished his debut campaign in fourth.
Dan Streckt/LAT

Below right: Freshman Ronnie Bremer earned a top-five spot in the standings.
Michael Levitt/LAT

THE 31st season of the Toyota Atlantic Championship Presented by Yokohama featured another talented crop of young, promising open-wheel stars battling for supremacy on a blend of road courses, street circuits and ovals in 2004. In all, 29 drivers competed in the 12 events, and the field produced nine podium finishers, three pole winners and four racers who enjoyed trips to Victory Lane over the course of the highly-competitive season. But as the year progressed and points became harder and harder to come by, the race for the championship boiled down to a battle between a pair of series veterans.

Jon Fogarty and Ryan Dalziel put on quite a contest. Both encountered problems in the early going, but when it came to the crunch they and their respective teams, Pacific Coast Motorsports and Sierra Sierra Enterprises, knuckled down to the task at hand. Either would have made a worthy champion.

After finishing as series runner-up to Champ Car graduate A.J. Allmendinger in 2003, Scotsman Dalziel began the season as the odds-on favorite to take the next step up and claim his first Atlantic crown. The colorful 22-year-old set the tone early in his third Atlantic season, convincingly winning the first race of the year on the streets of Long Beach in the #28 Pro-Works entry.

Consistency early on in the season proved to be a problem for Dalziel, however. He did not find the podium again until Round 5 in Portland and didn't win another race until the midway point of the campaign when he took the checkered flag in Cleveland.

Fogarty also started the year slowly. After winning the 2002 Toyota Atlantic crown with Dorricott Racing, the talented American sat out most of the '03 season due to a lack of sponsorship. His career was granted a reprieve and he returned to the grid on a full-time basis in 2004 with Pacific Coast Motorsports, but the 29-year-old stumbled out of the blocks. He finished no better than sixth in the first two events of the year, stricken by an engine failure at Long Beach and then a first-lap incident in Monterrey.

The cagey veteran settled into a groove with his new team in Round 3, however, and began a remarkable run. He turned in a dominating performance to win the lone oval event on the schedule in Milwaukee, beginning a string of four victories in five races that vaulted him to the top of the point standings. After the wire-to-wire win at the Milwaukee Mile, Fogarty swept a doubleheader weekend in Portland and then won from the pole on the streets of Toronto as a duel with Dalziel for the series crown began to take shape.

The twosome dominated the second half of the season. Dalziel won at Vancouver and Road America, and Fogarty had to elevate his game to hold off his hard-charging rival. Ultimately, his championship experience paid off as he captured the final three poles of the season and won the last two events in Montreal and Monterey, California, to secure his second Atlantic title in three years.

While it took both Dalziel and Fogarty a while to find consistency early in the season, talented female racer Danica Patrick looked strong and produced solid results immediately in her second Atlantic campaign for Rahal-Letterman Racing. After finishing sixth in the standings in 2003, Patrick was ready to contend for the Atlantic title and she showed it, posting top-five finishes in the first four events of the season, including a pair of podium results.

Patrick, the only woman to ever finish on the podium in an Atlantic race, made more history when she took the series point lead after finishing second behind Fogarty in the first race of the Portland doubleheader. The effort enabled her to become the first woman to lead a North American racing championship; but her weekend was far from over.

The 22-year-old captured her first Atlantic pole position in the second race of the weekend as she looked to claim her first victory in the series. Unfortunately, she was hit from behind at the start of the race heading into the infamous Festival Curves and was relegated to seventh, surrendering the points lead to Fogarty and snapping her string of six straight top-five finishes dating back to '03. Patrick remained in the hunt for the title until the penultimate round of competition, and eventually finished a solid third in the overall standings.

North America's top open-wheel development series featured a very talented rookie contingent and from the very outset of the season it was clear that the freshmen had no intention of settling back and learning the Atlantic ropes quietly.

Fresh off a Fran-Am series title in 2003, highly-touted Canadian teenager Andrew Ranger served notice in the very first event that he would be a force all season long, storming to a second-place finish in Long Beach. The event marked a strong beginning for the Nevada-based Sierra Sierra team as the gifted Québécois racer guided his #27 Tide/Charmin/Mr. Clean/Snugabye Swift home behind teammate Dalziel.

Another promising first-year pilot also made waves from the first green flag of the season. Competing for the previously unheralded Brooks Associates Racing team, Denmark's Ronnie Bremer opened some eyes with three top-five finishes in the first three events of the season. Bremer made his first appearance on the podium with a second-place run in Milwaukee, enabling him to seize the championship points lead in just his third Atlantic race.

Funding proved to be an ever-present problem, however, and after the Portland weekend he grasped an opportunity to join the Polestar Racing Group, beginning in Cleveland. The 25-year-old Copenhagen native clicked immediately with his new team and the battle for top rookie honors between Bremer and Ranger began to heat up.

Ranger ultimately scooped the BG Products Rookie of the Year award by a six-point margin but Bremer gained consolation by claiming the only rookie victory of the season in Round 10 in Denver.

American Bryan Sellers also showed a lot of promise in his first full year in the Toyota Atlantic Championship. The Ohio native made the most of his opportunity with Lynx Racing, recording five top-five efforts in his first seven races of the season. The 22-year-old Sellers went on to finish sixth in the championship, posting podium results at Long Beach, Cleveland and Denver, and establishing himself as one of the top American rising stars in open-wheel racing.

Another American who took advantage of his opportunities in 2004 was veteran racer Alex Figge. Competing in his third Atlantic season, Figge benefited enormously from the experience of Fogarty, his Pacific Coast Motorsports teammate, and the duo packed a solid double punch for the expanded second-year squad. Figge took advantage of a wild start to the Monterrey, Mexico, race in Round 2 and scorched to the front of the pack. The Hollywood resident never looked back and captured his first Atlantic win. Figge grabbed another podium finish in Round 11 at Montreal and wound up seventh in the championship as he finished the year strongly.

Competing as a rookie with the Rahal-Letterman team, American Chris Festa showed some promise as he posted nine top-10 results en route to an eighth-place finish in the series rundown.

Jonathan Bomarito started the season very impressively for Transnet Racing. The reigning Formula Ford 2000 Zetec National Champion enjoyed top-five finishes in four of his first six races, including a third-place effort in Round 5 in Portland. Sadly, Transnet pulled out of competition midway through the season, ending a promising campaign prematurely for the 22-year-old Californian, but he still managed to finish among the top 10 for the year.

Australian teenager Josh Hunt joined Sellers on the Lynx squad and matured considerably during his debut season, finishing 10th in the points with a best result of seventh at Road America.

Despite running a limited schedule, ex-FF2000 frontrunner Tonis Kasemets also exhibited some strong road racing skills. Driving an ex-RuSPORT car, the native of Estonia earned two top finishes in just six starts as a series rookie with John Brooks' team.

Canadian veterans Eric Jensen and Phil Fayer returned to the series and turned in solid performances in '04, while American road racers Chris Dyson and Adam Pecorari each ran selected events while looking to expand their programs in 2005.

The sadly under-utilized Rocky Moran Jr. (who finished an excellent second in Monterrey) and Venezuelan-born Alex Garcia both ran the first half of the season while Al Unser, Daniel Pappas, Joey Hand, Dan Selznick, Chris Souliotis and David Sterckx competed in selected events during the course of the year.

The 2004 season saw a return of the C2 class, for older Swift 008.a chassis. Veteran Canadian campaigner Cameron Binder captured the title with four wins from five starts. American youngster Tony Loniewski was the only man to beat Binder, driving for stalwart Atlantic entrant Ole Olsson. Tom Nastasi, Justin Sofio and Rich Zober also competed sporadically.

2004 CHAMP CAR TOYOTA ATLANTIC CHAMPIONSHIP PRESENTED BY YOKOHAMA

Final point standings after 12 races

Pos.	Driver (Nat.), Sponsor(s) - Team	Pts.
1	Jon Fogarty (USA), Umbrella Entertainment - Pacific Coast Motorsports	327
2	Ryan Dalziel (GB), Pro-Works - Sierra Sierra Enterprises	309
3	Danica Patrick (USA), Argent Mortgage Company - Rahal-Letterman Racing	269
4	*Andrew Ranger (CDN), Tide/Charmin/Mr. Clean/Snugabye - Sierra Sierra Enterprises	257
5	*Ronnie Bremer (DK), Brooks Associates Racing/PaySystems - Polestar Racing Group	251
6	Bryan Sellers (USA), Lynx Racing	227
7	Alex Figge (USA), Umbrella Entertainment - Pacific Coast Motorsports	201
8	*Chris Festa (USA), SpacePak/CareCentric - Rahal-Letterman Racing	172
9	*Jonathan Bomarito (USA), Dixien/Omnisource - Transnet Racing	134
10	*Josh Hunt (AUS), Wright Patton Shakespeare/Atkinson Core Group - Lynx Racing	127
11	Rocky Moran (USA), Healthcare Privileges.com/PaySystems - Polestar Racing Group	92
12	Philip Fayer (CDN), PaySystems - Polestar Racing Group	88
13	*Tonis Kasemets (EST/USA), Flexovit Abrasives/MK Ind./TMI/Redline Oil - Brooks Associates Racing	81
14	Alex Garcia (YV), Dixien/Omnisource - Transnet Racing	71
15	Eric Jensen (CDN), Penn Capital/Konica Minolta - Jensen Motorsport	61
16	*Al Unser (USA), 200+ Marketing - P-1 Racing/Brooks Associates Racing	40.5
17	*Adam Pecorari (USA), Penn Capital/Konica Minolta - Jensen Motorsport	21
18	*Dan Selznick (USA), The Room Store	19
19	*Chris Dyson (USA), Thetford/Norcold - Dyson Racing	17
20=	*Chris Souliotis (CDN), Trident/Speedway/Spinnakers - Jensen Motorsport	13
20=	Joey Hand (USA), PaySystems - Polestar Racing Group	13
22	*Daniel Pappas (AUS), QLD Group/Vagelis Café and Bar - Brooks Associates Racing	10
23	*David Sterckx (B), Penn Capital - Jensen Motorsport	6
C2 CLASS		
1	Cam Binder (CDN), Avmax/Western Avionics - Binder Racing	155
2	*Tony Loniewski (USA), Margay - Olsson Engineering	144
3	*Tom Nastasi (USA), USG Sheetrock/Mactank - Jensen Motorsport	54
4	*Justin Sofio (USA), Bare Elegance/Valley Ball - Binder Racing	31
5	*Rich Zober (USA), Zober Industries/zober.com - Comprent Motor Sports	27

All drove Swift 014.a (C2 = Swift 008.a) chassis with Toyota 4A-GE motors and Yokohama tires.

*** denotes rookie driver**

Performance Chart

Driver	Wins	Poles	Fastest laps	Most laps led
Jon Fogarty	6	6	4	7
Ryan Dalziel	4	5	5	4
Alex Figge	1	-	1	1
Ronnie Bremer	1	-	-	-
Danica Patrick	-	1	1	-
Tonis Kasemets	-	-	1	-

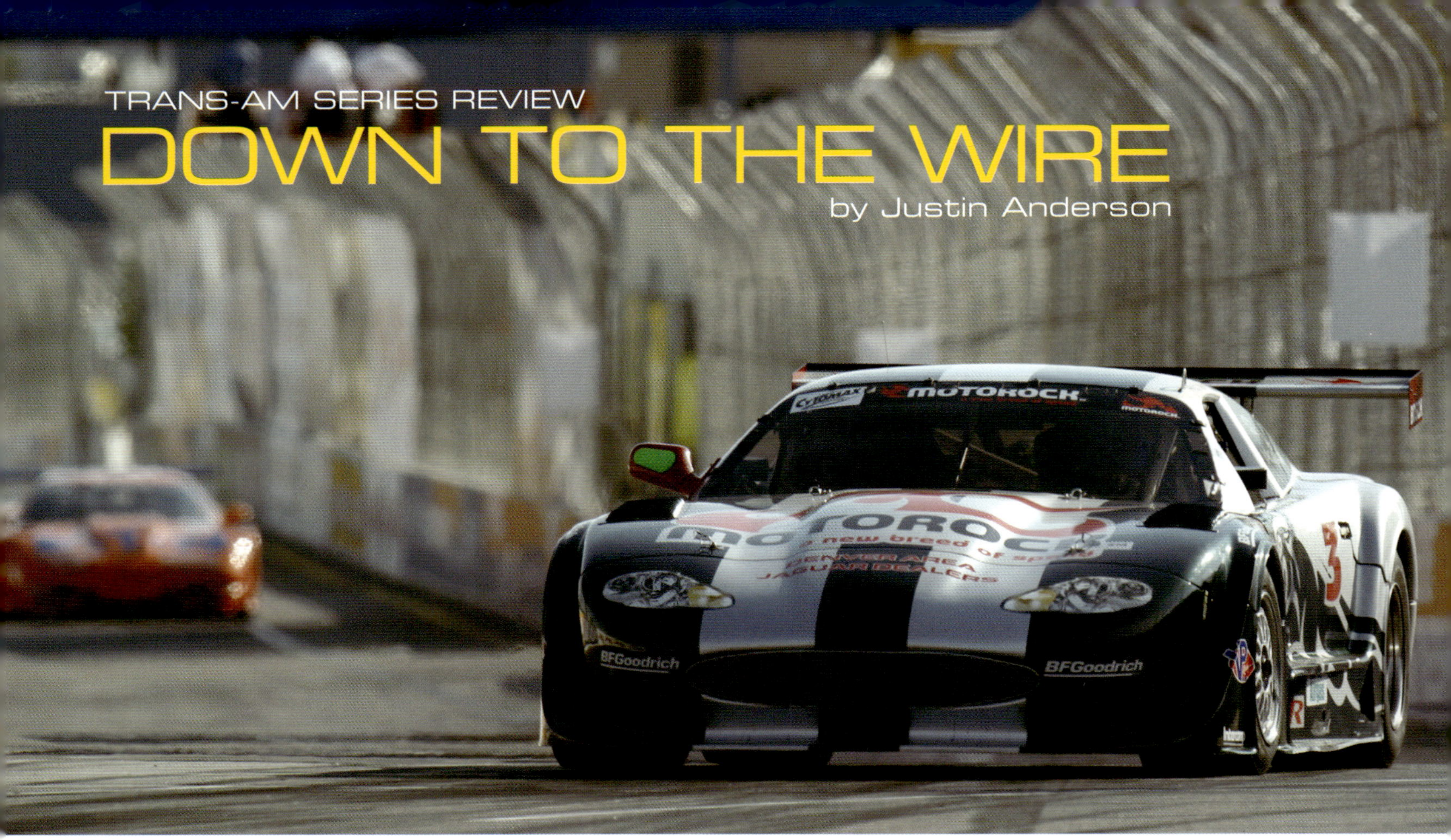

TRANS-AM SERIES REVIEW

DOWN TO THE WIRE

by Justin Anderson

Top: Paul Gentilozzi drives to the Trans-Am title in his Motorock Jaguar.
Phil Abbott/LAT

Top right: Boris Said makes one of his guest appearances in the series.
Phil Abbott/LAT

Above far right: Ross Murray (GT) and Gentilozzi (overall) celebrate their titles with Rookie of the Year Philip Simms at Laguna Seca.
Lesley Ann Miller/LAT

Right: Tommy Kendall tied his boss on points, but lost out on the tie-break.
Michael Levitt/LAT

Bottom left: Randy Ruhlman (Corvette) leads Jorge Diaz (Jaguar) at Road America following his first-ever pole.
Michael Kim/LAT

Bottom right: Tomy Drissi navigates the Corkscrew at Laguna Seca.
Phil Abbott/LAT

THE 2004 Trans-Am road racing season proved that the age-old combination of exceptional drivers and fast cars can be relieved upon to provide exciting competition. That excitement reached a crescendo in a thrilling conclusion to the season at Mazda Raceway Laguna Seca as Paul Gentilozzi and Tommy Kendall, two Trans-Am legends in their own rights, battled on the challenging and historic Northern California road course. The result was virtually a draw as the two teammates finished tied on points, a feat never previously achieved in Trans-Am's 39-year history.

Though Kendall (#11 Jaguar R Performance XKR) did everything in his power to net his fifth title at Laguna, by snatching the pole, setting the fastest race lap, leading the most laps and winning the race, a fourth-place finish for his Rocketsports Racing boss Gentilozzi was good enough to set up the tie. Gentilozzi clinched the title by virtue of his five wins to Kendall's two.

Gentilozzi's fourth championship further added to his illustrious Trans-Am legacy, tying him with Kendall for the most titles in Trans-Am history.

"This is conflicting," said Gentilozzi following his narrow triumph. "I told Tommy [prior to the season] my job was to help him win the championship and win the championship for Jaguar. It wasn't my intention to be in the title hunt, but I did what we thought I had to do. I went to Tommy before the finale. I was really torn up about what to do. I told Tommy if he wanted, I wouldn't race. In the end, we thought the fans deserved a race to the end...and that's what they got."

Gentilozzi, driving the #3 Jaguar R Performance XKR, finished out of the top five just once, at Road America due to two punctured tires, and won after starting last in two races -- Portland and Cleveland. He notched his 29th career victory at Denver in August, tying the win record held by the late Mark Donohue. All this despite sitting out the Infineon race due to prior business commitments.

Kendall had been tasked with developing Jaguar's new production-based, overhead-cam, fuel-injected engine. He overcame many hurdles to net the engine its first victory, following a stirring drive through the field at Road America, as well earning six poles and five fastest race laps from the nine races. By season's end, the engine was truly competitive – and more importantly, reliable. A dominant performance in his home state of California wasn't quite enough to overcome the earlier mechanical woes but Kendall's second-place finish in the title chase still represented a moral victory for the Santa Monica native.

"I just had a ball in 2004," he said. "At the start of the year I knew I wasn't where I wanted to be. I had originally planned to compete in 2005 and was just starting my [physical] conditioning program when Paul called. The engine had only been on the dyno a few times, but it hadn't had much race time. I set the goal of winning an outright pole and to win a race. We've accomplished both. It might drive me nuts looking at all of the places I could have picked up a point this year. But I gave it my all and I did what I needed to do."

Randy Ruhlman ran his best season on record in 2004, finishing a career-best third in the Drivers' Championship. Piloting the #49 Preformed Line Products Chevrolet Corvette for stalwart Trans-Am driver-turned-owner Jim Derhaag, Ruhlman put together a trio of three podium finishes, including a runner-up effort after earning his first Trans-Am pole at Road America.

"The car and team and I really started to click in 2004," summarized Ruhlman. "We were consistently in contention. We had seven top-five finishes in a row, so I think that says a lot about our program. The Derhaag Motorsports crew has done an excellent job. Our performance this season was virtually flawless. I couldn't be happier with the progress we have made during the season."

Tomy Drissi also had a season to remember. Finishing a career-best fourth in the championship, Drissi's #5 Twentieth Century Fox Movies Jaguar XKR was often seen charging to the front. Drissi was buoyed by three second-place finishes, as well as his first Trans-Am pole.

Jorge Diaz Jr.'s season was bittersweet. The young Puerto Rican learned just prior to the first race that his sister, Monique, had cancer. And while the 2003 Rookie of the Year battled it out on the track in his #8 JD Racing Promotions Jaguar XKR, she fought the disease. Both of them won, as Diaz netted his first Trans-Am victory at Toronto and claimed three other podium finishes en route to fifth in the championship. He dedicated his season to his sister, who is now cancer-free.

Boris Said made a trio of guest appearances, winning once at Infineon Raceway and rounding out the four race winners on the season. Said, driving the familiar #33 ACS Express Ford Mustang, never failed to reach the podium, finishing third at Long Beach and second at Laguna.

Charlotte, N.C.'s John Baucom once again was an ever-present contender, his #86 MAP Quality Engineering/Software Toolbox.com mount reclothed in Ford Mustang guise for the new season. Fourth place in the opening race at Long Beach remained his best result. Fellow East Coast racer Joe Scarallo again posted some promising results in his tightly budgeted #06 Toyo Tires/ROH Wheels/Autotrend Corvette, while veteran Greg Pickett was a strong contender whenever he appeared with the Cytosport Energy and Recovery Drink Jaguar XKR. Second at Long Beach was his best finish.

Jaguar earned its fourth Manufacturers' Championship after winning eight races and finishing second in the one that slipped away (Infineon). The marque's XKR brand moved to fifth on the all-time win list, while the Fast Cat's fourth title moves it into a tie with Lincoln-Mercury for third on the roster of all-time championship winners. Chevrolet was second in points, ahead of Ford, Dodge and Qvale.

Philip Simms comfortably won the Rookie of the Year title in the #24 Simms Motorsports Chevrolet Corvette, finishing ahead of Ross Murray (#01 Greenberg Cheese Company Dodge Viper) and Brandon Davis (#99 Spy Optics/ACS Express Ford Mustang). Simms competed in eight of the nine races and earned five top-ten finishes.

While Gentilozzi's run to the title was somewhat expected, Murray's winning the concurrent GT-1 Championship was certainly the Cinderella story of 2004. Murray, who has crewed for the likes of Boris Said and Michael Lewis, didn't expect to even compete as a driver. He begged, he borrowed, and he won. Murray only contested four races but topped the GT-1 class three times, capped by a fourth-place overall finish at Infineon and a sixth at Laguna Seca.

A dozen drivers participated in the newly expanded GT-1 Driver Development Program, which recognized lesser-funded, less-experienced drivers and gave them an opportunity to participate in victory circle ceremonies, receive their own trophies and take part in post-race interviews in the media center. The series-within-a-series program also offered competition support packages to the winners of the SCCA June Sprints at Road America and the Valvoline Runoffs at Mid-Ohio.

Jon "Chevy" Leavy (#18 MLEYE.COM Racing Chevrolet Camaro) finished a close second in the GT-1 chase, ahead of his teammate B.K. "Kenny" Bupp (#17 BankUnited Chevrolet Camaro), Garrett Kletjian (#20 UpscaleLingerie.com Qvale Mangusta) and Moneca Kolvyn (#78 West Coast Hot Rods Chevrolet Monte Carlo).

The #11 (Kendall) Rocketsports Racing team won the Team Owners' Championship by 11 markers over the sister #3 (Gentilozzi) Rocketsports outfit. The #49 (Ruhlman) Derhaag Motorsports team was third, followed by the #5 (Drissi) Rocketsports team and the #8 (Diaz) JD Racing Promotions squad.

Rocketsports Racing also won the Engine Builders' Challenge, ahead of Huffaker and CRD.

In terms of the number of entrants, 2004 might not be remembered as a banner year for the Trans-Am. But the quality of the competition, especially at the front, once again lived up to the series' proud heritage. Long may it continue.

2004 TRANS-AM DRIVERS' CHAMPIONSHIP

Pos.	Driver (NAT), Sponsor Car	Points
1	Paul Gentilozzi (USA), Jaguar R Performance Jaguar XKR	222
2	Tommy Kendall (USA), Jaguar R Performance Jaguar XKR	222
3	Randy Ruhlman (USA), Preformed Line Products Chevrolet Corvette	200
4	Tomy Drissi (USA), Twentieth Century Fox Movies Jaguar XKR	180
5	Jorge Diaz Jr. (PR), Puerto Rico Grand Prix Jaguar XKR	170
6	John Baucom (USA), MAP Quality Engineering Ford Mustang	156
7	Joey Scarallo (USA), Toyo Tires/ROH Wheels Chevrolet Corvette	150
8	Greg Pickett (USA), Cytomax Jaguar XKR	145
9	*Philip Simms (USA), Simms Motorsports Chevrolet Corvette	130
10	Mike Davis (USA), ACS Express Ford Mustang	87
11	Boris Said (USA), ACS Express Ford Mustang	85
12	Ron Fellows (CDN), Derhaag Motorsports Chevrolet Corvette	71
13	Bob Ruman (USA), Cenweld/McNichols Chevrolet Corvette	66
14	*Ross Murray (USA), Greenberg Cheese Company Dodge Viper (GT)	63
15	Jon "Chevy" Leavy (USA), MLEYE.COM/MurrayAuto.Com Chevrolet Camaro (GT)	61
16	B.K. "Kenny" Bupp (USA), BankUnited/Hamilton Safe Chevrolet Camaro (GT)	58
17	Max Lagod (USA), Hypermax Diesel Turbo Systems Chevrolet Corvette	56
18	Garrett Kletjian (USA), UpscaleLingerie.com Qvale Mangusta (GT)	55
19	*Brandon Davis (USA), ACS Express/SPY Optics Ford Mustang	54
20	Johnny Miller (USA), Eaton Corporation Chevrolet Corvette	48
21	Tim Cowen (USA), Cowen Truck Lines Ford Mustang	48
22	*Moneca Kolvyn (CDN) West Coast Hot Rods Chevrolet Monte Carlo (GT)	38
23	Charlie Webster (CDN), C.J. Webster of Canada Chevrolet Corvette	35
24	Michael Lewis (USA), Autocon Racing Jaguar XKR	30
25	Paul Fix II (USA), STOPFLEX.com/Hotel Monaco/Buca di Beppo Ford Mustang(GT)	30
26	*Cliff Ebben (USA), McMahon & Associates Chevrolet Corvette (GT)	19
27	*Blaise Csida (CDN), Csida Motorsports Chevrolet Camaro (GT)	15
28	*Wayne Hartzler (USA), Muscle Car Café/Mushroom Monday Chevrolet Camaro(GT)	13
29	*Edison Lluch (PR), Don Q Rum Chevrolet Corvette	12
30	*John Schaller (USA), Central Power Distributors Chevrolet Camaro (GT)	11
31	*Dan Downs (USA), Downs Motorsports Chevrolet Camaro (GT)	10

* denotes Rookie of the Year candidate

(GT) denotes GT-1 Driver Development Program participant

2004 Trans-Am Driver Performance Chart

Driver	Wins	Poles	Fastest laps	Most laps led
Paul Gentilozzi	5	–	2	3
Tommy Kendall	2	6	5	3
Boris Said	1	1	–	1
Jorge Diaz Jr.	1	–	–	1
Tomy Drissi	–	1	1	–
Randy Ruhlman	–	1	–	1
Greg Pickett	–	–	1	–

FOLLOW THE ROAD TO THE VANDERBILT CUP!

2005 SEASON SCHEDULE

April 10	Long Beach, California Street Course
May 22	Monterrey, Mexico Road Course
June 4	Milwaukee, Wisconsin Oval
June 19	Portland, Oregon Road Course
June 26	Cleveland, Ohio Road Course
July 10	Toronto, Ontario, Canada Street Course
July 17	Edmonton, Alberta, Canada Road Course
July 31	San Jose, California Street Course
August 14	Denver, Colorado Street Course
August 28	Montreal, Quebec, Canada Road Course
September 24	Las Vegas, Nevada Oval
October 16	Ansan, South Korea Street Course
October 23	Surfers Paradise, Australia Street Course
November 6	Mexico City, Mexico Road Course

BRIDGESTONE PRESENTS CHAMP CAR WORLD SERIES POWERED BY Ford™

www.champcarworldseries.co